Scout
A Memoir of Investigative Journalist Michael C. Ruppert

With

Against the Dying of the Light

Jenna Orkin

For my son, my family and Adele

Felix qui potuit rerum cognoscere causas.
Fortunate [was the one] who could recognize the causes of things.

Virgil

"I feel like Galileo. They couldn't kill him because he'd figured out how to navigate."
"It's all about maps."
"It's all about maps. Right."

Conversation between the author and Mike Ruppert

Contents

Acknowledgments

To Heidi Dehncke, whose unfailing professionalism eased what is normally a hellish process.

To Wes Miller and the staff of Collapsenet.com, Mike's final website, as well as those who carry on his work on his Facebook page(s.)

Introduction

On April 13, 2014, investigative journalist and subject of Chris Smith's documentary, *Collapse*, Michael C. Ruppert, shot himself in the head.

The following account was published blog-style in the aftermath of his suicide for the benefit of his thousands of shocked fans and less shocked circle of close friends. It is reproduced here with minimal editing in order to preserve the hectic sense of those days which echoed the hectic sense of the collapse of the newsletter he'd founded a decade and a half earlier, www.fromthewilderness.com, an event which is recounted within. In one or two places, identifying details of private people have been changed.

Thus, inconsistencies emerged as the blog evolved. At first, in the interest of clarity, I cleaned up some of the typos in Mike's emails. Then the better part of valor seemed to be to leave them but flag them with the usual "[sic.]" That effort quickly showed itself to be on the way to absurdity so the rest are presented as is, or was.

This account is in no way a full depiction of Mike. It does not touch on his accomplishments, for its audience when the blog first appeared was steeped in knowledge of those. Any reader who chances here without an awareness of why there was such keen interest in and mourning for a relatively little known figure is advised to seek out Mike's original work: www.fromthewilderness.com; his book, *Crossing the Rubicon: The Decline of the American Empire at the End of the Age of Oil;* his video, *The Truth And Lies Of 911*, among others; and Chris Smith's aforementioned documentary, *Collapse.*

Scout is followed by a different sort of end-of-life saga, *Against the Dying of the Light*, about the decline and death of my mother, the former Broadway dancer, Gisella Svetlik Orkin.

A Brief Comment on the Death of Mike Ruppert
By Self-inflicted Gunshot Wound

We always knew it could come to this.

To write about Mike requires the tranquility of recollection but at the moment, all is turmoil.

Mike, you told us, "Evolve or perish." Yet in *Apocalypse Man* you merged them, speaking of death as the ultimate evolution. One day we'll all find out whether that is, in fact, the case but it's not the message you used to impart!

Among the emails that cascaded in last night is a wonderful link, which is sorely needed at such a time: Hope and Courage.[1] Accompanying it, the following quote from Thomas Keneally's *Schindler's List*:

"Where's the electric fence?" Clara asked the woman. To her distraught mind, it was a reasonable question to ask, and Clara had no doubt that the friend, if she had any sisterly feeling, would point the exact way to the wires. The answer the woman gave was just as crazed, but it was one that had a fixed point of view, a balance, a perversely sane core.

"Don't kill yourself on the fence, Clara," the woman urged her. "If you do that, you'll never know what happened to you."

It has always been the most powerful of answers to give to the intending suicide. Kill yourself and you'll never find out how the plot ends. Clara did not have any vivid interest in the plot. But somehow the answer was adequate. She turned around. When she got back to her barracks, she felt more troubled than when she'd set out to look for the fence. But her Cracow friend had -- by her reply -- somehow cut her off from suicide as an option.

---

[1] http://www.oilempire.us/hope.html

Mike's Suicidal Tendencies

In response to the internet sages who have concluded — in the face of all known evidence from the people who were most intimately familiar with him as well as with the admittedly real dangers that had faced him over the course of his life as an investigative journalist — that Mike did not kill himself but was, in fact, murdered, his suicidal ideation goes back at least eight years. As a small example, below are excerpts from a few of his emails sent from Venezuela in 2006. In addition, he would call at any and all hours to be talked out of jumping from the roof or offing himself in some other way.

A foray into the seedier barrios of Caracas during a protest was one part journalistic adventure but one bigger part, courting danger. For a hero's death was devoutly to be wished. Failing that, he'd settle — as happened in the end — for death by any means available. On one occasion, he confessed to having tied his necktie around his neck as part of an effort to hang himself — and you can be sure I would not put forth such an implausible notion if it were not true — from the shower fixture. He said that he didn't go through with it because he wished to spare his roommate at the time, Carlos Ruiz, the trauma of finding him the next morning.

He finally left Venezuela in November, ending up, after a detour to Canada, at my apartment. But his reprieve from the alien environment that had not welcomed him the way he had dreamed brought only brief respite. For the next fourteen months, he contemplated suicide on an almost daily basis so that whenever I went to work or the grocery store, I made him promise not to kill himself before I came back. His word — his "honor" — mattered to him more than anything so we took it one day at a time, a notion that was familiar to him from AA.

More on this period in due course.

September 24, 2006 From Mike to Jenna:

...Every day I long for death because I just don't see how this current limbo is ever going to end. I just keep waking up and going through motions. I wrote a new

3

article today and start another tomorrow. I do miss the US and especially my loved ones but I know I can't ever go home. That would betray my moral decision and put my life at greater risk than I feel it is here.
I may wind up being the writer that no country wants. Then what?
Sigh. I've been doing the anger thing, especially at those close to me who betrayed me so deeply. That's what's really taken the heart out of me...

September 26, 2006 From Mike to colleagues at fromthewilderness.com:

...I am flat out of energy, spirit and hope now...
I am ready to die and the only thing I want to know is that I am totally clean with all the people who are FTW.

I saw a great documentary on Socrates last night. They made him drink hemlock because he kept throwing peoplés [sic] bullshit and sloppy thinking in their faces. Sounds a little familiar. I am not trying to torment or worry any of those who love me and care for me. I am hanging by a thread here. best, Mike

October 19, 2006 From Mike to colleagues regarding plans for dissolution of fromthewilderness.com and Mike's possible return to the US:

...anythng I do now will be out of the public eye. Guidance yes, but I need to get offstage for a good long while. That is both a pressure and a drug I need to detox from...

With the push of a button [referring to the 'send' key] the world leaves my shoulders.

October 19, 2006 21:32 From Mike to recipients unrecorded:

...The bridge is still calling. I say that not to threaten or pressure. I share it just to get it out of my head. I have had two close suicides and the breakup of an engagement in less than three years. Only now am I coming to grips with all of that and much more...

Mike's second suicide note, to Jack Martin:

Jack,
Am so sorry. It could not be helped.

I make a final offering of flesh for the children.

It is all I have left inside.
There is no more time.

I have tried to make it as easy as I could.

Rags [Mike's dog] should go to Jessy Re & River.

You will be able to deposit my royalty checks.
And you have been an amazing friend & are
a wonderful man.

I do this for the children. May it bring
love and light into the world.

Mike

Please make sure that Jessy Re gets
her letter. I love her more than
I can say.

Please return my body to Mother.

Part 1: Mike's Story

Mike left us an abundance of gifts, not least of which was his story. As an investigative journalist, he loved a good story even more keenly than the next man. And perhaps the one he loved most (as we all do, or would like to) was his own.

It was indeed a fascinating story, which goes some way to account for his thousands of friends and followers around the world, both "Facebook" and otherwise. Whether uncovering dirty dealings between politics and Wall Street that even Matt Taibbi wouldn't touch or enduring the flip side, "I'm done in; I'm about to jump off the roof," the Mike Show was a production which a certain kind of reader — a thinking man's action junky — yearned to be part of.

It is left to us now to piece together that story and it's an obligation which his friends and admirers are undertaking with a thoughtfulness that would make him proud. Some of the insights on the net, particularly at Rigorous Intuition, are as illuminating as Mike's detractors during his lifetime were maddening. (Beyond a few snarky headlines about the "conspiracy theorist's" suicide, the latter have been lying low this week, no doubt biding their time.) By pooling recollection, we may come to understand better how he could be such a hero to one group of people while at the same time appearing to another as a lunatic. This in turn may lead us to recognize how the whole concept of "hero" is a dangerous drug, not only for the "Leader" who becomes infused with his own importance and deaf to the insights of others but also for his followers, who sell their birthright of independence of thought.

In fact, no one was better acquainted with his "lunacy" than his inner circle. We got the hard-to-deal-with side of his personality in our face as long as he stayed close. I believe this is one reason he moved so often, living with no one person for much longer than a year — a trait he and I shared, by the way. His marriage, to a woman almost two decades younger, lasted eighteen months; his sojourn in my apartment, fourteen. My marriage lasted twelve years but shouldn't have.

He had long since outstayed his welcome in my one bedroom, but he was even more desperate to leave than I was to go about my business without worrying about his disapproval (as I would with anybody.)

Not, I hasten to add, that we often argued. There were one or two blow-up fights but mostly, in spite of profound differences of taste — (he hated New York on principle; the machismo of the West, where he felt most at home, left me cold,) — we got along smoothly, frequently slipping into a George and Gracey domestic routine complete with New York accents. Mike was a razor-sharp impersonator and I wish someone had taped his Russian, French and German personas.

Re Mike's story, reading Wesley Miller's account of how Mike came by the gun with which he shot himself is one fascinating piece. Another is Charlton Wilson Cht Ccht's description on Mike's Facebook page of Lakota traditions of giving one's body "for the children" as Mike said in his suicide note to his friend and landlord, Jack. "[I]n Native ways, we don't have money or animals or whatever to give. we have our flesh and our blood." If Mike is going to be cremated, as some recent reports said were his instructions, I don't get how the earth will benefit and will be watching for clarification. Anyway, Mother Earth receives our body no matter when we die; in the modern society in which Mike lived, however deploringly, hastening the process doesn't help anybody. But since he was not Lakota by birth or upbringing, though he revered Native American culture and became steeped in it once he moved out west, and since, as shown at Collapsenet.com, he'd been suicidal for years, a psychologist might opine that the Native American references were a cover for a longstanding suicidal drive.

Here's another piece of the Mike puzzle:

He was born DOA, "dead" on arrival. The doctor who delivered him told him, when they met twenty-five years later, that the medical team had done everything possible to revive him but to no avail. Mike's mother had already had one stillbirth so a second was not much of a surprise.

As Mike was being carried to the morgue, he cried. The rest, as they say, is history...

Part 2: Newborn

One morning a few weeks after he'd settled in to my apartment in Brooklyn, Mike said, "Honey? I'm having a hard time this morning."

He was supposed to call his therapist but the prospect was causing him such anxiety, he broke down in tears. I comforted him until the storm abated — at which point he said, "Would you make me breakfast?"

Is that what this was about? An appeal for pity so I'd make him breakfast?

"Why?" I asked suspiciously. I provided the first B of B&B since he was otherwise homeless, and the ingredients for the second since he was living on donations from his long-time followers. But why in God's name should I have to make it? Was he seeing how much he could get away with?

Mike's lifeline was honesty. A legacy of AA, it was what had bought him his sobriety from which flowed his connection to other people, their affection and help, his sense of belonging, his credibility, his integrity.

"I want to feel taken care of," he said, but it was not so much an explanation as an admission. The question had brought him up short and he was retreating with the grace that marked his many apologies, both public and private.

We sat down with our respective breakfasts, obtained by our respective selves.

"How does it feel to be taken care of?" I continued, veteran analysand that I am.

"Loved. Indulged. Worthy."

Indulged. Exactly.

"Those feelings may come more readily to those of us whose birth was not met ambivalently by our parents," I commented.

"My parents weren't ambivalent about me; they wanted me. My father did, anyway. My mother may have wanted me in order to please him."

On another occasion, Mike had said that he believed his mother married his father in order to escape her own father.

"They'd tried for a long time to have a child," he went on now. "I was two months premature. My mother spent the two months before that in bed.

'I was pronounced dead at birth. I cried on the way to the morgue."

It was my turn to cry now.

"Who are you crying for?" Mike asked.

"Your mother... I don't know." I believe that in addition to losing a baby before Mike, she also lost one after him.

"I met the doctor who delivered me when I was twenty-five.

'He remembered it. I had no pulse. I was blue. They tried to get my heart going. Then he handed me over to the nurse and I cried."

As he put his dishes in the dishwasher he continued, "Some spiritual people have said I'm a take-over, a soul waiting for a body to enter."

Perhaps it was this entry into the world, or at least his awareness of it, that accounted for his upset when we once happened upon a news article about terminally ill newborns.

In light of these beginnings, read Mike's last Facebook post:

I pray to all things seen and unseen, known and unknown, for we are all One.

The prophecies are being fulfilled. The hour of birth is at hand. The waters break and rend. There is blood. There are screams of pain. There is death and much anxiety in the air. Things look very bad for our Mother and all of her children.

The Truth awaits just on the other side of the ever dissolving veil where all the screaming and the mess is going on. The Truth opens its arms wide to lovingly receive the newborn and to comfort it.

"Isn't it wonderful?" The Truth exclaims.

I am your scout and this is my report.

Mitakuye Oyasin.
[Lakota for, "We are all related" - JO]

Part 3: Dad

"My dad had a great life," Mike said one day. "War hero in two wars. Fought in one; was a [I didn't catch the term] in the other. Made money. Died taking a shit, which he loved. So do I," he added, with a defiant smile. "But what did he do to make the world better? Paid his taxes; took care of [his second wife.] He just kept the system going."

On another occasion: "My dad was so in control, even after he had a cerebral hemorrhage while taking a shit, he managed to get himself to his favorite chair."

A major reason Mike worked so fiendishly to finish *Crossing the Rubicon* in 2004 was that he wanted to present it to his father before he died. (The other reason was that he hoped to sway the 2004 election.)

He succeeded with the first goal and got the satisfaction of watching his father's entrenched Republican views transform into an acceptance of Mike's. And he got to bask in the pride his father felt about his achievement.

"He did love me, though," he reflected.

"When I was five, I had my first eye operation. When I woke up, I had a patch on my eye. And next to me on the pillow was a teddy bear with a patch on his eye. I think the doctor put the patch on.

'My father did do some things when I was very young. We went to a Baltimore Orioles game... He took the cub scouts to something.

'That lasted 'til I was ten. He abandoned me to my mother. He was never there; he couldn't stand it. He was always traveling. I thought if I was just good enough, he might come and get me." His father only showed up, he said, when Mike had won something and Dad could preen.

One night at a party, Dad made Mike, who was in his teens at the time, a screwdriver. Under the influence, Mike told an anecdote, which ended, "...and then Dad beat the shit out of me."

His father was furious.

"He gave me a drink, then got mad when I acted the way people act when they've had a drink."

10

From the diary I kept during the period Mike stayed in my apartment:

January 21, 2007

This morning, he awoke with a start from a nightmare that black-clad guys in jackboots were coming to get him. This had followed two other dreams in which his father was beyond reach.

In a fourth dream, Mike was going on a trip, leaving his wife [he named a former female employee by whom he'd initially been dazzled] with their two daughters, ages five and nine, who were in the bath. He had chosen that moment to leave so the children wouldn't make a fuss.

In discussing the dream, he said that his father used to leave that way when he went away on business, without saying good-bye, and leaving defenseless ("naked") Mike in the hands of his mother.

Long time Ruppert aficionados may remember the female employee as the plaintiff in a sexual harassment suit against Mike, which she would eventually win. However, she was never able to collect. More on this (though it's not worth much time) later.

"He was a war hero; he worked hard, made a lot of money. But he didn't do his duty by me."

"Not only that," I added. "He left you to do *his* duty." (In many ways, some of them unhealthy, Mike took over his father's role in the household.)

"Son of a bitch." He looked towards the ceiling. "Dad, you're fired. That son of a bitch. I used to have a shrine to him in my office in Ashland, with all his war medals. It's time we execute my Dad."

Part 4: Friends

Mike's father's job with the Air Force required the family to move so often that Mike changed schools virtually every year. It's notoriously hard to make friends under those circumstances and it left him lonely and angry, especially after "Dad" started staying away from home for longer periods. He took out his frustration on the family dog, kicking and abusing it. When Dad returned, he immediately got the lay of the land, understanding he was the root cause of the problem. But he also realized that for everyone's sake, the dog had to go. I always felt that Mike's yearning for a "dawg" when he moved to a sustainable community was partly to make amends to that childhood pet. He needed to prove to himself that he could care for a dog since, as no one questions, he loved them so much.

One day shortly after the family moved to Denver, a kid in Mike's class said, "Hey, Mike! We're all down by the pool. Love it if you could join us. Bring some cookies!"

Mike got excited — Could it be he would finally have some friends?

"I said, 'Ma, quick — get some cookies!'" he remembered.

"She drove me down there. They just wanted free cookies. They laughed at me..."

As he relived this story, Mike looked like the miserable kid he had been that day.

This is the background to the pride that shone from him in recent years when he would say with awe, "I have five thousand Facebook friends!"

Part 5: Jobs

When Mike first arrived in Brooklyn from Canada, he was still shell-shocked by the death of fromthewilderness and by his failure to obtain asylum in Venezuela. He was physically unhealthy and, as he had been for several months, obsessed with thoughts of suicide.

Sensing that he needed a break from this endless cycle of horror but that he'd be unwilling to venture too far from familiar territory, one day I asked him about his childhood; specifically, what he'd wanted to be when he grew up.

"'Til I was twelve and found out how bad my eyes were," he said, "I wanted to be an airplane pilot." That was what Dad had been and what accounted for his war-hero stature. "But I didn't have any depth perception."

(Eyes were still a source of some anxiety as he needed treatment for a cataract. He couldn't understand why I wore glasses of lesser strength than the doctor prescribed [because I didn't want my eyes to get lazy.] And he couldn't stand it if they had smudges on them.

"But what if you have to drive?" he exclaimed.

"I don't have to drive; I take the subway."

When he couldn't take it anymore, my glasses received a polish worthy of the Hubble telescope.)

"After that, I didn't know," he went on, "except that I didn't want to be a businessman. Law? Nah.

'Then when I was seventeen, a captain came to my high school and talked about police science."

"You mean fingerprints? Things like that?" I asked guilelessly.

"No. You're being a girl. About being a cop. The badge and the gun. The camaraderie. The humor. I knew that was what I wanted to be."

Ah... Friends at last; even a fraternity.

His years at LAPD have been written about extensively but some events are not so well known. He never killed anyone, he said, even when, on one occasion, doing so would have earned him a commendation. (The perpetrator turned out to be more crazy or high on PCP than criminal.) But he did once break a prisoner's skull when the guy, also high on PCP and being carried on a stretcher, bit Mike on the testicle.

After leaving LAPD, he had a series of low-level positions: Selling guns (he loved guns but not the job;) putting together amplifiers; working a UPS route where he met a man who became his hypnotherapist.

"I don't like thinking about my past except for the years of FTW, LAPD. The rest was just so much loneliness and poverty."

He also acted as a security guard at the Oscars, escorting Vanessa Redgrave the night she gave her controversial acceptance speech for *Julia*.

When he recounted that episode, I mentioned that she was doing a one-woman show on Broadway, in Joan Didion's *The Year of Magical Thinking*. We bought tickets and Mike left a copy of Rubicon for her at the stage door with an inscription saying how they had met and how her speech that night had given him courage to write the book.

Her assistant called the next day to say that Ms. Redgrave thanked him and would definitely like to meet. But we never heard further. We imagined she had looked into his background and been advised to stay away from the "conspiracy theorist."

Part 6: Jackboots

I didn't let Mike smoke in the apartment when I was home so he would go downstairs in front of the building and talk to the doorman or tenants walking their dogs. But when it was too cold for that (he was a California kid after all,) he simply slipped into the stairwell.

One night, after returning from his last cigarette before retiring, he said, "When I was out in the hall, all I could think about was men in jackboots kicking the door down and taking away everything. I think it has to do with Denver."

Of all the moves Mike had had to go through as he was growing up, none had hit him so hard as Denver. For the first time in his life, he'd established roots. He was on the football team and he had friends.

"When we left Denver," he elaborated, "my dad didn't explain, didn't ask how I felt. He just said, 'Get your stuff ready; we're leaving for Los Angeles in two weeks."

"The way you left Ashland," I observed.

From conception to realization, that plan to close up shop after the computers were smashed and flee the country for the terra incognita of Venezuela where again, he knew nobody, had taken all of eighteen days.[2] And like the move from Denver, it involved divesting himself of everything he held most dear; leaving family heirlooms, which I will not describe, for his closest friends, with the stipulation that in the unlikely event he should return, (see his article, *By The Light of a Burning Bridge*) they would be restored to him. (For the most part, they were.) One of the signs of suicidal intent is giving away one's possessions.

---

[2] On the night of June 25, 2006, someone — or more likely, two people -- took a sledgehammer to all seven of the FTW computers. Initially, Mike believed that the burglary had been perpetrated by elements within the US government who opposed the website's ongoing investigation of Pat Tillman's death in Afghanistan by friendly fire. (He later speculated it had been carried out by resentful employees.) Having been harassed by the government before, he took this latest attack as a warning and fled the country.
FTW OFFICES BURGLARIZED by Michael C. Ruppert July 5, 2006
http://www.fromthewilderness.com/free/ww3/070506_offices_burglarized.shtml

"That's true," Mike said in wonder. He was not accustomed to the insights of psychotherapy. "But why would I want to repeat Denver?"

"That's one of the weird things about the psyche. We repeat old behavior because it's comfortable and fulfills predictions; we're not taken by surprise. It may suck but it's a case of, 'The devil you know is better than the one you don't.' Also, we may want to get it right this time."

I'm sure this constant upheaval as he was growing up was one reason that even as an adult, Mike never stayed in one place very long: After leaving his home of Los Angeles, he moved to Ashland followed by Venezuela, Brooklyn, Los Angeles again, Sebastopol, Colorado, (where he must have been thrilled to return,) Calistoga.

Like anyone else who'd been close to Mike, I assumed the men in jackboots taking away everything to be government thugs. It's only in rereading this account that I see that they also represent his father. But in the end, they became Mike himself.

Part 7: South of the Border

The morning of July 12, 2006, Carolyn Baker called. "Are you sitting down?"

"Yes." Then I did.

"Mike's in Venezuela. He got there this morning."

August, 2006 From Jenna to Mike:

when carolyn told me where you were, i was shocked but not surprised. you had left a trail of breadcrumbs: the line, "there are few things that could make me think of leaving this country but the loss of internet independence is one of them." i knew from the very denial that you were thinking of leaving this country. it was a snap to figure out where you would go; you'd mentioned it at petrocollapse [the first Peak Oil conference in New York City, which I'd moderated] in october.

but there was no way i could have known this was all happening at that moment.

i cried "no" nine times. (a pesky sense of rhythm keeps track of such things.) i thought that even if you survived (as you obviously had) you were saying, "i'm making a new life, turning my attentions elsewhere." [That was indeed what he was saying.]

she described your final days here. i was with you in your garden of gethsemane (on your porch with michael and carolyn, complete with wine.) [Despite the ironic turn, I now cringe to read the groupie-like idolatry of this. And it gets worse...]

i cried for three days, the chorus in this greek drama. the hero acts. the chorus moans, "woe. oi weh." would your life be an orson wells movie in which you play the joseph cotton role in a panama hat, pursued down nightmare alleys?

would i see you again? would you think of me in the past tense? [Yup. Sure would.]

she said that you had said, 'i want you to think of me as dead."

having passed thru the valley of the shadow of death you have been reborn on a brave new continent. the ultimate calvinian tumble down the hill, tada!

you will thrive there. you will finally be appreciated by the powers that be and financially secure.

you may want a child.

fantasy: in a few years i come to venezuela. your wife refers to me as 'esa mujer.' i sing the fishy song with your child. (boom boom diddun daddun wannum - choo.) your wife and i bond.

the fourth day i threw up all day on an empty stomach and thought, "so this is the origin of the word 'wretched.'" i have never before thrown up for emotional reasons, not even during the 17 months my father was dying of a brain tumor.

the gods of vomit were not appeased by my exertions; they wanted work product so i drank some tea which helped...

I adjusted to Mike's being on another continent — one I'd never been to —particularly after Carolyn, his liaison at the time to his past life, said that once he got settled, he planned to make a place for his closest circle.

I oriented myself to moving there too, by brushing up my self-taught Spanish. Learning a foreign language was a more familiar task than trying to build a house out of grass (a pastiche of the sort of advice that was given to people worried about Peak Oil.) I watched Spanish-language soap operas and religious programs as well as a stream of surreal movies in the tradition of Don Quixote, El Greco and Dali.

Mike's leap into the unknown seemed an act of either the greatest courage or nuttiness. I didn't know him well enough to understand the impulse but trusted that he knew what he was doing. It wasn't so crazy for him as it would have been for anyone else to think the Chavez government would welcome him. Within a couple of weeks, he had a radio interview with Chavez advisor Eva Golinger. However, there were more things in Heaven and certainly earth than were dreamt of in his philosophy...

Part 8: Orinoco

As mentioned in previous posts, before Mike left the US, he disbursed his worldly effects among his loved ones, his FTW (Fromthewilderness) colleagues who were the closest thing he had to family, with the stipulation they be returned to him should he ever come home again; and that for the most part, they were.

The exception was me. My gift, which Mike never asked me to return, was, to all appearances, a small envelope, of the size to hold a key, from Riverton Jewelers in Sherman Oaks. On the other side of the store logo was the legend, "Thank you — It has been a pleasure serving you;" then, in Mike's scrawl, "For Jenna. Two diamonds." I smiled uncertainly when the gift arrived in the mail, thinking it was an obscure joke. But accompanying this envelope was another one from Carolyn marked, "Please read first."

Carolyn explained that the two diamonds enclosed, which, having no idea of their worth, she'd insured for $1000, were from Mike's father's wedding ring.

It was a while before it occurred to me to look at the diamonds but I knew what they meant: Not real love; he didn't know me well enough for that. But when he fled the US, he needed to feel he was leaving behind someone to whom he was truly close. I fit that role at that moment. The gift was an expression of what might have been.

Like everything else he'd ever known, I had receded into his past while he set about to remake himself as a hero of the Bolivarian Revolution.

If anyone could pull that off, it would be Mike. But one day, I sensed, his past would catch up with him.

From Jenna to Mike:

what you leave behind will not sink in 'til you've established new roots. a joke will occur to you which no one around you will appreciate. or you'll see a favorite American movie dubbed into Spanish and you will be overcome. by the waters of the Orinoco, you will sit down and weep as you remember us.

but you are home. it is we who are homesick.

That moment by the waters of the Orinoco came sooner than I had anticipated. During the radio program with Eva Golinger who acted as both interviewer and translator for the show's two hour duration, Mike finally broke down in tears when a call-in came from his Portland buddy, renowned blues singer and bass player, Lisa Mann.

September 10, 2006 From Mike to Jenna:

I couldn't function for hours after that interview... I had a serious crush on [Lisa] for a while and she is very, very special. She didn't even know that [his fiancée] and I didn't get married or why.

Months later, at my apartment in New York, we were talking about the Venezuela episode.

"Why didn't somebody stop me?" Mike asked, not entirely rhetorically.

First of all, because almost nobody knew. But of those who did, there was at least one effort to take Mike through what such a move might mean, step by step.

"Carolyn tried to slow you down but you brushed her off," I said. "You weren't in the mood to listen to anybody."

"Yeah," he agreed. "I knew that as soon as I asked the question."

Part 9: Limbo

Despite his growing recognition of what he'd lost by burning his bridges, Mike's spirits must have risen when a reporter from an influential US newspaper flew down with the idea of doing a feature on him. But emotionally, the conversation itself seems to have been a precursor of the movie, *Collapse*:

"[S]even hours with the [newspaper] reporter yesterday. I´m writing a seperate [sic] email which you´ll get. It was in detail and he was serious. [Mike had been burned by mainstream features before, as a colleague was reminding him] *but it went back through all the most painful parts of my life. At the end it was like someone had stuck a vacuum cleaner in my ear and all the tastes and smells got tasted and smelled all over again.*

Not only that, but he'd gleaned that some of his colleagues weren't handling the press the way he would have liked.

"Could people please stop saying, 'Mike can be a real asshole but...?' Because otherwise, that'll be the lead of the story."

On the political asylum front, too, his needs were meeting with obstacles followed by false hopes and setbacks. And then there was the barren solitude of his living arrangement. Advised to keep a low profile while his case was pending, (hard to do when, with his Germanic coloring, he stood out in a Venezuelan crowd) he remained virtually confined to his hotel room.

September 24, 2006 From Mike:

...Life is very unhappy. Three days ago two drug dealers staying at the same hotel I am were gunned down on the street a block away. I´m in an upscale neighborhood where stuff like this never happens.Funny thing is, I picked them out for drug dealers the moment I laid eyes on them three days before that. I don´t have time to elaborate but I am getting indications that [an American pundit] may be actually trying to prevent me from getting asylum. That´s not for publication.

In a phone call, he named two other men (activists I'd met and had never taken seriously) who, he said, should be investigated if anything dire happened to him in Venezuela.

Every day I long for death because I just don't see how this current limbo is ever going to end. I just keep waking up and going through motions. I wrote a new article today and start another tomorrow. I do miss the US and especially my loved ones but I know I can't ever go home. That would betray my moral decision and put my life at greater risk than I feel it is here. I may wind up being the writer that no country wants. Then what? Sigh. I've been doing the anger thing, especially at those close to me who betrayed me so deeply. That's what's really taken the heart out of me.

He signed off with a forlorn, perfunctory, "Love you."

An email of September 4, 2006 reinforces this sense of alienation on both the cosmic and comic levels:

"This seemingly endless limbo vis a vis the gov't is a real drag and the tiny beds in my little fleabag suck big time."

La Hojilla, a popular TV show that was Chavez' favorite, invited Mike on but when the appointed day arrived, the show was postponed.

The next day on which he was scheduled to appear, he was pre-empted by a baseball star. Or so he was told. Two friends who watched the show said the baseball star didn't appear either.

Finally, he reached the conclusion he'd never get in to see anyone who could arrange for asylum.

"I'm a bargaining chip," he sighed. At the end of the day, Mike was a gringo from a CIA family whom Chavez would have had a hard time justifying to his people, regardless of Mike's street cred.

Part 10: Burundanga

Mike had fled his country in haste; now he was repenting in sorrow. With the exception of phone-calls to FTW colleagues, he was reduced to approximately one conversation a week in English. To save money and avoid explaining his status as asylum-seeker to inquiring strangers, he cooked his meals on an electric burner in his hotel room. At night, the car horns honked incessantly.

Not only that, but he'd learned that Chavez had made statements implying he wasn't sure that an actual plane had hit the Pentagon.

Mike had tried to warn the government against adopting this widely-touted but easily refuted conspiracy theory (as opposed to conspiracy fact.) Over 130 eye-witnesses had confirmed that what they saw was a plane rather than a missile. To focus on a debatable theory is to draw the attention away from actual smoking guns.

He'd had it; he was throwing in the towel. One night, with a "Fuck it," attitude he went out for a drink.

And then things started going sideways.

The following excerpt is from a confidential email Mike wrote on September 26, 2006 to a few colleagues:

I could not sit alone in the room one more night with Spanish TV. I went to a night club and had a few drinks. I was soon approached by two women. What happened after that is both a blur and a mystery. There's no doubt I got intoxicated but I suspect that something was put in my drink. At about 6 AM the next morning I came to in my hotel room. All of my pocket cash was gone and there were a number of credit card receipts strewn around. I have no idea how much was run on the credit cards that night.

Remember that current tensions between Venezuela and the US are very high. I am obviously a "gringo" in a city where fleecing gringos is something of a pastime. Because of the intense pain and other symptoms I believe that something was put in my drink. Maybe a "roofie". They are here too I'm told.

I don't know if I got laid or not. For all that I certainly hope so.

There are those in Ashland who know (as do all of the pre-Ashland FTW staff) that I spent 21 years in AA and resumed normal drinking in March of

2004. The uninformed backyard gossip, the ignorant, and those who achieve superiority by taking other people's inventory, will quickly assert that I am just an alcoholic who went out, went into a blackout and is now trying to make excuses.

But Ken, Carolyn, Mike, Stan and Jamey have all seen me drink moderately, without cravings or any aberrant behavior for more than two years. There are people who leave AA and do resume normal alcoholic consumption.

However, it is largely because of what I learned in AA that I am writing this 10th Step. I have never stopped practicing AA's steps or the deep spiritual program I acquired through 21 years of intense work.

We later learned that Mike's symptoms were consistent with the ingestion of burundanga, "an extract of the brugmansia plant containing high levels of the psychoactive chemical scopolamine."[3] While not impairing some cognitive functions, (Mike retained a dim memory of going to the ATM and withdrawing money, then doing it again until his account was depleted,) the drug does seem to remove "free will," whatever that philosophical enigma might be.

The lapse was to have what the British call "knock on" or ripple effects.

---

[3] Mind controller: What is the 'burundanga' drug?
03 March 11 by Vaughan Bell
http://www.wired.co.uk/magazine/archive/2011/04/start/mind-controller

Part 11: Apprentice Devils

The reason Mike felt impelled to confess the burundanga episode had to do with an event that had taken place back home.

FTW subscribers (and of course, staff) used to get news updates on a daily basis, if memory serves. One afternoon we opened the email to find a long account, supposedly from Mike, describing his life in Caracas as one of debauchery — drinking, whoring and blowing money which had been raised from those same subscribers after the computers were smashed and FTW's fate hung in the balance. This chronology, too, is drawn from memory and may be inaccurate in some details. But it is widely known that subscribers or, in later years, Facebook friends, donated funds when Mike or the site was in trouble. Given the nature of the work, these financial difficulties were inevitable rather than the result of any incompetence. See this email written by Mike, though it's stored on a site that is hostile to him, concerning the FBI's seizure of his bank account:

The FBI has – within the last three days -- used agents and illegally raided my bank account and taken $5,200. Someone filed an appeal to a court case I had previously won, signed my name on the subpoena while the FBI intercepted all mail notifying me of the court date. I never even knew about it. When I failed to show up for a hearing I had never heard about a judgment was issued and my bank account looted yesterday. Sure, I can win this but it will take maybe two years and thousands of dollars in legal fees and I'll probably never get the money back... [4]

The bizarre email, which appeared to have been sent from the usual FTW address, was skillfully written in Mike's style. However, veteran subscribers recognized it as a hoax. Newcomers were more inclined to find it alarming, as the sender intended. Beyond that, no one knew what to make of it. FTW and the blog were besieged with inquiries, all variations on the theme of, "WTF?"

Mike knew that the credit card expenses he'd run up the night of his burundanga exposure, as well as the ATM withdrawals, would

---

[4] http://thetruthaboutmikeruppert.blogspot.com/2007/10/piece-of-blushing-past-still-crazy.html

eventually have made their way to FTW headquarters. He also knew he'd offended some employees, even physically pushing one of them. He surmised that someone was getting back at him by playing a humiliating joke, showing him who was actually in charge.

His coming-clean email (the real one) written in AA tradition to his closest circle was in effort to keep FTW from falling apart. He'd left it in the hands of capable people but you can't hand over a company after a two week transition, no matter how thorough, and expect it to continue running as it did when you were overseeing it. The staff you've left it to don't have the same investment. They're doing a job; the company is not their baby.

Mike had to tell the whole story in order to prove that while his foray into the underworld of burundanga was not his finest moment, it was also far from the sleaze that the fake email was smearing him with. His explanation was offered as a figurative bowed head, in order to hold onto those few friends he still trusted as well as bring back the ones he'd alienated.

(After FTW closed up shop for good as an active site — though the archives remain online — other high jinx took place which undoubtedly originated with weightier enemies than the bogus email: For a while, clicking on certain links led not to FTW articles but to WING-TV.

This was the website of Victor Thorn, aka Scott Makufka. One of Mike's nemeses during the heyday of FTW, Thorn is the author of such masterworks as *JFK & UFO*, *Hillary (And Bill:) The Sex Volume* and *The Holocaust Hoax Exposed*.

Mike's suspicion that Victor Thorn had been tasked by the government with being a thorn in Mike's side may have proven justified. As soon as FTW closed for good, so did WING-TV. Their last show aired in November, 2006.)

Part 12: Blog Readers Weigh In

News of Mike's flight to Venezuela had become public in August, with Carolyn Baker's description of the days leading up to his departure. That, along with Michael Kane's account of the same period, makes interesting reading in light of Mike's final exit on April 13 of this year, 2014.

Since the blog had been assuming a greater role as FTW contracted, finally freezing into an archive site, a deluge of comments rushed in.

Some bore the telltale marks of disinformation. Just as when the computers were smashed, the blog was besieged with messages that attempted to deflect the conversation away from FTW and towards the purported harassment of another "activist" whom FTW followers don't even mention by name, when Mike left the country, "news" flooded in about a journalist from a Neo-Nazi website who'd supposedly also, coincidentally at the same time, had to go into hiding.

I allowed some of this spam through: first, because the blog at that time aspired to be a forum for a broad spectrum of opinions; second, because I'd posted a prominent disclaimer in anticipation of such an onslaught, to the effect that publication of comments should not be construed as endorsement, etc; finally, to show we weren't afraid of them. These days, I'd be more Draconian. But in any case, the chaff was outweighed by expressions of genuine dismay:

All I can say is Wow! I am sorry it had to happen the way it happen, but I am very happy for you to be moving on and having the intestinal fortitude to do what needed to be done... Give em Hell... but find some peace. Howlin_Dog.

...I have to admit, that I am bummed... FreeAcre

A salute from a follower with the eye-catching handle, "Allbetsroff."

My husband and I have been following you and FTW for many years............ In our 2 hour commute home from work we would always read a printout from FTW and discuss the various issues presented.I think it's safe to say we love you... Mary Brown

.... I couldn't help but cry when I read your latest messages... I had this odd feeling... not even knowing all that FTW had been through, somehow I just knew [Oregon] was temporary. I guess it's all temporary. Anyway now I'm just bawling!... Mrs. P

My only regret is... that I wasn't in your large suitcase. casecore

To alleviate his growing despondency, I forwarded the messages to Mike who was heartened, writing, "It's kind of like the final scene in *Miracle on 34th Street* when the mail bags come in." His isolation and Herculean efforts were finally bearing the fruit of appreciation.

He responded via the blog:

...I wish I could tell you all more about what my life is like here at the moment but I just can't for reasons that maybe someday I'll be able to 'splain to you.   These are terrible times for the planet and I fear they are going to get worse. Right now I am in something of an unavoidable limbo that seems to have no end. But it will, I'm sure. I mean, who the Hell am I to say, I'm 55 and have been through enough. I don't need no more freaking evolutions. As always, my arms are too short to box with God."

The word "'splain" was an allusion to Ricky Rodriguez in the *I Love Lucy* show, the pre-eminent sitcom of the 1950's. Mike had used the term at least once before, in his article, "Lucy, You Gotta Lotta 'Splainin' To Do," essential reading for anyone interested in the red flags known to the US government in the months leading up to September 11, concerning an attack on the World Trade Center.[5]

---

[5] ...**4. Feb. 12, 1998** - Unocal Vice President John J. Maresca -- later to become a special ambassador to Afghanistan -- testifies before the House that until a single, unified, friendly government is in place in Afghanistan, the trans-Afghani pipeline needed to monetize the oil will not be built. [Source: Testimony before the House International Relations Committee: http://www.house.gov/international_relations/105th/ap/wsap212982.htm]...

28

6. 1998 - The CIA ignores warnings from Case Officer Robert Baer that Saudi Arabia was harboring an Al Qaeda cell led by two known terrorists. A more detailed list of known terrorists is offered to Saudi intelligence in August 2001 and refused. [Source: Financial Times Jan. 21, 2001; "See No Evil" by Robert Baer (release date February 2002)]…

9. 1998 and 2000 - Former President George H.W. Bush travels to Saudi Arabia on behalf of the privately owned Carlyle Group, the 11th largest defense contractor in the U.S. While there he meets privately with the Saudi royal family and the bin Laden family. [Source: Wall Street Journal, Sept. 27, 2001. See also FTW, Vol. IV, No. 7 – "The Best Enemies Money Can Buy" http://www.fromthewilderness.com/free/ww3/carlyle.html]…

12. August 2000 -- Suspected Al Qaeda operatives wiretapped by Italian police made apparent references to plans for major attacks involving airports, airplanes and the United States according to transcripts obtained by the Los Angeles Times. The Times suggests that the information might not have been passed to U.S. authorities (hard to believe), but it did report that Italian authorities would not comment on the report. The Times also noted that "Italian and U.S. anti-terrorism experts cooperate closely." [Source: The Los Angeles Times, May 29, 2002]

13. Oct. 24-26, 2000 - Pentagon officials carry out a "detailed" emergency drill based upon the crashing of a hijacked airliner into the Pentagon. [Source: The Mirror, May 24, 2002]

14. January 2001 - The Bush Administration orders the FBI and intelligence agencies to "back off" investigations involving the bin Laden family, including two of Osama bin Laden's relatives (Abdullah and Omar) who were living in Falls Church, Va. -- right next to CIA headquarters. This followed previous orders dating back to 1996 that frustrated efforts to investigate the bin Laden family. [Source: BBC Newsnight, Correspondent Gregg Palast, Nov. 7, 2001]

15. Jan. 30, 2001 - Sept. 11 hijacker Ziad Jarrah was questioned in the United Arab Emirates (UAE). A number of UAE, Middle Eastern, European, and U.S. sources were cited in this CNN report, which said the CIA requested Jarrah be interrogated because he had been in Afghanistan and was suspected to have ties to terrorists. An unnamed CIA spokesman said the other sources' claims that the agency knew anything about Jarrah before Sept. 11 were "flatly untrue." Jarrah's Jan. 30 detainment at the airport in Dubai, UAE came six months after he took flying lessons in the U.S. Jarrah was released because "U.S. officials were

satisfied," said the report. [Source: CNN, Aug. 1, 2002
http://www.cnn.com/2002/US/08/01/cia.hijacker/index.html]...

19. June 2001 - German intelligence, the BND, warns the CIA and Israel that Middle Eastern terrorists are "planning to hijack commercial aircraft to use as weapons to attack important symbols of American and Israeli culture." [Source: Frankfurter Allgemeine Zeitung, Sept. 14, 2001; See http://www.fromthewilderness.com/free/ww3/f_a_zeitung_story.html]...

21. July 2001 - FBI agents in Arizona write a memorandum warning about suspicious activities involving a group of Middle Eastern men taking flight training lessons in Phoenix. The memorandum specifically mentions Osama bin Laden and warns of connections to terrorist activities [Source: The New York Times, May 14, 2002]...

25. summer 2001 - The online newswire online.ie reports on Sept. 14 that an Iranian man phones U.S. law enforcement to warn of an imminent attack on the WTC in the week of Sept. 9. German police confirm the calls but state that the U.S. Secret Service would not reveal any further information. [Source: http://www.online.ie/news/viewer.adp?article=1512332. http://www.fromthewilderness.com/free/ww3/online_ie_story.html]

26. summer 2001 - Jordanian intelligence, the GID, makes a communications intercept deemed so important that King Abdullah's men relay it to Washington, probably through the CIA station in Amman. To make doubly sure the message got through it was passed through an Arab intermediary to a German intelligence agent. The message: A major attack was planned inside the U.S., and aircraft would be used. The code name of the operation was "The Big Wedding." "When it became clear that the information was embarrassing to Bush Administration officials and congressmen who at first denied that there had been any such warnings before Sept. 11, senior Jordanian officials backed away from their earlier confirmations." This case was authenticated by ABC reporter John K. Cooley. [Source: International Herald Tribune (IHT), May 21, 2002]...

30. July 4-14, 2001 - Osama bin Laden receives treatment for kidney disease at the American hospital in Dubai and meets with a CIA official, who returns to CIA headquarters on July 15. [Source: Le Figaro, Oct. 31, 2001] http://www.fromthewilderness.com/free/ww3/Le Figaro_osama_dubai.html...

37. Aug. 11 or 12, 2001 , U.S. Navy Lt. Delmart "Mike" Vreeland, jailed in Toronto on U.S. fraud charges and claiming to be an officer with U.S. naval intelligence, writes details of the pending WTC attacks and seals them in an

30

envelope, which he gives to Canadian authorities. [Source: The Toronto Star, Oct. 23, 2001; Toronto Superior Court Records...

50. Sept. 6-7, 2001 - Put options (a speculation that the stock will go down) totaling 4,744 are purchased on United Air Lines stock, as opposed to only 396 call options (speculation that the stock will go up). This is a dramatic and abnormal increase in sales of put options. Many of the United puts are purchased through Deutschebank/A.B. Brown, a firm managed until 1998 by the current executive director of the CIA, A.B. "Buzzy" Krongard. [Source: The Herzliyya International Policy Institute for Counterterrorism (ICT), http://www.ict.org.il/, Sept. 21, 2001 (Note:The ICT article on possible terrorist insider trading appeared eight days *after* the 9/11 attacks.); The New York Times; The Wall Street Journal; The San Francisco Chronicle, Sept. 29, 2001]

51. Sept. 10, 2001 - Put options totaling 4,516 are purchased on American Airlines as compared to 748 call options. [Source: Herzliyya Institute - above]

52. Sept. 6-11, 2001 - No other airlines show any similar trading patterns to those experienced by United and American. The put option purchases on both airlines were 600 percent above normal. This at a time when Reuters (Sept. 10) issues a business report stating, "Airline stocks may be poised to take off."

53. Sept. 6-10, 2001 - Highly abnormal levels of put options are purchased in Merrill Lynch, Morgan Stanley, AXA Re(insurance) which owns 25 percent of American Airlines, and Munich Re. All of these companies are directly impacted by the Sept. 11 attacks. [Source: ICT, above; *FTW*, Oct. 18, 2001, http://www.fromthewilderness.com/free/ww3/oct152001.html]

54. 2001-2002 - It has been documented that the CIA, the Israeli Mossad, and many other intelligence agencies monitor stock trading in real time using highly advanced programs reported to be descended from Promis software. This is to alert national intelligence services of just such kinds of attacks...

59. Sept. 10, 2001 - San Francisco Mayor Willie Brown receives a call from what he described as "his security people at the airport" eight hours before the terrorist attacks "advising him that Americans should be cautious about their air travel," as reported by the San Francisco Chronicle. Brown was scheduled to fly to New York from San Francisco International Airport.

http://www.fromthewilderness.com/free/ww3/02_11_02_lucy.html

The outpouring of support allowed him to admit a desire he'd been suppressing, perhaps in the belief that it would jinx his chances of achieving asylum status: He wanted to come home.

Part 13: Amateur Shrink Gone Wild

If cities had the equivalent of national pastimes, New York's would be psychotherapy. While no match for Woody Allen, I've put in my share of time in therapists' offices and been grateful for what one or two of them had to offer; (the others ranged from indifferent to dishonest to insane themselves.) A well-known side-effect of such therapy is an eagerness to put one's newly acquired knowledge to use with, or on, friends, acquaintances and anyone else who asks.

Mike was fertile ground for this amateur "shrink*age*," as a friend who's an actual Clinical Psychologist pronounces it, with an ironic French accent. He was both beset by problems and unfamiliar with the M.O. of psychotherapy, which meant he did not consider the observations offered to be clichés. In addition, his loneliness rendered him more open to any lifeline that presented itself.

I responded lightly to his burundanga confession:

"2 hail maries. if you don't know the words, you're surrounded by people who do, albeit in spanish."

But when he wrote about watching with more than passing interest the TV program in which Socrates was forced to drink hemlock because he threw people's bullshit in their faces, my background in the psychotherapist's office went into high gear:

would you stop the fuck please thinking about fucking hemlock for fux sake? the reason you got into that mess is that you're leading a life of extremes; like a kid who was overly disciplined, reaches adolescence and goes fukkin berserk. you've been leading an overly disciplined daily life, beyond the monastic. at least monks have other monks to commune with. i'm told even the silent ones are acutely aware of each other and communicate with looks — like characters in a silent movie, i suppose. [Actually, silent monks find other ways to communicate: It is they who invented the tactile manual sign language which Annie Sullivan used to teach blind and deaf Helen Keller.]

your berserk adolescence was the night with the floozies or whatever they're called these days. (putana?)...

it must seem as though whatever pleasure you seek, you get punished for. there's also a whole self-punishment element to this...

Indeed. If he couldn't go out via a hero's death, next best was *la nostalgie de la boue*, yearning for the "mud," the urge to debase oneself. And what better way to do that than via women?

I pointed out the link between the two women at the bar who presumably drugged him (a South American doctor says that in order to avoid exposure themselves, women can transmit the drug by wearing patches or adding it to their nail polish) and the ex-employee who had filed a sexual harassment lawsuit against Mike, which she would later win.

I remembered when that ex-employee had first been hired. Mike was excited about the graduate with a Masters' Degree and a 3.9+ average who spent her weekends rock-climbing. She had it all! Within weeks, the twenty-five-year-old was given her own byline and was included in meetings among the most trusted staff members — those dedicated scribes who sometimes stayed at the office after hours.

It was during one such evening that Mike and his new employee kicked back, sharing personal stories which led to the employee's showing Mike a porn site. Mike thought it terrific.

When he relayed this drama on the phone as it unfolded (in large part to show me his enthusiasms lay elsewhere, lest I get any false ideas,) the phrase, "sexual harassment lawsuit" wafted through my mind. But he was in no mood to listen to such scolding so I held my peace. (Mike's and his former employee's clashing versions of these events have been a matter of public record for a number of years.)

When I brought up his former employee in the email to Venezuela, he responded:

I understood what you meant when you wondered about my stated attraction for [his former employee]. [I had not wondered anything; my memory of his phone-calls from that period remained intact.] *It was purely physical, but I think it was also a product of having loved women who abused me.* [He mentioned two.] *I wasn not attracted to her intellectually* [Yes he was, but no one, at least, no guy, is going to condemn him for taking this tack] *and certainly not emotionally. It was like Dracula's victims were usually drawn to him. I was a moth fighting a light intent on destroying it (and others) and resisting my own attraction at the same time.*

Got it?
Smooch

Part 14: Spinning Out of Control

After leaving the US in rage, sealing the deal by writing his Burning Bridge article, Mike was forced to face the possibility that he'd made a mistake. Owning up to mistakes was not new to him. AA had taught him that to do so was honorable so he apologized more frequently and fully than most people, whether for an editorial inaccuracy or an explosion of temper.

But Venezuela was different. He couldn't just slink back home with his tail between his legs, as anyone else might who was doing so out of public view. He needed a "valid" reason that his followers would accept. (Actually, it was none of their business and being aware of that, they would have accepted anything. It was his enemies who needed to be neutralized. The prospect of their gleeful taunts in cyberspace was unacceptable.)

One of his enormous gifts, which should not be underestimated, much less belittled, was for PR. Presidential candidate Ross Perot knew what he was doing when he hired Mike to manage his press campaign in LA. Mike had an innate sense of how to spin a story; not lie, but simply present it as vividly as possible so the audience would be captivated. This was the charisma factor and it's a large part of how he got as far as he did. It wasn't just what he was saying (others may have borne the same message) but how he was saying it: Cutting to the heart of the issue; encompassing the length of world history and the breadth of world geography to reveal the contours of the big picture. This is a vital ability if the average person is to understand your message. A little P.T. Barnum helps the medicine go down.

So when he complained of illness in Venezuela, I sensed this was to be the platform of his "Mike Ruppert Returns" campaign. But it wouldn't be simple. For Mike was like one of those people who don't allow themselves a vacation unless they're truly incapacitated. Somehow they get into real accidents or have genuine breakdowns, which allow them some respite. (A friend of a friend said in wonderment, when she received a diagnosis of cancer, "I did this so I wouldn't have to move to Baltimore.")

Thus, as usual, Mike was playing with fire — his health — driving himself to death's door so he could leave Venezuela honorably.

From Jenna to Mike undated:

...your foremost moral decision is to survive. aristotle said the prerequisite to the good life is just life period ... the excellent is the enemy of the good... on airplanes they tell mothers to put the oxygen mask over your own mouth before you put one over your baby's. if your best (or even equal) shot at survival were the u.s., (i wish) and if someone made fun of you for it, fuck em. HAPPINESS PROMOTES LONG LIFE.

From Jenna to Mike undated:

there's a bi-polar aspect to recent events, from chavez' potential new best friend to writer-in-self-imposed-strait-jacket-living-out-his-retirement-in-obscurity, a living-on-the-edge, 'the world loves me; it loves me not' aspect that's got to be wearing on the nerves. do you pace yourself? maybe that's what you're starting to do but i'm skeptical. it sounds more like balancing being on top of the world with being in the pits.... must it be the gold ring or nothing?

But there was still another complication: Evidence from his test results that he was being poisoned.

[Note that the typos in the following emails are partly a result of his growing cataract.)

October 25, 2006 From Mike to colleagues:

Thanks to a referral from an well respected activist who served with Allende I got to a Cuban clinic today. What an amazing difference from US medicine. I was treated like a... human being. All tests done in one day but more are needed. I will be filming a testimonial for Cuban film makers tomorrow... gladly. My friend Carlos and xxxx traded off babysitting for me all day. The kindness of the Cubans was just amazing. "You're a human being? You're sick?... Let us help. Preliminary results: Kindney stones in both kidneys. Not ready to pass yet.Heavy calcification of an enlarged prostate gland.Low blood pressure and hypoglycemia. (That´s right). I almost collapsed walking back from the clinic to the doc´s office. Heavy blood toxicity from known and unknown sources. There´s a lot of toxic backup from the calcification that may have affected a lot of things throughout my body.Elavated cholesterol and triglicerides. I will be referred to a urologist tomorrow for discussion about how to treat the stones. (Please God, I have already had third degree burns and peritonitis. Can I miss passing kidney stones?) We still have to do a chest X Ray. All treatment and prescriptions will be free of charge and an appointment for the worsening cataract. This is medcicine as it should have always been. I start a massive cleansing and detox program with prescriptions and natural remedies. No cost. I may be almost extinct in the US but I guess I am about to be famous in Cuba. Go figure. The doc said, you have not been well for a while. We can see this. Am saving all the paerwork for the day whenI write a story about it. Hopefully on FTW...

October 27, 2006 From Mike to colleagues:

I am writing these detailed updates because I want an historical record, just in case.

Today didn´t go that well. Carlos took me to Bolivarian Univeristy for a chest x-ray. On the supercrowded morning subway my camera was stolen out of my backpack. I´ll live.

After a not too long walk, maybe 3/4 mile to the clinic I nearly collapsed again. Walked thru the doors sweating like a stuck pig and it wasn´t that hot. The docs gave me 2 liters of dextrose IV for very low blood pressure (90/65) and put me on oxygen. They wouldn´t let me move for two hours. That threw everything else off. The chest X´-Ray showed some damage from smoking (I have had little else to do here) and I have agreed to taper off and quit. the Cuban doc says not to go cold turkey.

Carlos Ruiz, my roomi and great angel is photographing my visits to clinics and some of the great Cuban medicos.

There´s also something else wrong with my blood and they want more tests on Monday. There´s some kind of chemical thing they cannot identify. Only Ray Kohlman will remember the infamous ¨chemical toxicity of unknown etiology¨ from the Al Carone case. Too soon to tell. -- Search for that phrase onthe web site if interested. [A well-informed friend] has confirmed my burundanga experience and given me some much needed grounding there.

I have a writing assignment for a prestigious local magazine.

I will spend the weekend working on that, several things for FTW and resting.

Mike's autobiography states: "I was poisoned twice. Once with a native drug called burundanga, the root drug of scopolamine and also – according to an intelligence source – with a form of methyl mercury, which was causing all of my glandular and lymph systems to shut down."[6]

---

[6] http://www.collapsenet.com/free-resources/collapsenet-public-access/item/681-michael-c-ruppert-autobiography

Part 15: This Isn't Working

As so often happens with people who live dramatically as Mike did, his initial enthusiasm for the Cuban-style medical system of Venezuela quickly gave way to a realization of its limitations:

From Mike, undated:

Major difficulties with doctors today. No urologist available until january. we'll talk tonight. It feels like all is closing in.

c. October 30, 2006 From Mike to colleagues:

Aside from other symptoms I have paresthesia or tingling which is not good. [A friend in the US] hit some nails for me.

We're closing in on a diagnosis of adult onset diabetes but there are some other complications that [his friend in the US] called a cascading effect. I went back to the Cuban clinic at 10 AM. Just got home before 3 PM after nothing but waiting and travelling. Was sent to another clinic some distance and told to make an appointment with a urologist. After waiting till 2 I was told no urologist until January.

I'll go back to the Cuban doctor tomorrow and ask for help on blood sugar and pressure. The language difficulties are very tough as i don't speak enough Spanish yet to be able to answer med history or symptom questions or to understand most directions. X, my friend here in Vz has been going with me but today i cut off going back to urologist or pursuing that because it's just eating up too many lives and I sure feel like I've done enough of that lately.

The diabetic symptoms (blood sugar crashes, low bp), are known causals of major mood swings and they were appearing even b4 I left Ashland.

I will be a non-smoker by the end of the week. Tapering off at direction of Cuban doc. Eliminating all refined sugar and most fruit. Going heavy veg. Anybody who knows me will understand that I must be sick to be doing that. Still very weak.

VENEZUELA

One of the new contacts here has really opened some doors. People at ministries of culture and education are talking about translating and publishing Rubicon through the Vz gov't . The gov't would give me 10%. New Society would be free to sue Chavez if they wanted. But this is Vz and things move slow.

The package from Ken arrived today and i might be able to meet the Minsiter of Culture as soon as this weekend.

As for FTW, I just wish they could get the subscriber section fixed again. I realize how difficult it is for all.

Am working on my Gauntlet story. Just passed 3,000 words but can't push too hard. This one has to be right.

End

From Mike undated:

I am very sick. We don't yet know the full causes. My blood pressure suddenly drops very low along with my blood sugar. My urine is extremely cloudy and smelly with calcium. Kidney stones have formed. My urinary tract is calcified and the prostate is enlarged and calcified. I have nearly collapsed several times and am very weak. Onset of adult diabetes is likely but there are other things we can't explain. Poisoning has not been ruled out.

I sent Mike some Google links concerning these symptoms and possible diagnoses.

October 30, 2006 From Mike to Jenna:

I have all of these symptoms. I did not know the information about the seizures but that meshes perfectly. Have had four since January.

The Cuban doctor is not first rate, except in attitude. It's going to make people think she's prescribing meds. etc. when she is not. That's going to make people think she has given me dietary instructions when she has not. I am not getting any care at all right now. She's a Gen Practitioner at an overcrowded clinic full of poor people. I am not getting first-rate care. I got basic tests and first aid, that's it. [His

41

friend in the US] has been a better doctor thus far. The Cuban doc hasn´t even mentioned diabetes when we all have seen that it´s obvious even if it doesn´t explain everything.

I am very weak.

Part 16: Honeypot(?)

Meanwhile up north, FTW was wandering in the wilderness. Mike's account of the unraveling of the company may be found in *By the Light of a Burning Bridge.* A key figure is an unnamed "female employee." In the article, he presents a scenario in which he played along with her sexual provocations in order to make her "show her hand." We won't stoop to any glib jokes about what else he might have wanted her to show. He claimed to have been secretly taping her all the while. Later, he would say that the tape was destroyed in the burglary.

When he got to New York and talked about the case, he told me that there had, in fact, been no tape. I don't know if he also revealed this to other people. If the case was still on his mind, he might have, because he needed, as we all do, to be free, natural and honest with the people close to him.

The "missing tape" meme, he believed, would help him win the lawsuit for sexual harassment which the female employee brought against him. Why this case meant so much is a matter for conjecture, which is an otiose waste of time. For the case was marred from the get-go by her own "unclean hands," as legal lingo has it. She was no pure, young thing who was traumatized by Mike's antics, however "inappropriate" for an office setting. If this was not, technically, an example of entrapment — since Mike was so easily drawn in — it certainly was entrapment in some more ideal forum in a more just world.

She did show him porn sites, as he was quick to report in his phone-call afterwards. On the other hand, he responded with the enthusiasm of the protagonist in *The Devil and Daniel Webster.* Then he appeared in the doorway of her office in his underwear. (When he showed me and his lawyer, Ray Kohlman, his stance — in profile — and added, "No erection," we decided it would be best to leave out that detail, if possible.)

All this was more recklessness to the point of self-destructiveness on his part, given the context of a boss/employee relationship. But the female employee, whether honeypot or not, had given him good reason to believe she wouldn't mind.

In my experience, Mike respected lack of interest on the part of a woman. (Of course, I wasn't twenty-five.) Once or twice when I was at the computer and he was getting undressed for a shower, he appeared in the doorway naked, with his fists clenched at his sides like a wrestler striking a tough pose. This was during a period when he was recovering from his depression. Probably he'd been looking at himself in the mirror and thinking, "Not bad!" His naked posturing wasn't an invitation; psychologically at least, it revealed nothing beyond the wish to be admired. But there's no question that if the female employee had been willing, she would have had one happy employer.

After Mike got his inheritance following the death of his stepmother — approximately $200,000— and paid the FTW staff and everyone else whom he or FTW owed, (as well as sending $1000 to an activist in need, remarking, "It felt so good to do that,") he spent $35,000 fighting the sexual harassment lawsuit. It was a matter of honor which is odd, because the sort of behavior he'd been accused of was the sort he continued to engage in without guilt, since it was not uncommon for men of his generation and upbringing. Though there's no question that he went too far in his response to the female employee's overtures, it's absurd to think his honor is deeply affected by this case; it's a farce.

This account will probably offend some people who are of the, "Don't speak ill of the dead, and particularly, of Mike," school of thought. While it's true that historians bear a special burden because history is written by the winners, or at least, the survivors, in Mike's case, it's especially important to tell the whole truth, to the extent that one knows it. First of all, if we don't do it, the enemy will. To relay this story in context, as is the intent here, can serve as an inoculation against the sort of outlandish accusations which have been leveled against Mike in the past. This is a flesh and blood, warts-and-all portrait written in the belief that in the end, Mike and his transcendent work and critically important ideas will prevail. He lost the lawsuit and everyone finally forgot about it.

Part 17: Fallout

Back at FTW, another fire erupted: Readers were placing product orders that could never, under the current administration, be filled. When Mike learned of the situation, he emailed those in charge that it could constitute fraud; they were to return whatever money had come in and freeze the sales portion of the site immediately. (If I remember correctly, the same problem later arose with respect to subscription renewals.)

A trusted friend and colleague offered to buy the site. Mike thought this might prove to be a way out of what was devolving into an unworkable arrangement:

First of all let me say that it has become apparent to me that the chief obstacle to a way out of the current predicament, is me. I apologize to all for my outburst yesterday and B.'s depiction of me as an angry Panda was pretty appropriate although the bear looks better than I do. As a result of Carolyn Baker's message to me yesterday, a couple of things have become clear. Once I accepted these facts a way out began to appear. I emphasize that I think there's a way to get everyone paid, close up FTW and do so without leaving a mountain of debt and resentment. We might actuall make some money.

TWO REALIZATIONS THAT MADE IT ALL CLEAR

1. After nearly 30 years of fighting these intense fights I no longer have then energy, or the will, to continue to do what I have done. I have never doubted my judgement until yesterday. After 30 years I am burned out. Very soon, I will announce my permanent retirement from political and economic journalism. That opens all the necessary doors to the successful and equitable dissolution of FTW.

2. [A friend/colleague] has sent some profound messages to me lately. I thank her for both her personal counsel and business smarts. But it is clear that she sees the same very real assets that I do. These assets have serious value and they can be sold in a proper way to pay off all of FTW's debts (including credit cards) and get all employees all back-owed monies. As always I will wait at the end of the line.

The basic plan is to turn as much over to [the friend/colleague] as possible, as she wants to structure it.

ASSETS

1. EMAIL SUBSCRIBER LIST " *This list CAN be sold to a consortium headed by [the friend/colleague] because all of our subscribers love her any way.That would never be viewed as a ale to a list company of the government. [The friend/colleague] would keep it as secure as I have. The way to do this is to make a public announcement of FTW's closure and liquidation with an announcement of that sale and by giving subscribers 30 days to request that their information be removed from that list. Very few will ask for it. That alone is worth at least $50,000 but I will leave valuations to [the friend/colleague] since she does that better than anybody.*

2. The FTW ARCHIVES are also worth a lot of money. All of those could be purchased and I would relinquish copyright ownership of them to a group headed by [the friend/colleague] to satisfy debts.

3. The copyrights to all FTW DVD´s also have great value. They go into the package.

4. All of my FTW computer research files, 9 years worth, would go to [the friend/colleague]. There are more than 800 (est.) separate files here divided between Research and FTW business. The FTW bBsiness file are not accounting files but rather files on all pesons, corporations, media outlets and entities with which FTW has had inerraction or correspondence. these range from Alex Jones, to ASPO, to the Pentagon, to AIG, to hundreds of major and minor figures throughout our little universe, both good and bad. These also include the files on all previous emploees, writers, researchers and lecturers we have encountered. There are more than 400 research files loosely divided between pre 9/11 and post 9/11. There are more than 150 files on people alone. I am, after all, German. All of these files are a great intelligence and analytical research base and I know that [the friend/colleague] would use them to their fullest extent possible. Carolyn has copies and she can attest to what's in them.

5. *Carolyn Baker and Mike Kane would be free to write for the new entity that would preserve a substantial portion of FTW's legacy and make it useful to all of those who want and need t keep it alive. [The friend/colleague] might not be able to pay them as well as FTW did, but I know she will honor and treasure them as I have. Maybe even Stan Goff could get in later. We will all miss Jamey.*

POWER OF ATTORNEY

I had already begun to have a new Power of Attorney drafted giving NY attorney, international lawyer and longtime close friend Ray Kohlman, full authority. It is apparent that Ken's many other obligations will keep him from participating in this in a meaignful way but that does not spell the end of the world. This should actually relieve Joe. The rest of this message might want to make him at least ensure a smoother transition.

DEBTS

Under this plan I would be out of all future decision making over these these assets. I have no idea what our current debt status is because I've seen no financial statements and recieved no reports in three months. However, I would estimate that our total debt (including all back salaries, wages Ken's royalties, Joe's ees and credit cards), could not posibly exceed $70,000. The lease is a separate issue but I think it can be negotiated and settled.

Clearly, and I pray that [the friend/colleague] will agree, we have a lot more value in assets than debts. Now the question is how to keep the office running long enough to pull it all together. MARION, what would really help me, [the friend/colleague], and Ray Kohlman enormously is an itemized statement of debts including credit cards that I used to finance FTW over the years. If I am going to walk away losing most of my equity then I need to walk away debt free.

I am specifically authorizing MARION to give the friend/colleague anything shes asks for, hopefully understanding that [the friend/colleague] is someone who can help.

I want to stress that should it become necessary for me to temporarily return to the states to execute all of this I will do so, regardless of the risk, but only after I have formally announced my retirement from public life. I cannot and will not leave all of you hanging in the lurch. I only wish that I had known how far things had gone south long ago. It was not until yesterday that someone finally told me that Marion was not even getting paid. We cannot undo the lack of information sharing until now, nor should we take time to condemn it. We must deal with things as they are today.

IMMEDIATE

From my limited knowledge of the financial situation my undestanding is that $5,000 would see us through the immediate crisis. With one single essay I can raise more than twice that amount easily provided that it goes up on the web site and the blog.

What I need to know from [the friend/colleague] ASAP (before I write it) is whether she sees merit in these ideas and has any suggestions, directions or other requests. [The friend/colleague] can structure this transition with ease because that is exactly what she does. I would also need to know from Ray Kohlman whether he sees any impediments.

All I need is a basic yes from both [the friend/colleague] and Ray and we´re on the way. Had I fully known and understood the true situation sooner it wouldn´t have gotten this far. But I want to emphasize that this is far from over and no one´s going to get financially screwed if I can help it. I founded and ran the company for almost nine years, taking it to peak earnings of just under $600,000 a year, and overcoming a multitude of obstacles other businesses never face. I have learned a thing or two and I am here now to use that experience.

But, personally as a journalist and earth shaker, I am burned out beyond belief. The smashing of our computers took something out of me that will never come back. Things are looking up here in Venezuela with the government but it is starting to look like they want to create a Mike Ruppert here doing the same thing he has done for 30 years already, with the same energy, and even more dangerous risks. I think I need to give myself a choice here and I am. I have done enough for one lifetime.

So, I ask everyone to please accept my amends. I accept responsibility for leaving FTW the way I did, even though, on a hundred levels, it was absolutely necessary to leave when I did. Please accept my apologies for any personal insults made in retaliation. One of my favrite books contains a passage about self-will and the observation that sometimes we can become producers of confusion, rather than harmony. Mea culpa.

FTW is me, was me. As I went into the confusion, soul-searching and change that marks all spiritual and personal evolutions it was obvious that FTW would have to mirror that confusion. The remainder of my amends will be amends of action rather than words. Please bear with me on a couple of things. I have a prgressively worsening cataract in my left eye that is impairing my vision and I have another unknown medial condtion that I don´t want to discuss via email. There is no free health care here for people who don´t have official status and that may take as long as year for me. As you all know, I am almost out of money but we all will make it. I´m quite sure of that now that I have some calrity.

Please do whatever is necessary to protect my personal library, my research files, whatever remains of my photographs nd the Ruppert Family Trust.

I will await your feedback and suggestions from anyone in the top addressee line. Mike

October 18, 2006 From Jenna to Mike:

ok your nobility is scaring me a little. also the fucking unknown medical condition you don't want to discuss in email. before i make an asshole of myself commenting on what the vz gvt might want, i need more info. but it looks as though you're considering returning to the u.s. permanently, with the proviso you not write anymore???

... we need to talk, in a RELAXED way. what do those calls cost? is that the problem? or that you don't want to be trackable? i am so fucking clueless. i don't need answers to the logistical stuff but your email, well thought out as it is, has an 'in sound mind' quality that makes me think you might be in danger of throwing out the baby with the bath water...

From personal experience years before, I'd concluded that suicidal ideation could result from the wish to extinguish one part of oneself that was causing distress. But not knowing how to do that, one contemplated doing away with the whole.

...got to go see a [young] woman in a wheelchair and oxygen mask who's one month away from getting evicted...

49

This was a patient with a crippling case of chemical sensitivity who'd been in a film by Alison Johnson in which I also spoke, regarding the enviro-disaster of 9/11.

...talk to u, email or otherwise, soon.

October 18, 2006 From Mike to Jenna:

Medical problem is cloudy urine coupled with chronic fatigue.
I'm not sure I want to return to the US permanently. What contacts do we have in New Zealand?
Will try to call u later.
The Venezuelan thing is just for me to be Mike Ruppert. To lecture, give speeches, write, become public for the revolution. That's both dangerous and exhausting when battling inherent Vz suspicious natures and the language barrier. I would be a sitting duck here for covert ops.

October 18, 2006 From Jenna to Mike:

...the [young] woman i just got back from seeing has been diagnosed with, among other things, 'hydrocarbon poisoning.'
your email disposing of ftw's assets must have taken a lot out of you. it had the ring of those post-burglary 'i'm throwing in the towel' articles...

October 19, 2006 From Mike to colleagues:

Apparently, the FTW stalwarts are refusing to let me retire and pull the plug. I am in control of nothing it seems. If you want to know what's happening with me and FTW, wait five minutes.

Part 18: Decision

Looking back, one purpose the Venezuela interlude served in Mike's life was that of expiation. Any potential friendship threatened with the most guileless of questions, "What brings you here?" He couldn't answer truthfully, that he was seeking political asylum (which on the phone, we referred to as "the 'a' word.") When the reporter from the US newspaper interviewed him for seven hours, Mike acknowledged only that he was requesting permanent residency. Thus he was forced into solitary confinement with its attendant pastime, contemplating the sins that had brought him to this point.

September 26, 2006 From Mike to numerous recipients:

I have had much time to think about those horrible events and what I feel so utterly ashamed over is the fact that I was so terribly attracted to a very sick woman whose intent I clearly saw and understood was to destroy both me and FTW. I never crossed any lines through my actions, but I certainly did in my head and this is my great shame and embarrassment to which I now freely admit.

But, as a wise man once said, "They don't put you in jail for thinking crazy. They put you in jail for acting crazy".

c. September 27, 2006 From Jenna to Mike:

if you feel like shit promise you'll email first before even thinking in terms of 'my public life may be over.' [a phrase he'd used in his email.] this is why god invented the internet.

September 27, 2006 From Mike to Jenna:

It is clear to me that the memo [the fake email] *originated from within the FTW offices. we have at minimum a leak there and at worst a traitor. I'm just sick of betrayals.*

To be honest I was talking about life, life. not public life. [I had realized that but wanted to steer Mike's thinking away from it.] *That's how depressing things are. I am beginning to suspect that I may be too hot a political potato for Hc*

51

right now and they're just hoping I'll tire and go away. That would be a humiliation. The Bolivarian revolution embodies every belief I have acquired for all my years of study.

God bless [a woman who was helping him in Venezuela,] I truly believe she's doing everything she can and she is one of those wonderful women, like you, Carolyn, Fitts and McKinney who have saved my life.

One day he called, his breathing labored, and said, "I've got to get out of here. I've got to write a notice for the blog and the website asking for emergency donations for Mike Ruppert to leave Venezuela, and to solicit offers from other countries."

Offers flooded in from England, Canada, Italy, South Africa, Thailand, Hawaii, Australia, the Philippines... all variations on that of "quarquin" who wrote... "*hi Mike you can come here to Spain i have place for you You are welcome.*"

Along with them, health advice, mostly from holistic practitioners or patients. Many readers took pains to write at length and in detail, as per the notice's request for information on health systems in the countries where they were offering their hospitality.

One person wrote about a cottage on their property where Mike could hole up; another, about her extended family who lived down the road.

A writer from Hawaii described a tent city whose inhabitants were fugitives from justice living simply off the land, undisturbed by the authorities.

Mike held out hopes for Germany. The culture wasn't so alien; it was his family heritage. (And although he was a California boy, his deteriorating health in the Venezuelan heat had perhaps induced a longing for cloud-cover.) Andreas von Buelow, the former German cabinet minister who had written a blurb for *Crossing the Rubicon*, had once taken him to a concert of Janacek and Dvorak which had made Mike cry.

"That's not German culture; it's Czech," I thought obnoxiously but had the sense not to say. He wrote to von Buelow whose delayed response, due to travel, was polite but understandably cautious.

A correspondent from Costa Rica piqued Mike's interest with a description of the colony of intellectuals there working on alternative energy. But an article in a local paper described the boredom of the ex-patriots, who found a life of playing golf unfulfilling, despite the idyllic surroundings.

"I'd be a pet," Mike said, "and I don't want to be a pet."

"No. You want to be among peers."

However, another lesson Mike had learned in Venezuela was that dabbling in a foreign culture may be fine for a holiday but in the end, one wants to be surrounded by familiar people who speak one's own language.

Most people know this intuitively but Mike had been banking on a warmer welcome in Venezuela, which would have compensated for all the differences. Failing that, he'd rather nurse his unhappiness at home.

I don't remember how the possibility arose of his coming to stay with me. Much as I valued the connection to him as well as the conversations, having him live with me was another matter. I'd been divorced for ten years, relishing every moment of freedom. Being in his inner circle was all I wanted; the adage, "Familiarity breeds contempt" seemed all too apt. And he was the last person from whom I wished to earn that contempt.

But I was a known quantity, which mattered to him. He knew I wouldn't treat him as a guru and ply him with questions.

Another known quantity was Barry Silverthorn, the producer of *End of Suburbia*, who lived in Toronto.

Although Mike was (and remained for the rest of his life) too much of a gentleman to say so, at a level beyond his control, he must have felt disappointed, even betrayed by Venezuela.

c. October 30, 2006 From Jenna to Mike:

beneath your admiration for chavez and the bolivarian revolution, your unconscious could be having this conversation with venezuela: "don't you understand i'm your friend? i could help you; i've been fighting drugs in the u.s. all my life and gotten persecuted for it. now i escape here and the first night i venture out on my own, you drug me."

i don't know why you need to tempt fate. maybe you want something awful to happen so you won't have to fear it anymore. maybe it's your way of punishing yourself for something 'even worse' (according to your child-self) that you don't remember and don't want to, hence all the running.

you are not lot's wife or eurydice. you can come home again if you want to, at least while the planes or even the trains are still running. you need to accept the entirety of yourself and live in equilibrium so you're not buffeted from one extreme to the other. don't wait for your body to wrestle you to the ground. acknowledge its needs the way you did when you went to macdonald's today, by walking slowly.

talk to u tomorrow

October 30, 2006 From Mike to Jenna:

God, you know me so well.
I really want to come home and just rest but it seems so impossible. No money. Homeland Security. No place to live if I got there, not even a bed. Here, Carlos and xxxx are banking on getting me going with lectures and writing. I can't tell them these feelings.

Meanwhile, a plan was taking shape.

Mike Ruppert Subject: My AA Sponsor and Ray KohlmanSent: 19 Oct '06 21:32"stgeorge119@gmail.com

is XXXX. He lives in XXXX not far from XXX. His wife, XXX, is talking to some folks about trying to get me home. I think both of you should talk to them and coordinate. Their number is XXX-XXX-XXXX

> On the issue of how I re-enter, I strongly suggest that we all defer to Ray Kohlman. I cannot walk accross the border lugging a huge suitcase, an overflowing backpack and a laptop case without getting searched. I know those rules. My passport will get swiped and the net result would the same as if I had landed at LAX on an American Airlines flight only I

would be at the border and close to nobody, with no chance of help anywhere around. We will do what Ray says and nothing else on that point. I have to insist on that. On legal matters we MUST listen to Ray. The bridge is still calling. I say that not to threaten or pressure. I share it just to get it out of my head. I have had two close suicides and the breakup of an engagement in less than three years. Only now am I coming to grips with all of that and much more. I am relieved that you guys are taking the intiative. That makes me feel as if someone actually saw all of the emergency flares I have been sending up. Mike

But a powerful faction didn't want Mike to return.

Part 19: Suspicion

Several colleagues in Ashland had become increasingly annoyed by the latest developments at FTW. They felt that writing the Burning Bridge article was in itself an act of burning the bridge home; if Mike came back, particularly so soon, FTW's credibility would be trashed.

Now that he'd relinquished his role as CEO, Mike could best serve the website, they maintained, by acting as its Latin American correspondent.

Among their complaints was the appearance of alleged "compelling evidence" that Mike himself had been the one to wield the sledgehammer on the seven FTW computers, the act of burglary which had precipitated his flight to Venezuela.

Mike was accused — not by law enforcement, nor by any government agency but by some of his own colleagues — of staging the burglary himself, then high-tailing it several thousand miles south, taking the insurance money with him the day before he was to have a lie detector test with the Ashland Police Department.

October 20, 2006 From Mike to colleagues:

On my life and on my soul, I swear that I did not smash my own computers.
On my life and on my soul I swear that not a penny of the insurance money ever entered my pocket. I left with $2,100 and my gold. [Carolyn] and Mike Kane saw it in the silver box from which I took my Great Grandfather's pocket watch for Mike. The cash came from one subscriber who saw what was coming and told me to use it personally, for anything I needed. I told you that.

Would I have been stupid enough to commit such an elaborate fraud for just $2,000? The only insurance check I ever saw for $7,000 went straight into the company account to pay bills.

On my life and on my soul there was no appointment for any polygraph test in Ashland. That's absurd. I was asked if I was willing to take one within a week after the burglary. I said sure. For three weeks I never heard another word. I would not have left with that appointment hanging knowing that it would instantly condemn me for failing to appear. I had/ have nothing to fear from a legitimate polygraph test. Why do we learn of this now? Where is the record of the appointment? Who found it?

As it is I have been tried, convicted and sentenced without having been given the right to examine or challenge the evidence against me. That is a fundamental human right. George Bush signs a bill and everyone starts acting like a fascist. This so-called evidence surfaces four months after the burglary and three months after I leave the states. Does anyone think that I would be stupid enough to leave such evidence if it existed?

Mohammed Atta's passport has just been found in the wreckage of the World Trade Center. Case closed. Ruppert is guilty. No trial needed thankyou.

Where did this evidence come from? Who found it? What is it? Who told you about it?Answers to these questions are my fundamental rights as a human being.

If the evidence was strong enough to convince [he named three colleagues,] then I now know that this entire thing was very well orchestrated and executed.

If I hear nothing from anyone within ten days then you guys can assume that – not knowing who I can trust -- I have gone to a new level of operation. Suicide is out now. [XX] you make me want to come back more than ever to clear my name. Someone does not want me to come back and they are obviously very afraid that I might. Who?Why? Who benefits?

We'll see.

Ray, we need to talk ASAP please.

At this point, the ante was upped: Apparently, further evidence had been unearthed to show that Mike himself had written the "phantom" or fraudulent email to subscribers.

October 20, 2006 From Mike to colleagues:

I am innocent on all counts. I have been shown none of the so-called evidence or afforded an opportunity to comment on it. At least in a US court I might receive a little mopre justice than I am receiving here and now.

From Mike to colleagues, undated:

Who in the hell believes that I could have possibly sent that email message? Has everyone lost their minds?

From Mike to colleagues, undated:

I again request that this "evidence" be shown to me, or at least described. What is it? Where was it found? Who found it?

The new allegation that I sent the bogus email is beyond ludicrous. Everyone who works with me knows that I absolutely lack the technical know-how to do that. I have never directly posted to our list even once, from the FTW offices. That's why I paid IT people $900 a week.

This is like Kafka, you talk of evidence and then produce none. Then you ask me to defend myself against somethng unspecified and undescribed. How can I prove evidence to be false if I am not even told what it is? When is my day in the FTW court? How can I disporve something that isn't on the table.

If it is evdience I can't possibly tamper with it from here. Wrap it up, take it to Ashland PD and then tell me what it is.

I repeat, I am innocent of all of these charges. I have admitted to my mistakes but that's all there were. On every one of these allegations I am completely and utterly innocent. You have become sadly like Joe McCarthy with his list of known Communists. When do we get to see this list?

Part 20: Snafu

October 20, 2006 From Jenna to Mike:

...be careful of email trails. a few days ago a sequence got forwarded to X in one email of which u said he was 'full of excuses...'
[And, since Mike was no longer sure whom he could trust among the FTW staff]...remember that it's possible to set up a blog in the name of mike ruppert2 any time for free.

October 22, 2006 From Jenna to Mike:

after the conference call, it occurred to me that even if [the webmaster] were fired, xxx could replace him with, say, her best friend's niece and you'd have the same problem of sabotage again. so the underlying issue is control of the webmaster...
your [political] arguments speak for themselves. where you live is your fucking business. ftw's credibility is based on the innate truth of ftw's work.
i understand that it would be hard to explain coming back after the burning bridge article. but so what? you've learned things. there were factors you hadn't known about. these are complexities that readers would understand. your enemies would jump for joy in their netherworld; that is what they do for a living. but allowing that to guide one's behavior is truly 'letting the terrorists win...'
i'd like to talk to your unconscious for a moment. i'm concerned that your unconscious could think, 'if i come home after having written the burning bridge article, my fans will be disappointed. but maybe that would turn into sympathy if i came home because i was sick and couldn't get healthcare otherwise. even X would relent and give me money for a ticket.' then you might allow some sickness to get the better of you...
please be on guard against this. you're vigilant against exterior enemies. but they have a mole in you whom you have to watch out for too.

October 25, 2006 From Mike to colleagues:

My US cell phone was shut off today, I guess the hopeful message from X yesterday did not impact what was really a fait accompli.

These are tough questions. I can only offer my two cents and suggest my priorities.

1. I would like to get a new power executed to Ray ASAP. Ken, you shouldn't be troubled. How do i do that without going to US embassy.

2. Ray, in Ashland is a box with all of the Ruppert Family trust documents and records. That's worth $300,000 to me-us. >From that I can pay you, Ken, and eventually the creditors. My stepmother may already be dead. I don't know. But if we don't have that box and the original trust docs we have nothing. This needs to get accomplished fairly quickly.

3. We still have asstes. Ken has the mailing list and the archives are worth a lot. I will keep the copyrights to DVDs.

Beyond this I am helpless to advise and can only rely on you two.

Going to the doctor now.

FTW was now insolvent, with 200-250 orders unfilled and no credit left with Fedex or UPS. Staff were working for no pay, some with thousands of dollars owed. If the website was taken down, the newspaper article would no doubt be scrapped.

October 25, 2006 From Mike to colleagues:

How do you evaluate archives etc. I should retain copyrights for DVDs in case of future miracles. There are lots of intangible assets and valuation but I don't think the mailing list should be put up as equity due to privacy concerns. That's the biggest asset of all though. X in the Ashland office knows exactly where the box with the Trust docs is and can put her hands on it almost instantly. What we don't know for sure where the ORIGINAL trust docs are. Y sent something to the Portland firm. Don't know what or if it has come back. You already have the name and contact info. The key is that my stepmotrher may have died a months ago. As soon as she dies, it's split 50/50 and there's nothing her family can do about it. She's past 90 and nuttier than a fruitcake. Her family wouldn't dare put her on the stand now with her Alzheimer's. The trust was always a 50/50 split between me and her heirs... Medical report to come soon.

October 27, 2006

Ray Kohlman wrote that as of the previous day 1445 east coast time, the Ashland police had no interest in Mike, except as a victim of B&E. [breaking and entering.] They had no idea when or where rumors of "person of interest" began.

October 27, 2006 From Mike to Ray Kohlman:

God, thank you Ray!!!!!!!!!
Now where did all this bs originate.

Meanwhile, Michael Kane, for personal reasons, announced his resignation as Energy Editor.

October 27, 2006 From Mike:

I think we have to let FTW die. Mike

On the phone he added mournfully, "I'd only been keeping it alive for him, because he loved it so much."

October 29, 2006 From Jenna to Mike:

[a propos of something else which I no longer remember] I can't help thinking that at some level you do what you do for copy...

October 30, 2006 From Mike to Ray and Jenna:

CONFIDENTIAL

Ray, I've cc'd Jenna becasue she's my only real sigificant other, aside from you. Stop laughing.

(Jenna, you may share with Mike Kane if you wish)

Details you need to know.

I am very sick. In my heart of hearts I just want to come home and stay out of public sight but would have no place to sleep if I did. There may be some breaks in Vz soon, but there have been a lot of maybes lately.

As for FTW, it's so fucked up I can't describe it. X cannot sign checks because there's a new bank account that Y walked out on. She's sent paperwork to Z in LA and is waiting for its return so she can even write a check. She cannot ship product until she has those. She cannot ship you the Trust docs because she apparently can't access any money. Catch 2222.

X's cell phone number is XXX XXX XXXX. She takes calls, is no nonsense and straightforward. She'll talk to you. You can cut through to simple solutions quickly.

I don't know what the balances are in Ashland. And I just cannot figure out why the subscriber stories are still free. It is not that people don't want to buy, it is that they can't. I understand there have been glitches in converting to the new system (which was needed), but I have heard about four times now over more than a month that the store would be fixed and subscriber stories no longer free any day.

I really don't know where Y's head is at these days and he's just not going to take charge. As soon as I get the new PofA from you I'll find a way to have it notarized properly, but please understand I am also almost out of money down here. Jenna's made a deposit of $400 for me. I'll sell my watch and last few little gold pieces if necessary but there is nothing more important for me right now than getting a new PofA into your hands.

If you just get me the PofA, I'll get it back to you. But it's got to be fast. Make sure I have a street/delivery address. I have no idea how to solve the unable to write checks problem in Ashland. Y can solve that quickly if and when he sends X the paperwork that will allow her to write checks on the new Ashland bank.

Ray, the Ruppert family trust is my ONLY hope right now. When you want and are able I will hook you with the LA attorney, a Yale grad and glacially slow W, who I retained after Dad died. Big mistake. I can give you all the background. Technically we're supposed to wait until "[Mike's stepmother]" dies but the trust can be dissolved earlier.

Dad left an amendment saying that it was to be dissolved immediately after his death. They're contesting it and saying I ain't entitled to nothing, even the hafl he

*brought into it. The original deal as 50-50 split after [Mike's stepmother's] death.
"XY" is my mother nickname. Her full name is YZ. If alive, she is 90, has
Alzheimer's and is nuttier than a fruitcake. But no one has even verified she's
alive in more than a year. Dad died in May
of 05.*

Remember "Psycho?"

*FOR THE RECORD -- If I do not live to see the money my father left me,
I want you to use it to pay off all debts, pay all the writers, Carolyn, Stan, Mike
Kane and all staff. Pay Ken and, or course, yourself (very well). I have no family.
With Y solo on the PofA all I can imagine is that it will just sit in a bank or go
to my stepmother's... niece who is an Alabama Democrat for Bush.*

*Whatever's left (might be a chunk) please split between Jenna Orkin and
Mike Kane.*

*This is not much of a will but when you have an executed PofA it will be all
you'll need.*

Please hurry Ray. Please. Please.

*I have no intention of doing anything irreversible as soon as it's done. That's
not the point. But I just might be able to sleep one night without worrying about it
being lost due to the fact that no one went after it and saved the documents. My
share is probably over $300,000 right now. Even a negotiated half or a quarter of
that could save my life.*

October 30, 2006 From Mike to an ally:

*...my friend, I must trust that you can completely adhere to what I have asked
here. My life is in danger and on the line. I need to come home. It is also possible
that people who are not FTW's friends are planning on taking the web site down
soon. We are developing a plan.*

*Please do nothing. You will here more from me, Mike, and Jenna soon
enough...*

October 31, 2006 From Mike to Ray:

Ray "

*You're going to have to read between the lines, but we know each other well
enough that I know you can do that.*

1. The bad guys... fucked up. They let Mike Kane get his story up describing my health problems which are not getting any better. The Cuban doc has prescribed nothing. The response is overwhelming and now we see that there can be ample financial aid to accomplish two things A), get me back to the States, NYC for medical treatment and B) save the FTW web site. BUT NOTHING CAN GO THROUGH THE FTW WEB SITE. WE'LL NEVER SEE IT.

2. X has outed himself as one of the sources of the unfounded rumors. We already know that Y was hostile before I left the country and helped spread them... [One of the offers for the website] would have destroyed FTW and castrated me. At minimum X should be asked to take a polygraph exam by Ashland PD, but that's much further down the road. We should squeeze X, but never directly. jusy keep working around him.

3. Y is coming back around and we must leave the door open for her. [She] was mind fucked and she's worth every effort to save.

4. We have no gauarntee that we will see any money donated through the web site. Yesterday, X said she couldn't even write checks until Y sent her back papers for the new bank. But still she sees every penny coming in through the store and none of us have any idea how much money is coming in or where it is going. (She can move it electronically) That includes Y. Why is the subscriber-only section still free????????????????????????? Where is a freaking sales report? how much money is coming in? Ray could really help here with timely phone calls to Y and X that mentions nothing of these plans.

5. Y's loyalty is questionable. What can I say about his competence? At present I don't think I can write ANYTHING for the web site because of the fraud issue. I am on record as opposing any fruadulent behavior and there's a clear record showing that I had nothng to do with these decisions. However, Y was on the original PofA and now he is the ONLY person with Power. Ray, maybe we can use that. So if the web site goes down and the store closes, etc, the fraud charges kind of roll in his direction, don't they? The point is that they can't close the business yet. They're laible and I'm not.

I (and Mike Kane) are leaning towards a guerilla web transmission of an emegerency message from me, Mike and Jenna that will call for rescue monies to be sent to a brand new account in NY that comp`letely bypasses FTW. Between Mike and me, we can reach maybe 20,000 people in 24 hours and that will propagate to maybe a million within a week. This will only acknowledge the war that we already know has been underway for some time. But then, if in retaliation, X shuts the web site and walks out it only confirms their agenda in the first place, proves we were right and lets me, Mike and the good guys off the hook on fraud. It would increase sympathy and donations.

X has got to understand all this but I am not the guy to persuade her. We need to do everything possible to get her completely back in the fold before the message goes out, but we can still do it without her if we have to " leaving the door open. X is a rescue mission, not an enemy.

The question is how to structure this and do it quickly. Ray, if this works I can sign the new PofA in NY. It is to New York that I must come first.

GETTING ME HOME

I have no doubt that we´ll raise a lot of money. maybe over $100,000 that must not go anywehere near Y's hands. That can cover medical care and hopefully some place to stay in NY while Ray and I put the next phase together. I had already compiled a list of heavyweights and miks kane´s story has shown me how to reach out to them.

Once we have money, which might be as soon as 3-4 days after the notice goes out and we
have a place for me to stay, we should plan on flying me back via American Airlines. Here´s why.

1. We´re going to have to plead for a one way ticket on medical emegrency grounds. For years I was an AA frequent flyer, member of the Admirals club and a VIP. They know me. I know they can make exceptions based on those grounds for a one-way ticket purchased with a credit or debit card. That will eliminate a lot of computer generated DHS problems but probably not all.
2. Before buying the ticket Ray should call DHS and find out if I am on a no-fly list as a dissident author. By then our guerila web plea will be making world news.

3. When we have the ticket, the flight and the date, I make a cell phone call to Ray or Mike in NY as I board the plane and am sure I´m onboard. We make sure

that all o our friends and lots of Indy media know what the flight number is. Then, if I don't emerge at JFK the noise can start and Ray will know where to start looking for my habeased corpus.

Ray, I think you'll be able to fill in blanks from here. This just might work and get us FTW back in better shape than ever, with friends in VZ, and having eliminated what I am sure have been some long time, behind the scenes very nasty problems..

But most important is my health. I am very weak and seemingly getting weaker. I have to go rest for a while before i can come back to the web.

Ok, I'll pray for a quick response from Ray.

Mike

Part 21: Death Throes of FTW

November 1, 2006 From Jenna to Mike and Ray:

seconded re need for holding pattern. remember ray's in pittsburgh and not on email so if we don't hear from him for a couple days, don't think anything sinister. anything else i say will be obsolete by sundown.

November 1, 2006 From Jenna to Mike [in response to his expression of abject failure:]

what would you say to a person who announces, at twenty, 'i'm going to be a billionaire by the time i'm forty.' at fifty, they've made a mere couple million dollars and let's hope, done something worthy meanwhile. is this person a failure or was the goal too narrowly defined?

November 1(?), 2006 11:47 AM From Mike to colleagues:

We have to all just stop and see how the dust settles.
I pray that I hear from Ray who may have both the common sense and the special knowledge to find a solution.
It is not wise to arrange things in the middle of a tornado and a tornado is clearly in progress.
...We all have to just chill until we hear from Ray.

November 1, 2006 2:03 PM From Mike to colleagues:

Have been dealing with medical issues this AM and yesterday. Hope to have my story complete and sent by tonight. This [an account of Mike's illnesses and attempts at treatment] *is by FTW subscriber and my roomie Carlos Ruiz. If you need to ask editorial question of him you can contact him directly. he also has your email. He pretty much hit the nail. My story will take a broader, more global look and relate that to our subscribers in a way that will prove useful in that context.*
These two stories, when combined should open the door to some serious cash inflow. My rcommendation is that some of it, maybe $1,000 or more --based upon

availability-- be put aside for me in the Bof A account and that all of the rest be used to pay bills, ship product, etc.

November 3, 2006 9:55 AM From Mike to colleagues:

Hey, why doesn't everyone chill. I am not scapegoating Ashland and am not fanning these flames at all. I haven't touched that subject for a while, my recent conversations with X were polite and cordial. I never mentioned aliens or accused X or anyone there of being on CIA payroll. Ken will confirm all of this. X should also confirm that our recent contacts have been cordial and respectful.

I am too sick to have time for this so... please chill just a bit. At present you are the only one acting hostile and accusatory here. You seem to be impersonating me.

To me it is clear that without Mike Kane, FTW is no longer sustainable in any form. [Not having gotten to these emails yet, I was off by six days in yesterday's post. Sorry. JO] *I think Ken is in complete agreement as we spoke about this yesterday. As brilliant and dedicated as you have been, Carolyn, you just can't carry it all on your own. No one human being could. The heart of what made if FTW is gone. The heart of what we sell to subscribers is gone. That is no offense at all to you Carolyn, a great and brilliant writer. But it was me, Jamey, Stan and Mike who made FTW great and known over the years. We were the investigators and field reporters. All of us are now gone or neutralized in one way or another. Mike Kane is the last tree shaker, investigator to go. It was the tree shaking and investigating that made FTW.*

I don't see how we CANNOT tell subscribers that Mike Kane has resigned. We can't sell subscriptions based upon the presence of phantom writers that we know aren't going to be there. Mike has a very large following in his own right. They deserve to know.

Whatever is said as our final word it will be said by me. I gave FTW birth. I held it together at the price of my health. Respect for almost nine years dictates that I be the one to pull the plug. No one should say anything publiclly until I do. (See below)

My immediate recommendation is that we take down all parts of the store except the donation page. Ray, please take note of this.

I am weak, still very sick, and must go back to doctor's soon. Am working on a very large piece which will be FTW's last. It will NOT be accusatory. It WILL be an essay on Post Peak sustainability based upon my lessons here. It WILL be a tribute to Mike Kane and it will explain why we are shutting down. It WILL be a very large fundraiser which is our only hope now to achieve many things. It will NOT blame Ashland staff. It WILL provide options that might raise enough money to satisfy our creditors, pay staff, establish good faith on fraud allegations which should concern ALL of us and is the ONLY way I can see to get all back salaries paid, keep a permanent web presence and get my library and files shipped to Carolyn for posterity. I don´t expect I will ever get to see them again anyway.

It WILL recognize that we all must accept defeat now. I totally understand and support Mike Kane´s decision and why he made it. He has family. I do not.

Carolyn and all of you will have it before Monday unless I am hospitalized.

...I am NOT accusing anyone of anything. I am ill and with olive branch in hand. What all of us need now is a little teamwork. I know how hard this is on you too. You loved FTW almost as much as I do. But we must accept that this patient is dead and wtihdraw life support. It was my only child and it is my decision. It is my legal right.

The way we pull the plug will determine a great deal. Can we call a truce until that is accomplished.

I will try to get back online later today if physically able. My US cell phone will be shut off in a couple of days at most.

X, please expedite banking papers and my trust documents to Ken ASAP. If you want to pay bills and to recieve what may be sufficient money to zero the books, it will come from and through him and Ray Kohlman who will be in charge of receiving donations. Since the office in staffed only one day a week and the store should go go down, this is the only option that makes sense. We are really stuck until Ken gats those papers. This is the ONLY way we´re going to get everyone paid.

I know it´s a big request but there may be some donation offers in the phone messages and emails that no one has been able to check.

Thank you

Mike

From Jenna to Mike:

ray says checks can be sent to

c/o

    ray kohlman [address]

    we're assuming they can go into the bank of america account whose number i gave to ray. ray thought there might be a different number in ny from oregon but i told him... the only thing they said about its being an oregon account was that that meant it would take a few days longer to get to you.

November 3, 2006 10:01 AM From Mike to Jenna:

No. NO!

    X has access to and can drain the BofA acount in a heartbeat. Ray and I must control how the money gets handed out, not just dump it in X's lap! We talked about that. A few hundred is fine becasue I can get that. But thousands and tens of thousands will disappear. They will never go for my health care or relocation. Ray should endorse the checks into his account if possible. What we need is instructions on how checks should be made out. Please hurry.

    I am real sick today and very little is going right.

    love,

    Mike

November 4, 2006 12:25 PM From Mike to Ray, Dr. Faiz Khan, Jenna, cc Andreas von Buelow:

    Last night it became clear that I need for you three to look at the situation and make a decision as to how to get me out of here ASAP. I'll follow whatever you figure out, just please keep me advised. The where's and how's I'll leave up to you four. Ray is best qualified to evaluate logistics and legal needs. Faiz has an eye on medical issues and Jenna is the rope that is keeping me tethered at the moment. I just sent out our last article which I know will raise money.

    Med updates. Diet change has pretty much cleared up urine. But nights are very difficult. Blood sugar (guessing) drop during night caused me to wake up severely depressed. Am improving accessibility to carrots, crackers, etc for use by bedside. Heavy, heavy day sweats in tropical heat, more than normal. Weakness continues. Had paresthesis of lips and fingers on awakening this AM after very troubled night. Freuqent, almost non stop urination at night is adding to already troubled sleep.

...I have the med documents copied and ready to fax... Don´t have enough spare money yet for glucometer.

Small cash deposits of $500 or under can be made to BofA and I can access directly. Large ones run the risk of being appropriated by X. Am certainly OK for time being.

I know that FTWs last article will bring in money.

Thanks to all and especially to... Jenna. Thanks for your labors on my behalf. Jenna now knows about possible third country. That knowledge should be kept close in this circle only. Ray can share what´s needed with AVB. Ray, could you please explain why Faiz needs to avoid contact with Y or having any contact with Z who will funnel it back to Y. It´ll make more sense coming from you.

Mike

November 4, 2006 4:12 PM From Mike to Jenna, cc "A:"

A, will get back to you as soon as a plan firms up. I am very sick. Do not post this yet because I must make changes to show you getting library and files. you might have to make a quick dash to Ashland but not yet.

This is real serious. I am through at FTW and FTW is through. It really is aout saving my life now, which a lot of people seem to think is worhwhile. That´s reassuring.

jenna, you did fabulous with this [briefing A on the unraveling of FTW.] I donñt know why you think you´re not good at it.

MESSAGE AUTHENTICATOR -- The last time i saw you A we were in the Black Sheep English Pub in Ashland. We went off for a sidebar about how fast things were deteriorating. We were right.

Someday we´ll catch up and I hope get to meet again. And yes, in spite of all my troubles here **I did get a convincing message through to the right people about no planes and building collapse. At least I got that done. That is not for publication.** [Emphasis mine. - JO]

November 5, 2006 From Mike re steps to be taken medically and offer of funds to do so:

WILL GET THERMOMETER TODAY

fUNDS CAN BE DEPOSITED INTO BANK ACCOUNT FOR WHICH JENNA HAS INFO. WILL TAKE 3-4 DAYS TO POST. IT'S SUNDAY BUT WILL TRY TO PRICE ONE TODAY IF ENERGY PERMITS. IF NOT, TOMORROW

[Re recommended tests:]

GOT IT. NEED FIRST TO IDENTIFY AND LOCATE A CLINIC, THEN PRICE TESTS, THE GET SUFFICIENT FUNDS. WILL REACH OUT FOR HELP ON THIS TODAY.

November 5, 2006 10:34 M From Mike to "A:"

A, I want you to have the books. That's a huge library. No risk there. Could you get my clothes. There's nothing I can do to get the research files to Ray in NY. I am too sick, too broke and too far away. nobody has time or money. But the library is my gift to you. I know you'll take care of it.

A. did not end up with the library. Mike speculated that A. might indeed have felt it too hot to handle.

Part 22: Adios, Venezuela

November 1, 2006 11:18 From Mike to colleagues:

...X has indicated that there is a trust settlement offer. Ray had begun the process of confirming this. Soon he'll be able to start executing on my behalf. I'm already personally trashed, my company is destroyed, so I don't give a rat's ass what people will say. I am "radioactive" as they say, but I am not dead. [Responding to the rumor that he'd smashed the FTW computers and taken the insurance money before fleeing the country and sending the fake email to subscribers.] *I can still move and that makes me dangerous.*

MESSAGE FOR [WEBMASTER]

You have labored well without pay. Although you have not said that you were going to quit, you certainly would be justified and have every right to do so. However, if you were to quit without leaving me and Ray Kohlman all necessary codes for upload to the web site, that would absolutely constitute theft/misappropriation of company property. There are about a zillion instances of case law supporting that. I know you would never intentionally do something like that being the "straight up" kind of guy that you are.
When a corporation goes out of business its assets are normally liquidated to satisfy debts. When in bankruptcy the court does it. Before bankruptcy the stockholders do it. The codes to the web site are probably FTW's single most important asset at the moment.
I am the sole stockholder of FTW. In other words those codes and protocols are my property.
So I am instructing you to provide a copy of all web access codes and complete instructions for upload to Ray Kohlman and to me. Once these have been checked and verified for functionality you can quit any time you want. I should think that Wednesday is a sufficiently generous window for what should amount to less than 30 minutes of your time t get us this information.
Now everyone think for a minute. I am proposing a solution in my article that may not solve everything but will do the most to get money in the shrotest period of time and leaving everyone (except me) walking away clean, with no strings and without having to look over their shoulders for me or Ray.

We will not post the article I sent to Carolyn yet. It will be edited. But that article does represent a serious way to get everybody at least some payment and end this all as quickly and cleanly as possible with the best possible outcome for the greatest number of people. Any other negative actions merely risk lengthy legal entanglements for EVERYBODY.

As I said, I got nothing to lose and after I get my health back I'll have a lot of time on my hands.
Mike

November 1, 2006 2:58 PM From Mike to colleagues:

One step forward, two back.

Walked and travelled for 30 min in heat. Waited, only to find out that the free clinic did ot have the quipment for the tests. The travelled 30 min back and almost crashed. Have loctaed private lab close to apt. Here will go tomorrow and make appointment for tests.They'll cost about $200 I'm told but don't know yet. Money thin but cannot wait. The only other free lab was almost an hour away and no guarantee that they have right equipment.
Also found out I need Yellow Fever and Hep A&B vaccines to leave country. Can't get those until doc sees what current prob is, of course.
Thanks to all,

November 1, 2006 From Mike in response to an irate email from a loyal FTW reader who hadn't received his order:

If Ray can take this from the money earmarked for my health care and relocation and refund it directly I would appreciate it. I will sleep better. I am very ill but this is something I feel needs to be done.   I have no control over what happens in Ashland and haven't for months now. I am just trying to stay alive but I don't want my conscience eaten alive over this. I have tried so hard to never cheat anyone.What happened in Ashland has beoken my heart.   Ray, there should be enough from the donations for me to take care of just this one order and it would let me sleep better. Jenna, Ken, please help me make this one thing right.

On November 6, at 9:36 AM, Ray Kohlman wrote that he had submitted papers for a "show cause" hearing, stating that although Mike owed rent, he had a history of paying.

From Mike:

Ray:
Sorry, I am waaaay lost here. How can I pust in papers for a show cause hearing in Ashland from here in Caracas?? Who's going to do that??? I am just trying to stay alive and get med tests done.
That would have to be ken and he's not going to go to Ashland I don't think. Certainly not just for that.
X is the only one there and I don't know if she would/ can do this. If there was a show cause hearing who would appear??????????????

Starting November 9, I have no emails from Mike because I was giving a talk in Berkeley: *How Science Was Abused to Perpetrate Lies After 9/11: A Cautionary Tale for the Approaching Peak Oil Disaster.*[7] But on November 18 he pops up again — in Toronto. Given the choice between me in New York and Barry Silverthorn's place with a horse down the road, Mike opted for the horse. Ray and I met him at the airport when he changed flights, to make sure he didn't disappear.

I'd never met Ray so he described himself over the cellphone: Younger, thinner and handsomer than Mike... and wearing a baseball cap. Let's just say that the first two adjectives were objectively false.

Mike looked slim and happy to be "home" but at that moment, all he wanted was water. We were in an area without any nearby so, explaining he had kidney problems, he cadged a spare bottle from a sympathetic security guard.

The kidney problems also came in handy for bypassing some of the lines at the airport.

Months later, in a conversation about the National Reconnaissance Office, where a war game was conducted the morning of 9/11

---

[7] http://911review.com/articles/orkin/post911lies.html

involving a plane flying into a building (in direct contradiction of Condoleezza Rice's testimony to the 9/11 Commission that the administration had never dreamed of such a scenario,) I learned that the papers concerning the NRO that Mike had taken to Venezuela to show the Chavez administration had all been ditched before he headed back across the US border. He didn't tell me what they contained, thank God.

Part 23: Ah, Canada

End of Suburbia producer Barry Silverthorn's recollection of Mike's time at his house:

When Mike landed in Toronto he looked very thin — and relieved. All he wanted was some food that wasn't indigenous to South America, so we went to the nearest restaurant after leaving the airport.

We went shopping for clothes at a thrift store. Mike was impressed by how little they cost, and I got the impression that he had never shopped at a thrift store before. I had also bought him CDs by David Baerwald [a friend of Mike's whom we'd later meet in Los Angeles] *and Don Henley and they were waiting for him on his dresser.*

I put him to work chopping wood. He said it helped him work out his anger over some of the people that he felt betrayed him.

We took a drive to the hobby farm where I grew up. They had horses there and we stood at the fence by the road and spent some time with them.

He had never read "The Long Emergency", so he spent a couple of days in front of the wood-burning fireplace reading. He said the fireplace was better than TV and more informative.

We had many conversations over that week. One day, in the garden, I was asking "What is my place in all this?" How much responsibility do we have in "saving the world", not as public figures, but as people living day-to-day life? Is it important? I mentioned the Slowest Camper story, which Mike has attributed to me, but I read somewhere else – was it Ran Prieur?

My wife made a stack of ribs, which he dug into. We took him out to hear musician Jamie Oakes play at a bar. I bought him a CD to take home. He wanted to sing, which I had never been aware of. He stood in the kitchen one night and sang Bruce Springsteen's "Thunder Road". We downloaded a karaoke track of Elton John's "Burn Down the Mission" for him to sing to. Appropriate. I still have it on my iTunes. At times he seemed so relaxed. Mike wanted to watch season three of "Deadwood", one of his favorites, but it wasn't available in Canada yet. We watched Roland Joffé's "The Mission". When Robert De Niro threw off his bag at the top of The Falls we both cried. Although I didn't share the same burdens as Mike, I understand a bit of what he was carrying.

I remember him breaking down and sobbing at the bottom of the stairs one night. All my wife and I could do was hug him.

We tried to get paperwork to his lawyer in NY. It took a week by Fed-Ex. We tracked it all over the place. I never would have believed it if I hadn't seen it for myself. No organization could be that incompetent, and I am certain it was flagged.

I have memories of him sitting against the wall in my basement, looking so beaten. After that Mike decided he should take the papers to NY in person. I thought it was a bit soon, but we loaded up the Smart car at 10:30pm and drove all night.

I still have the Venezuelan Bolivars that he left on the dresser.

Mike later said Barry had given him a staircase to demolish and taken him to a holistic healer who knew his work. During the session, he visualized a peaceful scene of a leopard with a bird perched on its back. The image would later serve as the opening of his next book, which was intended to be an autobiography.

But well-appointed though Barry's set-up was, (as I would later hear when, at my typically cramped New York apartment, Mike expressed homesickness for Toronto,) his stay there could only be brief.

November 22, 2006 From Jenna to Mike:

tomorrow i'll tell my mother et al re xmas. i'd been waiting til your whereabouts were public but even though that hasn't happened, thanksgiving is the best time to tell her since otherwise, she'll invite someone else.

November 23, 2006 From Mike to Michael Kane, concerning another offer to buy the website. The prospective buyer had been asking about the rumors regarding Mike Ruppert, prompting Michael Kane to wonder what the prospective buyer had been told:

Mike --
Not telling him much except that X is not our friend and what she did. He understands that I did not do any of that shit she alleged and has always known me

to be honest like everyine else. He's done a lot of stuff with X but let's not get paranoid. [The prospective buyer] made a lot of money in his own right and is no idiot. He's made what sounds like a fair, even generous offer to buy FTW's assets and has agreed in principle to not alter or modify any of our positions on Peak Oil or 9-11; to guarantee lifetime acess and use of my own material which I would license to him, etc.

He would guarantee to keep the site online in perpetuity.

There are two possibilities here and we cannot arbitrarily dismiss or endorse either one. One is that he's working with X on some hidden agenda. The other is that he really does want to preserve the site, maybe bring on some new writers and do some good. He seemed really taken aback by what I told him about what X did.

The fact that he called you indicates that what I had told him... surprised him and he wanted to know more. Would he have done that if he was part of some evil plan? I don't think so. That was a good sign. He's investigating like we taught people to do. Let him.

I would not be upset if you shared with him...

If he and X were in bad cahoots he wouldn't have needed or wanted to ask you. I didn't mention anything about events not related to X...

Y really upset me. As sick as I am he was coming on with, "Mike, we'll have you back writing and on the stage in six months to a year."

Man, that fried me. I am done with all that. Mike, if you could see me you'd know. It took a long time to get it through to him that that is all toxic and would kill me.

I have just entered a heavy healing regimen with a holisitic physician who loves Gary Null. My adrenal system is just fried and collapsed. Liver damage from some kind of toxicity. Still finding out more. I start acupuncture next week.

I think what we have to do is to express the concerns we want addressed to Ray and allow him to structure the deal so that we don't get burned. [The prospective buyer's] offer is much better than X's was. 20 k up front to pay some bills and take care of me, He picks up all the inventory, gets 2,000 Rubicons out of past-due storage in LA and sets up royalties and licensing for me for future income.

...I had a relationship with him before X did and [the prospective buyer] said he has always known that I am an honorable guy. I am not going to throw what may be a life-saving offer out just because [he] and X also do business. A lot of people know and do business with both of us.

Y wants to stay away from the offer because Y just wants more money and hopes for a resurrection that isn't going to happen. Y will be advised and consulted but he is not my partner and he is not a decision maker here.

RE LOOSE CHANGE (Very important) -- In a previous conversation with A, before I left Venezuela, she said that she had just met with the Loose Channge folks and that they had REMOVED all no plane references from the newest edition. She said she liked the people and they impressed her as sincere.

So what do we do with that? Do we now throw A out too? Do we now accuse A od something?

We cannot be totally unbending here. Totally unbending is what nearly killed me and may still. I have to stop controlling everything and so do you. There's a way to draw a line, separate, and make it perfectly clear that we ain't responsible for what happens next. Our record is intact.

It will be up to Ray to structure enough protections so that:

1. The legacy is clear and secure; and

2. Neither I or anyone we love gets screwed with bad PR. That will be accomplished with a clear statement announcing the sale of the assets, change of editorial control and clear cut mission statement.

If the offer is good, we let Ray take care of us. I don;t have the energy to fight for months over this.

9-11 is waaaaaaay dead. Just hearing it now makes me physically ill. We cannot jump to a conclusion that [the prospective buyer] is the enemy. I am still pretty sick and need some money.

I don't think X ever had a hidden agenda with Loose Change like trying to spread disinfo. She's always been sloppy on those details. Her motive is to maximize profits by being as inclusive as possible. She never gave a crap or understood why the disinfo was so dangerous. She cares about market share, getting the largest number of people into the tent. We were the purist monks.

Again, it's up to Ray to protect us against a "straw man" sale. Neither X or [the prospective buyer] stand to gain much by trashing FTW or me or you. If we are out of the fight then we have to be out of the fight and trust that those we taught have an IQ of more than 50.

Gotta go. This took a lot out of me.

Mike

From Mike to Ken Levine regarding the prospective buyer's queries:

It's not what Kane told him. It's what X told him. Kane is right where he's always been, with me, with us. You're not reading correctly. I talked to Mike yesterday. Please slow down just a little bit.

...please just get the exact number of dollars it will cost to liberate the books. 900 was the last number you gave me. Please do not delay. I want to keep you included but will unhappily work around you if I have to.

We need to hear from Ray. Please include Ray in all messages.

take care and thanks

Part 24: Brooklyn, Ho!

It was time to move again, Mike felt, before he got on Barry's wife's nerves.

He was coming to Brooklyn where he'd be able to meet with Ray to sort out the trust, and be with me. I had become the next goal.

This was a dream come true: To have Mike on my turf and show him — Wild West guy in cowboy boots — the beautiful streets of nearby Brooklyn Heights.

But living with someone had always been something I'd been leery of; particularly when the someone was a person who thought nothing, for example, of calling at 7:30 AM. I am not a morning person. (Once he called at 4 AM New York time, claiming that he'd calculated the three-hour time difference in the wrong direction. That was not the sort of mistake Mike made and he later chuckled it had been a self-serving error. Cui bono? as he asked in *Crossing the Rubicon*.)

Still, he needed me, which would cast me in the best possible light.

I did not keep notes for the first three weeks of his stay in my apartment, because he was fragile as well as self-conscious about that fragility and the subject could not be broached. But one day, when he was coming out of his traumatized state and mentioned the possibility of a history of FTW or maybe it was of a biography of him, he mused that at one time, he'd thought Carolyn Baker the most plausible candidate to write it as she had all the files of correspondence. However, in recent months, her attitude towards him had changed dramatically. (They later worked out their differences, of course.)

This opened up the opportunity to ask his permission to keep notes of the conversations we'd been having.

Mike recognized the impulse, for he'd also thought those conversations worthy of recording. So he agreed to the project but didn't want to think about it anymore. I understood that I was being given permission to make notes so long as I was discreet about it. I didn't sit with him earnestly jotting our words in real time, interview style, but wrote them up as soon afterwards as possible and without ever discussing the matter. However, the first three weeks were intense and I regret the loss of a record. Before he finally left

Brooklyn for Los Angeles fourteen months later, when he was copying his files from my computer onto a thumb drive, he came across the notes and copied them as well (without asking permission but I understood his sense of entitlement about them.)

That thumb drive or a version thereof may or may not still exist. But in the unlikely event that someone stumbles upon it, it's missing some crucial elements. There were certain statements he made which I never recorded, knowing I wouldn't forget them. Or I recorded them in a watered down form to preserve the syntax, but omitted key words, again, knowing I wouldn't forget them.

Of course, I thought it more likely that this account which you're now reading would be written while he was still alive. Had that been the case, the vast majority of it would be the same while details like the fictitious nature of the tape recording of his dangerous liaison with his female employee might have been left out.

December 18, 2006

It will be three weeks ago tomorrow that he came. Barry Silverthorne drove him in a "compact" car covered in *End of Suburbia* insignia. When there was no place to park the old-fashioned way, they drove into a parking space head first and fit just fine.

Mike was exhausted, having been unable to sleep sitting upright. Barry, too, looked shell-shocked; Mike had not been a happy camper on the way down.

"I tried to get him to focus on landmarks, get his mind off himself," he explained in the kitchen while Mike was passed out in the living-room.

Then it was Barry's turn to take a nap for an hour before heading back to Ontario. (*"I don't want to get there at two in the morning."*)

Having so recently left what he had thought would be his permanent home of Venezuela, Mike owned no outer winter clothes, (he'd bought pants and shirts at the thrift shop Barry had taken him to) so we went shopping. Downtown Brooklyn offered a mall's worth of discount stores where we bought a winter coat for $20 and a fleece sweater which he exhilaratedly left behind when he ultimately moved back to sunny Los Angeles and which I'm wearing as I write this, not for sentimental reasons but because it's suitable for this stormy spring night as well as indestructible.

A sticking point in our living arrangement was my mother who, if she discovered the whole story, would consider it the embodiment of her worst nightmare: A penniless man holing up with me because the U.S. government had seized his bank account and threatened his life.

Thus Mike could not answer my phone. And when we went to my mother's for Christmas, we'd have to navigate carefully certain conversational shoals. Even if I warned everyone ahead of time that he'd been ill (a true and effective tack) they could, in all innocence, still poke at sore points: "So Mike, where' you from? The west coast? Oh, where are you staying in New York? What do you do?"

Then there was the question of public notice of his whereabouts. Would creditors show up? (Lest there be any doubt, let it be said again that in the end, everyone got paid in full.) For the moment, then, we decided he should lie low. Also, he had no one but me to talk to and nowhere constructive to go. So one afternoon when I came home from a meeting, he was playing backgammon on the computer with someone in Israel *("Language: Hebrew")* and was in despair.

The apartment was depressing, he said.

It was winter; the sky, a dull grey which underscored the grimness of the surrounding municipal buildings, particularly the jail.

"When we live together, we're going to have standing lamps that reflect off the ceiling."

We were already living together, but he insisted it was not living, only existing; he thought of it as Purgatory until we moved to a sustainable community. I told him about light deprivation depression which I'd had for years until I read of it and learned that other people had it too.

Initially, coming home to him had been like having ET in the closet, known only to me and a handful of others. But that fantasy dissolved in the recognition that without a vibrant, full-fledged, openly acknowledged life, my secret friend would die.

Part 25: Sinking

Having asked for some water, Mike inspected the glass dubiously, like a connoisseur of housekeeping; the fluted part at the base was murky.

"We're going to have some work to do," he laughed.

"I scrubbed and scrubbed," I protested.

"Don't you use the dishwasher?"

"I don't know how."

This was within two or three days of his arrival; we were still at the guest/host stage, which was why he hadn't gotten his own water. As for the dishwasher, I hadn't grown up with or ever used one and had read that they wasted water, so even though the apartment provided one, albeit with some sort of pillow stuffing erupting out of the bottom, I'd never bothered to figure out how it worked.

Months later, when we knew each other better, Mike admitted that this incident had convinced him I was simply stupid. My status as "queen of links," the research division of the FTW news section, was, like FTW itself, history.

At the time, however, he responded to the alarming insight by taking action. When I returned from grocery shopping, he said, "Come here," and led me to the kitchen whose counter was now clear, the glasses sparkling as in a detergent commercial, having had their baptism in the up-and-running dishwasher.

The next day, another milestone was passed on the road to achieving his domestic standards. Taking my sleeve like a kid, he tugged me towards the bathroom saying, "Look what I did!"

Half the contents of the shelves were gone; the tub fixtures gleaming.

"Now watch this!" He leaped from a floor panel next to the right wall to one on the left — like a frog among lily pads — avoiding the ones that creaked. He'd figured out a way to go to the bathroom during the night that wouldn't wake me.

From there he led me to the kitchen where he opened the door of the freezer, which looked unfamiliar; half its contents were gone.

Indeed, it had transformed into a showcase model of a typical middle-class couple's freezer.

His housekeeping ideal was order; mine, thrift. The latter quality had led to clutter which — to drop a loaded statement — reminded him of his mother. How much experience of women had he had besides her? As mentioned in an earlier post, his longest relationship seemed to have been his marriage of a year and a half.

"That's cheating," I complained about the newly organized freezer. He'd thrown away all the stuff I'd been saving because it's a mortal sin to waste food, but that I was secretly glad to be rid of.

However, the last remnants of a pint of Ciao Bella sorbet were also gone, and I didn't let that faux pas go unobserved.

The next day, he left an old tea bag floating in a cup next to a forkful of hard cheese on a plate.

"I didn't know if you were finished with them," he said, with a malicious glint in his eye.

I was a source of constant dismay, putting cereal in the freezer when the expiration date approached, and wearing two pairs of glasses — one for reading while the other pair, for the computer, perched on my head. When I didn't need either, they both ended up on my head where they did funny things to my hair.

His perfectionism made me nervous which made me even clumsier. For the first time in my life, I left the detergent in the communal laundry room downstairs and spilled coffee on the computer desk.

"There was a cop, Jim Jocquette," Mike remembered one day in his unrelenting tortured review of the past. "When we were ten calls backed up he would say, 'Chief, I love it when it's like this.'

'He died in a traffic accident. 2000 people came to his funeral.

'When I was in LAPD, I wanted to have a hero's death like that."

He was afraid that his life's work — Rubicon and FTW — were over.

I pointed out that this is how people often feel after they retire or their children leave home.

"What's new on the blog?" he asked. I had sent out a notice to the Peak Oilists in New York that he was in town. Had any of them responded? Did they want to get together?

"Everyone is forgetting me," he said anxiously.

"Don't be silly. They probably just skimmed the email. People don't focus unless you call them or address them personally."

He listed the former friends who'd fallen away for one reason or another: Fear of guilt by association; anger; believing the rumor that he smashed his own computers.

I called the only two NYC Peak Oilists whose numbers I had. Both did indeed want to see Mike.

Mike also emailed Emanuel Sferios who responded, solicitous about Mike's health; Mike was moved.

"He's one of those people I was always too busy for," he said softly. "He was always calling when I was on my way to the airport or something like that."

He had similar regrets about Marian Lewinsky, a BBC producer who called from England when she heard about the fate of FTW.

Sunday, at his request, I went with him to his first Al-Anon meeting where he was called on to "share" and cried unabashedly. Several members offered their phone numbers afterwards and over the next week, he consulted them often.

He also called a psychiatrist who was the sister of an old friend from 9/11 days. She prescribed Ativan after eliciting a promise that Mike would go to Bellevue for an assessment on Saturday when her friend would be on duty.

It was imperative for Mike that any shrink he saw understand that his tale of CIA harassment as well as his findings of US government involvement in 9/11 were true and that they not use those "conspiracy theories" as a weapon against him. The Bellevue doctor had heard Mike speak.

Each morning he took a long bath during which he read the Al-Anon book as others read a page of the Bible. Afterwards, the Ativan put him to sleep for another two hours, which made him feel calmer.

But after a few days of this routine, the Ativan had slowed his movements so that there was a zombie-ish cast to his demeanor. He excoriated himself for needing yet another nap.

"What have I accomplished? Got up, had breakfast, took a bath, lay down.

'I keep hearing voices telling me, 'You should do this; you've got to do that.'"

"Be careful about telling that to an intake shrink. That's one of the buzz phrases: Auditory or visual hallucinations." Of course, Mike's "voices" were those of conscience but psychiatrists tend to be vigilant about such reports.

The thought of being admitted to Bellevue was enough to drive him crazy.

"I'll end up in Bellevue, drooling, a basket-case."

"I know people who've been in Bellevue several times and are doing wonderfully. Bellevue doesn't want to keep you any more than you want to be there. You'll be out in a few weeks at the most."

"Rejected by Bellevue!"

Part 26: Pills

November 27, 2006 From Mike to Ray:

Ray --

I left with [a lawyer], [the] employee file [of the female employee who was suing Mike for sexual harassment] with the information that it contained large amounts of exculpatory evidence. X has reported that she has filed a sexual harrassment complaint with the Dept. of Labor but we do not have the information yet. [The lawyer]'s information is above and below.

We need to find out where that file is and respond quickly. I am clean on this. The web site has the full story which will be my testimony.

She is banking that my serious health issues will not allow me to respond and she'll get a default judgment. We can beat this case easily if we respond and [the lawyer] can help us locate the file. It will be harder without the file that was left with [the lawyer] but is still doable. That was one of the most important items I gave him before leaving. I hope it has not been misplaced.

December 2, 2006 From Mike to Ray:

Ray:

I'm concerned by some things you need to know about and feel that if I brief you a little bit it may make your job easier. Again, thank you so much. You have been a saint. Please stay very healthy. Speaking of which, do you know good doctor?

PROBLEMS RELATED TO THE SALE OF THE WEB SITE
…Someone has had a real patsy at my expense in Ashland.
Rght now I am fish in a barrel. To weak to do anything about anything. But you needed to know about this before closing a deal with [the prospective buyer.] And [the prospective buyer] needs to understand that we are kind of helpless to actually transfer the site to him unless you can find a way to get/make Z to cooperate.

Also, in the agreement with [the prospective buyer] it should be stipulated that no disparaging comments about me should go up after the sale. Easy language should do it. I think [the prospective buyer] really wants to help but I think you can understand why I'm a little paranoid.

In the batch of letters you gave me there was one from a very kind attorney in Salem, OR. Would it be worthwhile to le him know of our troubles and ask if he can help?
Thanks Ray. Mike

December 14, 2006 From Mike to Ray:

What does [the prospective buyer] mean by "non-compete". I hope that wouldn't prohibit me from writing for others at some point when I have something coherent to say.
Also want to ensure he wouldn't print anything disparaging about me. I'll leavethe rest of the contract with you until I get more stable. All of these little problems getting fixed are leaving the one big one glaring in my face.
Keep being wonderful.
Mike

"You scared me when you told Ray I was sleeping twenty hours a day," Mike said one day. "My mother did that right before my father divorced her."

"Was she on any medication besides booze?"

"She was probably on tranquillizers I didn't know about. For a while she took Miltown. That was nasty."

On another occasion, Mike said that his maternal grandmother had also been on tranquillizers until she was eighty.

"After my father divorced her, my mother just died. She didn't date, hardly went out. Just stayed home and slept and smoked," (as Mike had been doing for the previous week.) "She had lost the one thing that mattered to her," (as Mike had lost his company.)

"In some crazy way, she thought she was punishing my dad.

'I didn't talk to her for many years. Just called her once a year on Christmas. Some years I drove two hours to see her. Another two to see my dad. Then back home where I'd be alone. That's why I hate Christmas.

'Then in 1997 when she had her third heart attack, my uncle X called. I went to see her and took care of her for the next four years.

That was when FTW was going strong. Every week I had to go see her because it was my duty.

'Mike Ruppert always does his duty," he said with bitter irony.

"Why was your dad the one thing that mattered to your mom?"

"I can only speculate. But I think it was because he rescued her from her own father."

"Can you think of some good things about your mother?"

He thought for a moment. "She always believed in me. Even when she was crazy, trying to light a cigarette with a mascara brush, she believed in me." Then he relayed the story, previously described in the post entitled "Friends," about the time his mother found some cookies, as requested by a potential "friend" who'd invited Mike to meet a gathering of teenagers at the pool.

The invitation turned out to be a ruse and he, the butt of their cruel joke.

"When she was dying, they gave her a sedative, the one that would put her to sleep forever.

'She couldn't speak but she made the Elmo sign at me." With his fingers, he made the sign of Elmo the dog which, coincidentally, is indistinguishable from a sign that supposedly represents Satan. Certain internet outposts get into a state of high agitation when pictures surface of Obama or assorted celebrities thus saluting each other.

"There was one time in high school. I can't remember what it was about but something happened and my father didn't believe me. I didn't do it. But that taught me to keep records of everything. In LAPD I documented everything that happened....

'That's the way X sounded after she spread the rumors that I smashed my own computers.

'I said I didn't do it.

'I don't believe you.'" He imitated the former ally who'd turned against him.

"Exactly like my father."

Part 27: Voices

One night, Mike woke up at four AM.

"I was thinking about [two employees who he believed had smashed his computers, whether as part of a government plot or personal vendetta.] I'm *not* going to let them get to me. I'm *not* going to let them get to me."

"They're not here. You'll probably never see them again. If you do, it will be inconsequential.

'They're not doing anything to you right now; *you* are."

Another night he woke up hot, itching, a rash on his back.

"If it's a metaphor, it's of being uncomfortable in your own skin, itching to shed it."

Or, of course, it could have just been a reaction to his medication.

"Each morning, my mother and father wage war in me."

His father represented the active side of his personality, the one to which could be attributed his management of FTW at its height but which, taken to extremes, became manic; his mother he equated with passivity and, taken to extremes, depression. Knowing the depths of his ambivalence for his mother, one could understand why he so needed to be on the move, never staying still.

He had to run from the lure of lethargy, for fear of drowning there.

Worst, he said, were the mornings when his father's voice hammered, "Got to, got to. You should have..."

"We can work around that voice or undercut it," I said. "I think the way to do that is to talk about something that's different but relevant."

That was the tack I'd been taking with him. To think you could change the subject completely would have been naive; he was obsessed. So you entered his world with him and tweaked it a little to alleviate the torment of the same thoughts pounding relentlessly. Just seeing the problem from another angle was respite enough and the only kind he could take in anyway.

"The reason you don't let go of that voice is that you think it's responsible for what you've accomplished. On the other hand, it's driving you nuts, in the lay sense of the word."

He waved aside my concern that he might think I was calling him "crazy;" he had gotten my drift.

"My shrink used to say to me," I continued, "'You're suffering instead of doing the work you're supposed to be doing.' By that she meant psychological work, being honest with oneself at a deeper level."

I had also learned that punishing oneself psychologically, however torturous, could be a way of escaping an even worse memory or belief. But Mike wasn't ready to go there yet.

One evening, he wanted Thai food so we set out for Smith Street, Brooklyn's trendy restaurant neighborhood, and ate at the first Thai joint that came along.

He ordered Pongoon, which he pronounced excellent; almost as good as the one in Los Angeles. But in the middle of the meal, he had a panic attack.

The restaurant had brought up his pattern while at FTW: the lonely life, working long hours. The Thai place had been his treat to himself, very like the one we were in, only the one in LA had had a fish tank. Sometimes he brought dates there but usually he ate alone, came home, watched movies.

"The one thing I would like," I said when, in a more expansive mood, Mike expressed a desire to repay me for my hospitality, "would be if you could talk to Alex [the name I use for my son in writing] about what's coming."

"Not a problem," Mike replied. "But that's the sort of thing that has to come up naturally, organically."

Alex, who was in college, came over during the Christmas vacation, with tales of the *Daily Show*, the "moment of Zen" with Donald Rumsfeld listening to a question from a marine about why troops were scavenging in the garbage for body armor, then saying, "Could you repeat the question?"

When Alex left, I asked Mike, "You see what I mean about his being out of it?" Alex was a typical kid his age; "out of it" was Mike's and my shorthand for people who were oblivious to the direction the world is heading in.

"I wouldn't even try to address Peak Oil with him," Mike said. "He's one of those people going back to the bar on the Titanic."

While we prepared dinner, I started to cry. Mike looked at me, mystified.

"Back to the bar on the Titanic," I explained.

He was still clueless.

"Alex."

"Oh. Perhaps I should explain. We'll go prepare a place for him. He's smart. When things start to fall apart he'll say, 'Mom and Mike have a place in Portland,' and he'll get on a plane and come. You think I haven't been thinking about that? He's your flesh and blood. I love him almost as much as you do."

Part 28: Christmas

December 24, 2006

Mike came in from the stairwell where he'd been having his morning coffee and cigarette.

"Actually, today I think I'm going to start an outline. For the novel. And it occurs to me that your family....."

"Knows agents?" I thought. I knew one who'd achieved prominence by sticking with mainstream topics and literary fiction. My brother and sister-in-law knew others; my mother's connections in that field were all dead, retired or fallen away.

"...could be interesting material."

We were going to see them the next day for Christmas. Perhaps, knowing that they weren't interested in Peak Oil and all that it entails, Mike was trying to psych himself into finding the gathering useful.

"As an example of the clueless?"

"Yes."

The novel loomed as yet another mammoth undertaking.

"But there's a need for it," he mused.

"Forget that for a moment," I replied. "What do *you* need to write?"

What he needed, I felt, was a catharsis.

"'Help!'"

"Then say that. And fill in the details, the specifics."

"Whoa... I have to think about that."

If speculation were not the idle pastime it's known to be, I'd say that the soul-searching the novel would have required could have saved him. But I don't want to start a conversation thread about writers who've killed themselves as soon as the work was completed. Mike wasn't prepared to write that kind of novel anyway; he was thinking of a less personal Post-peak story.

No wonder the project never got off the ground.

He also wanted to do volunteer work but not with AA.

"What they do in AA is have you meet with someone worse off than you and help them out of it. It's a time-honored means of helping oneself. But I don't want to help turn someone into an acceptable member of a herd of lemmings about to go off the cliff because of Peak Oil."

Christmas Day

No abatement in the morning angst.

"Now what do I do?" he said, only half rhetorically.

He was like a method actor asking his director, "What's my motivation? What do I do with my hands?"

By way of response, he resorted to the method actor's fallback position: He lit a cigarette.

The Arts section of the Times featured an obituary of Mary Meagher, a literary agent who had died at the age of forty-seven of a heart attack induced by drugs and alcohol. A vivacious Holly Golightly type, she harbored a secret sadness which her brother, the only person with whom she remained in contact throughout her life, said stemmed from "a legitimate cause" in her childhood.

I did not mention the article to Mike who, to illustrate his torment, was putting his hands around his neck in mock strangulation. The gesture evoked his rehearsed suicide in Venezuela, by means of his necktie.

I reminded him of my former shrink's admonition: "You are suffering instead of doing the work you are supposed to do," by which she meant the work of looking inward.

In Mike's case, I continued, he was suffering by way of punishment for not making money, (a cause for much of his angst) and as a goad of the time-honored sort favored by his father. What's a tormented genius to do when he's not busy doing his geniusery? The only thing left is the torment.

Also it was a way of staying focused on himself.

He took this in, along with his Tropicana and Thomas' whole wheat English muffin with apricot fruit spread, no added sugar, from the farmer's market.

"I have two choices," he said. "Take a nap or have a panic attack."

The novel was too overwhelming to face.

"There are smaller tasks," I said. "You could write a Christmas —
no, — a holiday message to readers that we could post on the blog."

After an e-Christmas card from a loyal supporter in which you
clicked to create a cottage with a tree outside lit with candles, snow
falling, dog wagging his tail, he resolved to write the message.

"I always feel better after a nap," he said. So that would come first.

Evening

We're back from dinner at my mother's where Mike scored a hit
with his Ross Perot imitation: ("Now I'm just a short, floppy-eared
Texan with a big nose but listen while I tell you something straight:
When ya see a snake, ya kill it.")

"I hope some day I can get up without thinking about [the
employees he blamed for destroying FTW] or suicide."

"You will."

"The morning started out badly but just now, out in the 'den' [the
stairwell] I did some thinking: I'd like, today, to outline the novel, deal
with different snapshots at different points in time.

'But now I'm having a panic attack."

"The valium may have something to do with it."

"I think it was the second cup of coffee. That was a mistake. Good,
but a mistake. I only have eight Valium left."

"You're seeing [your doctor] Wednesday. It's enough if you keep
up your current pattern; not enough if you decide to crank it up to the
maximum you're allowed."

"I'll have to take half an Ativan. Half."

Ativan was scary, putting him to sleep all day.

"It's the daunting task you've set yourself. Remember in Venezuela
when you were all in a sweat because you 'had to' write your final

article for FTW, the article to end all articles — and I told you it didn't have to encompass everything?"

"*Evolution.* That was a good article."

"Right. Just take it one step at a time."

Part 29: Anxiety

"The two people whose pictures I had on the wall in Ashland were suicides: Jack Gubanc and Gary Webb. And Jack was bi-polar," (as Mike had been told by a psychiatrist might be his diagnosis as well.)

Jack, I believe, was the guy who had paid for FTW's Washington Post ad years ago. The headline was an allusion to the *Wizard of Oz*: "Who is the man behind the curtain?"

December 26, 2006

"You know what keeps churning in my mind now?"

I named the triumvirate of villains who Mike believed had precipitated the downfall of FTW.

"The [newspaper] article will come out in February and it'll be based on an indictment of fraud."

"Wouldn't you get a sense of this beforehand, if that was the agenda? Wouldn't [the journalist] have to ask you for a statement?"

"If the indictment doesn't come down until February, that's when they'd ask for a statement."

"But I don't think they'd be talking in terms of a cover story if this was their plan." They might if Mike were already famous but it's not interesting if someone whom most people haven't heard of gets indicted for fraud. The whole point of the newspaper article was that Mike had been unjustly overlooked.

"Neither do I."

So who, we wondered, was more likely to get indicted in February, Mike or Rumsfeld?

"If I had a panic attack like the one that just happened at breakfast, they'd put me in a straitjacket for seventy-two hours. I have a horror of being confined."

"I know. You feel confined here... That's why you love the wide open spaces, BLM land."

"Yes." He returned to a subject we'd discussed earlier. "You're right that I live in the moment. It becomes the whole world, forever. Do you promise me there's hope?"

"Yes."

"This won't go on forever?"

"No." I thought, *"But there are times when it'll seem like forever."*

"I feel so powerless."

We were talking about The Novel, "the monolith," as Mike called it.

"With FTW you worked one step at a time," I began. "The articles were a helluva lot shorter than a novel, you knew where you were going, what you wanted to say, and how to get from here to there. With a novel, no one's crying for you to write it. You have to make the whole thing up out of nothing."

He nodded, his eyes, widened. Boy, was he aware of that.

I had written one novel, which has not yet sought publication. Like most first novels, it was based on my life and was born of a need to tell a story.

Mike's novel, on the other hand, was not driven from within; it was yet another obligation and one that was oppressive not because it represented a volume of work but for the opposite reason: because it was so amorphous.

"Apart from that goal, you need something more mundane to do with your time," I observed.

The previous night, I had cc'ed an ally on an email to Ray about the lies in Mike's biography on Wikipedia. The ally emailed back that the Subscription link on the FTW website was still up.

Mike and I tested it. I subscribed yet again to FTW and got two confirmations, one from the bookkeeper, the other from "Administrator."

"I gotta send an email to Ray," Mike said, shifting into efficient mode. As long as the tasks were specific and of manageable size, he thrived.

He showed me how to log into his computer files. I didn't want to know. If something got lost, I didn't want to be blamed. But Mike was probably thinking that if he was hospitalized, he might want to ask me to go rummaging in his files for him.

"See? I have files on everybody," he said.

I did see. They were alphabetized by first name but they were formidable.

"You're in here."

"You said you had several files on me, one professional, one personal. Then the T-17's [the news articles I found and forwarded to FTW] went into their own file."

He looked for the personal file but couldn't find it.

"I probably destroyed it in Venezuela when they were after me."

"You thought they might go after me too?"

"Me! Psy-Ops! If they knew I had a vulnerability!" He calmed down. "That's how it works, Sweetheart."

"When I was twenty-seven and had just left LAPD, I said, 'I'm putting my life on hold 'til I figure this CIA thing out.

'After I wrote Rubicon, I wanted to pick up where I'd left off and be twenty-seven again... When am I going to stop these thoughts of [the three possible perpetrators of the burglary?]"

"When you stop feeling so powerless."

Part 30: Transference

"I accomplished five things today," Mike said, getting up from writing a memo to an FTW staff member requesting, yet again, the black checkbook for the Ruppert family trust.

But more work lay ahead. With $15,000 dollars, Mike and Ray could go to Ashland, kick ass and silence [the female employee suing him] forever.

Also, the prospect of giving up the intellectual property rights to his own work stuck in his craw.

"I'm going to ask Ray to stall the sale [of the website] 'til February," he said. That was when the newspaper article about him was scheduled to come out.

Why were they holding onto it until February? he wondered. What did the newspaper know? Was Rumsfeld going to be indicted over the Pat Tillman case? (In the end, Secretary of Defense Donald Rumsfeld resigned and nine officers, including three generals, were disciplined over the cover-up of death by friendly fire.)

That evening we watched Steven Spielberg get an award at the Kennedy Center. The parallels between Spielberg's life (an award ceremony, the reference to hope) and Mike's life as it should have been kept us both transfixed until the Bernstein chorus rose to its climactic finale.

I'd called two Peak Oil activists to widen Mike's social circle. He needed friends, he said, "besides you, no offense to you. So they'll call me up and say, 'Hey Mike, you want to go out?'"

It was the challenge of high school all over again, only this time, I was Mom. I provided shelter but he hated it; it represented everything he'd stood against. One evening he went to the roof and took a picture of the sun setting over Wall Street. The symbolism amused him and he stored the photo for possible use in a future article. He felt imprisoned in my apartment so that although on a conscious level, he knew he should feel grateful to me, on a deeper level, I was his jailer.

There's a phenomenon in psychology known as "transference." Say, for example, that a patient gets angry at the psychiatrist for a particular comment which was not especially inflammatory. This could be a clue to the psychiatrist that the comment has "pushed a button" for the patient; reminded him or her of similar comments that the patient's father or mother used to make. If this turns out to be so, psychiatrists say that the patient has "transferred" his or her feelings about the parent to the psychiatrist. Transference, then, may provide the psychiatrist with insight into the patient's family history.

In such a way did Mike seem to be transferring onto me his attitude towards his mother.

Once, when he described his mother's worrying, I asked him what she worried about.

"Same things you worry about," he answered. "'Should I stop for a yellow light?'"

I have a driver's license but no experience driving and had heard conflicting advice about what to do when approaching a yellow light. My driving teacher, whose greatest fear in life was whiplash, insisted you should speed up to sail through the intersection but that sounded suspiciously like the response of a cabdriver; other driving sages recommended the opposite.

One night, we were having roast beef sandwiches. This was not my usual fare; I'd bought them because after Venezuela, Mike craved familiar food and at that time, he was still a meat-and-potatoes guy. In fact, one of our running jokes was the "strange" vegetables I used to bring home which he'd never seen.

"You sound exactly like my mother," Mike said and with his usual pitch-perfect talent at impersonation, he imitated her chewing with her mouth open. The sound was moist and revolting.

I've eaten with many people, some of whom were not shy about expressing criticism but not since childhood have I eaten with my mouth open although I don't doubt Mike could hear my chewing that night.

I made sure we never ate together at home again. I ate what I wanted when I wanted and left some for him to do likewise. He never commented on the change, which meant he must have been relieved.

Even the apartment reminded him of his mother's. There were

colorful pillows on the couch and a bookcase in the middle of the living-room displaying artifacts from around the world — a marble box from a souvenir stand at the Taj Mahal inlaid, like the Taj itself, with blue and orange stones in a floral design; a pair of embroidered shoes, such as one might find in Arabian Nights, that the office manager of my ex-husband's law firm had given me when he screwed up my ticket home from Saudi Arabia — so I hadn't felt a need to hang pictures on the walls.

Mike found their absence so depressing, he told one of his psychiatrists who recommended that he pick out some pictures which would make him feel more at home.

In the bedroom, the reminder of his mother was that I had so many clothes, courtesy of my own mother or friends who'd gained weight. Eight months earlier, before he ever contemplated moving in and while we were just getting to know each other, Mike had said, "I bet you have a lot of clothes." I hadn't understood enough to be wary; that already, I reminded him of his mother.

Now that we were living together, he wanted more space in the closet so he suggested we throw away some of my paraphernalia that seemed to be out of circulation. We would play upbeat music and make a party out of it, a bonfire of the vanities.

I was not so excited as he at this prospect which reminded me of a previous partner who had once said in anger, "Get your shit out of here so I can put away my stuff."

Mike registered my lack of enthusiasm and let the idea go. And I rearranged things to make more room.

One afternoon he paced the living-room repeating, "You're not my mother; I can have an intelligent conversation with you."

I had no trouble understanding I was not his mother; it was he himself who needed to be convinced.

The two Peak Oil activists, X and Y, called back. X was a young admirer. I had my doubts about fifty-somethings hanging out with twenty-somethings but it was a start and X had advantages over the average twenty-something. Mike didn't want to be around strangers who didn't know his work or what he stood for. We kicked around some ideas of what to do. X had just bought a truck so it was hard for him to park in the city. He suggested we go to his house in the suburbs and hang out at the largest mall in the area.

The ironies were obvious — a trio of Peak Oilists seeking recreation at that pinnacle of unsustainability, a suburban mall — and Mike wasn't up for the trek. We did see Y several times but not X who, for reasons I never learned, if indeed it is ever possible to know such reasons, later killed himself.

Part 31: Prelude to Bellevue

We were at a pizzeria, killing time before Mike's doctor's appointment in a neighborhood run by the Mafia. I knew this because my husband had lived there when we met and when I had voiced misgivings about moving in, he had assured me the Mafia kept it safe since they didn't want any unnecessary visits from the police.

So when four guys stuffed into their shark-skin suits sat down at a table across from us, I was reminded of a story about a little boy whose first full sentence was, "My father is a respectable businessman."

"Dolphins are the only mammals that have recreational sex," observed one good fella.

"And monkeys," Mike interjected. "Baboons throw wild parties."

I wanted to show Mike the finer aspects of New York — the streets of Brooklyn Heights that evoked another era; the Central Park zoo where tropical birds flew freely overhead, alighting on the finger of anyone with the patience to wait. My hope was to melt his aloofness but he would have none of it, remaining determined to hold fast to his hate as though it was his last vestige of identity. Anyway, on Ativan, he subsided onto the bed before even getting dressed.

But one night after he'd been in all day so determination trumped lethargy, we went to see Apocalypto. The movie was great but when it ended, everyone poured out of their respective theaters at the same time, piling on top of each other on the narrow escalator.

"What would happen in a fire?" Mike exclaimed. "We're not going back there."

Saturday was grim as Mike described himself ending up in Bellevue, drooling, in a strait jacket.

"Dress up," I suggested.

He put on a black shirt and black pants.

"A little depressing, you think?"

"Yup."

He changed into his blue dress shirt over a red turtleneck.

Nonetheless, as he packed his bag (medical records, toothbrush, copy of *Crossing the Rubicon*,) he moved with the somber air of a man embarking on his final journey, just as he had before departing for Venezuela.

I went with him partly because he was afraid of the NYC transit system, but more because he was afraid of being swallowed up by the mental health system. As a backup witness with legal clout, Ray promised to meet us there.

Only one visitor was allowed in the waiting room so I accompanied Mike while Ray sat outside reading the Sunday Times Book Review before dozing off.

Mike was given no-stick blue slippers, an across-the-board policy against patients who kicked.

Ahead of us was a Cooper Union student, a slight girl with bloodshot eyes, flanked by two roommates. Over the next several hours, fragments of her story unfolded: Boyfriend troubles; boyfriend's father, feeling responsible, had called 911. The roommates knew nothing about the situation although the cops talked to them accusatorily.

Another woman was brought in with her hands behind her back. The handcuffs were removed, leaving indentations on her wrists.

("She's fat," Mike explained in a whisper.)

In an abusive relationship, she had finally lashed back at her boyfriend.

"Just my luck," she moaned several times over the course of the evening, "it was right in front of an FBI car."

The two female cops advised her to speak calmly to the judge and explain what she had just told them. They were attractive, particularly the blond whom I privately dubbed Brunnhilde and who captured the imaginations of both Mike and Ray.

"When I was young, I would have gone ten rounds with her," Mike said. "She must get chased around the station house."

Another prisoner was brought in, cuffed to a wheelchair.

"Smith and Wesson 45," [I'm not sure that was the brand] Mike said, referring to the cop's gun. "I was in LAPD," he continued. "I used to love the [he named another gun.]"

"Yeah?" said the cop.

"You were in LAPD?" asked Brunnhilde.

"Yeah. 'Til I found the government dealing drugs. I had a website where I published some articles about it. I also wrote this." He pulled out the copy of Rubicon.

"See? Here's my picture." He held it up next to his face, mimicking the smile in the photograph.

"Oh yeah," said Brunnhilde. "You wrote that? Wow. Can I see?" Then, perusing the book, "I'm going to get this."

The cop with the Smith and Wesson 45 shook Mike's hand.

"Yeah, the government is involved in a lot of bad shit," said Smith and Wesson's partner.

"If I had it to do over again," Mike said, "I wouldn't go into narcotics; I'd stick with homicide. You see some bad shit but at least it's clear."

Mike and I had discussed this. No matter which department he started out in, I maintained, he would have followed its path to its origin and uncovered corruption at the highest levels of government, where all roads lead.

He agreed, which seemed to alleviate one source of angst. *("If only I hadn't started out in Narcotics.")*

Bellevue was surprisingly reassuring; his doctor, who, although female, looked like a dark Apollo, was subtle and concerned; the bureaucracy, smoother than the Kafkaesque nightmare he'd envisioned.

He speculated that this was because New York ran on the labor of the poor. "Bloomberg knows this." Thus it behooved the city to take care of them.

The doctor, like a previous psychiatrist, proffered the tentative diagnosis of bi-polar.

"One thing she said clicked," Mike reflected later. "She asked me if I'd engaged in risky behavior, spending money I didn't have, risky sexual behavior. I did spend a lot of money I didn't have, but I don't know about risky behavior."

"The burundanga ladies," I reminded him, without raising the sore point of the female employee who'd filed suit.

"That was risky behavior. That was the day that Nicolas Maduro and Chavez endorsed the 'no plane' theory. I'd warned the government it was a trap so when that came out, I realized the upper echelons didn't even know I was there.

'I just didn't care anymore.

'And I used to walk down some pretty God-forsaken streets in Caracas hoping someone would say, 'Your money or your life.'"

He opened his arms wide in imitation of what his reaction would have been. "Take me."

Part 32: Therapy

Yesterday's post prompted an unusual crop of expansive and informed comments, among them, that people would either love the post or hate it. This was surprising because I had thought it more of a holding pattern, filling in details of Mike's daily life and preoccupations but providing no revelations. Perhaps that particular commenter thought that some people would be offended by the description of Mike's first foray into a mental institution. But there was no secret about that; he had written of it himself in 2007.

Anyway, today we have to backtrack because I came upon a cache of notes from a time leading up to his admission to Bellevue; my notes are not so organized as one might wish. In fact, I've found other omitted details, which, if this account develops into a book, will be tucked in at the appropriate moments, more or less. But today's find was too large to overlook.

"It would help you to see what role you played in this mess, but without passing judgment," I told Mike during one of his many bouts of angst. "You're agonizing, 'It's all my fault,' then reminding yourself it was also other people's fault and transferring your rage to them. You *did* play a role getting yourself into this mess and it would be enlightening for you to figure out what it was. It doesn't matter if it was 60/40 in your favor or theirs. But try to see it objectively without the cringeing guilt."

My best friend, a clinical psychologist, had taught me the salutary effect of taking responsibility, though without censure; it provides a greater sense of power over one's own actions and by extension, one's emotions.

I also wanted to head off a possible reaction Mike could have as he embarked on therapy so I said, "You have been suicidal and right now you are ambivalent about being alive. I talked you out of killing yourself in Venezuela and here. In the course of your therapy, as you go over the 'train wreck' of your life, [his words] you may find yourself resenting me."

"You mean for saving my life?" Mike asked.

"Yes. If this happens, let it happen. Don't necessarily tell me about it but tell your shrink and explore it."

"OK."

We changed the subject to Jamey Hecht, the editor of FTW and *Crossing the Rubicon*, wondering if he would call over the Christmas vacation when he came to town to see his parents and more pointedly, to bring his daughter to see them.

"I wonder where he stands these days," Mike said. "After [a close friend who now resented him,] nothing would surprise me."

"I don't think she turned as far as you think she did. She back-pedaled in an email to me, about how she wasn't 'accusing' you.

'There's something about email that makes people seem angrier than they are. All you read is what's in the email itself. There's a whole lot of ambivalence they don't bother to express.

'Also it may take them five seconds to dash off the equivalent of 'fuck you.' They forget about it but when you open it, it's like an explosion and you're left with the debris."

Dr. X. recommended a therapist who would be cheaper than a psychiatrist. *("This is New York. We can find one for you right in your neighborhood.")* Mike would check with his psychiatrist once a month so she could monitor his medication.

"I'd recommend you ask for the most intelligent therapist rather than the most convenient," I advised Mike, having learned that lesson myself the hard way. "It's not like looking for a dry cleaner."

"How do you go about finding a good therapist?"

"Clumsily. I once went through seven before rejecting all of them. One was sweet until the end of the session when she screamed that she didn't take checks. Later she called to apologize, saying she'd been 'picking up on all the anxiety in there.' That's a lousy excuse for a therapist.

'Another one explained why she thought my behavior was 'angry' by saying, 'Let's just say I've been in this business longer than you have.'

'A third, who was a full-fledged psychiatrist, wanted to hear about my mother's career in show business.

'I gave up. But nine years later, I was sitting on the park bench talking to another mother who described being suicidal after her son was born. She seemed enviably stable so I asked her how she did it. She told me the name of her psychiatrist and I called her. She was wonderful."

At least, as far as therapy went, Mike had landed in the right city.

December 27, 2006

Another bill collector called. Mike's house phone in Ashland was never turned off.

Sometimes when he tired of talking about himself, Mike asked about me. Like most people in a relationship, he wanted to know about his predecessors. He was particularly interested in one who had threatened abuse.

"The one article I wrote for the LA Times," he said, "was about battered women. I didn't have much respect for them because they kept choosing the same sort of men. But I recognize that those qualities that I looked down on are the ones that are saving me now, with you."

Another loaded statement, betraying his evolution from, "Blame the victim" to a more reflective response; not to mention what it revealed about his perception of our relationship.

"Will I ever get everything under control? Perfect? Will I ever be comfortable?"

112

"Honey chil', you can be comfortable loooong before you're perfect."

"I can be comfortable without being perfect," he marveled, incredulous. "I can be comfortable. Without being perfect."

[On one of his colleagues:] "There's a saying in AA: What do you have when you take a drunken horse-thief and stop him from drinking?"

Shrug.

"A sober horse thief.

'[The colleague] is an ex-heroin addict. But she still thinks like a heroin addict."

"One of my thoughts when I left for Venezuela was: 'You trashed my company; now you deal with it.' They wouldn't have extradited me for debts amounting to a few hundred dollars."

"I think your moves have been a form of panic attack," I answered. "'Gotta get outta here.' First LA, then Ashland, then Venezuela, then Canada, now New York."

"I never had panic attacks before I got here."

I ignored the implication that I or my apartment or New York or all three were to blame. "You always had some other emergency, your business or your health. You always had a goal. Nature and you abhor a vacuum. When you don't have something concrete and immediate to do, the panic rushes into the void. I think that's why you kept yourself lurching from one emergency to the next when FTW was going full throttle. And when you took a break, you smoked."

"Don't take smoking away from me," he warned defensively, his voice rising. "You're not going to stop me from smoking, are you?"

I thought, "I don't have that power." But I did. I could have given him an ultimatum about staying in my apartment. However, that seemed farfetched. Did he really think I'd do that?

He asked why no one had tried harder to dissuade him from running to Venezuela.

"You knew a helluva lot more about all this stuff than we did," I explained. "When you said the CIA were after you, what were we supposed to say? 'No, they're not?'"

He spoke of his broken relationships, the people he'd overlooked or actively kicked out of the way.

"Maybe you felt that your main relationship was not with an individual but with the world," I said.

"Wow. That's something to think about."

I'd come to that conclusion because it was a thought I'd entertained about myself years before. But he never asked how I arrived at my analyses.

Part 33: Alone

December 28 2006

Last night we talked about what sort of animals we'd have in Portland.

"How do you feel about chickens?" Mike asked.

I feel positively enough towards chickens.

"But no roosters," he continued.

"What'll we do for eggs? Borrow the rooster down the street?"

"You don't need roosters for eggs."

"What are you talking about? There was a komodo dragon that gave birth parthenogenically this week but it made the paper and she wasn't a chicken."

"Oh. I heard you didn't need roosters. Well, we'll keep him at the far end of the property. They crow 24/7."

The two city slickers, one from LA and Washington, the other from New York, are going to need some help with our sustainable farming.[8]

10 PM

A terrible night. A fellow in Ohio has Quikbooks Pro with which he can convert the accounting files to Excel.

Although I have put out a request for this on the blog at Mike's request, the response sends him into a depression. "I don't want to see it," he cries.

I remind him that when Michael Kane left FTW, Mike Ruppert was relieved. "I only kept it alive for him, because he loved it so much," he had said at the time.

He explains now, "There's the fact that it's dead and then there's the way it died. I can't face seeing the numbers, how they destroyed it. It's like watching a movie of your child being murdered."

I have a long-standing engagement tomorrow night to which I

---

[8] I've since learned that Mike was right in the sense that the eggs we eat aren't fertilized so no, you don't need a rooster.

can't bring Mike. I've suggested he call his AA sponsor or Barry. Tomorrow morning I will also suggest an FTW supporter with whom we've spoken several times.

But as he lies in bed, he confesses to thinking about how when I'm out, he might commit suicide.

"What am I supposed to do with this?" I ask. "Call [his psychiatrist?]"

"No, because then they'd put me in Bellevue and I can't stand being locked up. Now that I've said it, I won't do it. That's the purpose of having said it."

I remember, but don't bring up, that in April he told me and Monica Psomas about his fascination with the female employee who later sued him for harassment; the temptation to have an affair.

"Talking about it is a way to make sure I don't act on it," he had said at the time.

"Can I have your word that you'll tell [his psychiatrist] about this thought the way you gave her your word a few weeks ago that if she prescribed something for you, you'd go to Bellevue on Saturday?"

"Yes."

"Can we extend that beyond just tomorrow? If you did it, they'd ask me, 'Did he talk about suicide?' 'Yes.' 'Why didn't you call his shrink?'"

"I know I've put you in a tight spot."

But he didn't offer a way out. Instead he said, "Without a broken neck it takes four minutes for death from hanging; two minutes for permanent brain damage. That would be terrible."

"You wouldn't know."

"You could have brain impairment but the cortex would be intact."

"When you tried it in Venezuela, how did you know Carlos wouldn't have to go to the bathroom and find you?"

"Two bathrooms."

He thanked God out loud for the supporters who loved him as well as for me while giving me a sidelong glance to see whether I was touched.

Then he emerged from suicide mode and talked about a case that could be brought against his former employees in Ashland.

116

"Three to five years to bring a civil case," he said. "And at what price?"

I remembered the adage: *In any lawsuit, one person loses; the other person loses more.*

I also tucked into a corner of my mind the obligation to make sure his shrinks knew about his suicidal ideation. One of the questions they ask in order to determine if a person is serious in intent is, "Do you have a way?" Mike did. We don't play with fire. If Mike didn't tell one of his shrinks, I would.

December 29, 2006

By way of bolstering Mike's spirits to face the empty apartment this evening when I'm out, I suggested we play hookey and go to Manhattan for some "Kulture" or a walk down one of the magnificent side streets, what I had privately dubbed "Consulate Lane," off Fifth Avenue in the sixties. Some countries must have doubled their national debt to secure that real estate.

But as he got on email, "Whoa!" erupted from the computer corner.

"What?"

"[The prospective buyer] to Ray: He's gone ahead setting up the new site. All we have to do is sign the contract."

The problem is, if Mike backs out now, the prospective buyer can, whether successfully or not, sue him for the "good faith" investment he's made in setting up the new site.

He has taken a risk going ahead before the contract was signed.

"What's normal business practice here?" I asked.

"To wait 'til the contract is signed."

"So that's the reasonable man standard."

Mike nodded. "Another one bites the dust. He'll tell [an ally who'd turned against him,] 'You were right.'"

"Won't be news to her."

"I woke up thinking about her. [In the quasi-dream] she was trying to win over Cynthia."

Despite protestations that he is just responding to Mike's call for help, the prospective buyer is champing at the bit to close the deal. If Mike signs the contract, everything will be a fait accompli on Monday, New Year's Day. For $5000, the prospective buyer will own Mike's intellectual property, getting the proceeds for any movie deals in the future.

Also the contract contains a non-compete clause, which gags Mike from writing about the subjects on which he's expert — such as Peak Oil — for two years.

This makes no sense to me. If Mike wrote again, people would dash to his former website, now owned by the prospective buyer who would thereby gain readership.

This clause may prove to be the stumbling block for the deal.

Part 34: Hash Browns

Someone asked an intelligent question about the last post: Did the prospective buyer just want to shut Mike up? Of course, we don't know other people's motives but in terms of investigative journalism, shutting Mike up by that time was supererogatory. He understood that that was the condition on which he'd be allowed to survive in the U.S. and he accepted it; that was why he was selling the website in the first place. For all the speaking out he did after 2006 in the movie Collapse or the Vice series or on Facebook, he was reiterating already known facts or connecting them in a way that revealed underlying trends which was one of his greatest gifts. But, as he put it, "9/11 is so dead." The window of opportunity to act on the information he and others had exposed with respect to that disaster, and all that it implied, had closed with the 2004 election. The one in '08 just sealed the deal. On to today's post:

The Village Voice called for the second time about a prospective article on Senator Schumer's response, or lack thereof, to the environmental disaster of 9/11.

"I have two questions," said the writer, Kristin Lombardi. "First of all, do you have [an activist]'s contact information?"

"Let me look it up," I answered. "Meanwhile, ask me the second question."

"Do you think I'm being unfair to Schumer? Some of the other activists are saying that."

"I told you they would."

"Yes, you did."

"It's complicated. Hillary could have and should have done a lot more, a lot sooner. I called her about the barge at Stuyvesant [the waste transfer station directly outside my son's school where tens, if not hundreds, of thousands of tons of toxic debris was brought in violation of state and federal law] and so did the Stuyvesant Parents' Association. Her office said, 'That's a local issue.' You didn't hear a peep out of her until February when it started to become accepted that the environment was a major problem. She could have prevented some of this tragedy. Instead, she just opted to count the bodies."

"But still, she's done a lot more than Schumer."

"Right, when it was politically expedient, when the wind was already changing."

"Why are the activists telling me to go easy on him?"

I said something to the effect of, "Because they're clinging to the thread of hope that playing nicely will get them somewhere."

I told Lombardi to talk to Chief Investigator for the EPA Ombudsman, Hugh Kaufman, about how Schumer's wife, Iris Weinshall, was herself implicated in the environmental fallout from 9/11: She ran the city's Department of Transportation which placed the waste transfer barge at Stuyvesant's doorstep.[9] But lest anyone accuse the Schumer-Weinshalls of hypocrisy, their own daughter was also a student at the school at the time.

Afterwards Mike, who'd heard the conversation from the computer desk, said, "Boy, as a journalist, I'd think you're the real deal... and when you're passionate, you're scary." That was gratifying.

Three months after the article came out, Lombardi was fired. The Huffington Post[10] later reported on the irony of her winning a prize for her article, *Death by Dust*, on the environmental aftermath of 9/11.

"I have a lot of reading to do," Mike said in anticipation of his upcoming trip to Bellevue, "on bi-polar. By the time I go in, I'll be able to tell the doctors things."

"I hope you're not going to be one of those patients who hide behind intellectual understanding in order to avoid being honest with themselves, which is the real work of therapy."

"No," he answered, a little sheepishly. But he was a quick study: "That's why I'm not going to do any reading."

A day or two later, we were in the Happy Days diner where Mike was having ham, eggs and hash browns with Worcestershire sauce. After all the alien culture in his life recently, including Brooklyn, he was ravenous for his own particular comfort foods.

---

[9] http://web.mta.info/mta/leadership/weinshall.htm

[10] http://www.huffingtonpost.com/2007/06/18/fired-villagevoice-write_n_52663.html

He mused on a notice we could post on the blog: "I'm a mental case who just got out of Bellevue. Anyone want to read what I have to say about the state of the world? Please send donations."

Eulogy

Written upon request for one of several memorials for Mike and read at the Portland memorial by Collapsenet CEO Wesley T. Miller's wife, Cathy Breen Miller.

Mike Ruppert was a complex, brilliant, infuriating, funny, impossible, honest (usually), never boring, enraged, musical, competitive, generous, contradictory, dog-loving, horse-whispering, childlike giant who happened to be right about the most important problems facing the world today.

A psychologist once said, "You can't have just a baby's foot," meaning, you can't have the cute parts of a baby without the sleepless nights and dirty diapers. Similarly, you can't have Mike's unique gifts to the world without the upheaval he generated around him.

To lionize him does not do him justice; he doesn't need it. He had his demons, both internal and external. In fact, he epitomized the old saw, "Just because you're paranoid doesn't mean they're not following you."

He once said, "There is a deep flaw in me and that is the source of everything I've done." Driven to flee his own devils, he fought far greater ones on the global stage. And although he didn't succeed in single-handedly shifting the paradigm of the global economy, he got further than just about anyone else.

You don't have to perform the mind-bending feat of accepting death by self-inflicted gunshot wound as a peace offering in order to show him respect. To paraphrase Mike's own eulogy to Gary Webb who also killed himself, only Mike knows why he finally did it after threatening for at least eight years.

Some of Mike's accomplishments: From uncovering CIA drug-dealing, he went on to found fromthewilderness.com which revealed how the US banking system looted Russia after the fall of the USSR. FTW also published documents which helped secure the release of CIA spy Edwin Wilson who had been convicted on the basis of perjured testimony by a CIA Executive Director.

But one of his greatest achievements occurred around 9/11. At

FTW and in his book, *Crossing the Rubicon*, Mike showed that four months before the attacks, Vice President Dick Cheney had been put in charge of war game exercises; and that in spite of the multiple warnings from foreign intelligence agencies to the White House concerning a terrorist attack the week of September 9, at least five war games had been scheduled for that morning which drew planes away from the East Coast, where they would have been able to intercept the hijacked planes, to Alaska, Northern Canada, Greenland and Iceland. FTW also revealed insider trading – exorbitant numbers of put options on the airlines involved in the attacks; a sure red flag that a major disaster was about to take place. (*Added later: The US government monitors put options in real time.*)

The best way to honor Mike is to understand and educate others on the fundamental lessons he taught. First, his favorite line: "Until you change the way money works, you change nothing." An economy based on infinite growth cannot continue indefinitely on a finite planet. Resources are being depleted as population growth marches on. The population currently stands at seven times what it was when oil started being used to fuel the economy. No matter how smart our technology becomes, as easy oil inevitably wanes, the replacements cannot fill in at the same rate, certainly not without poisoning the air, water and soil as well as huge swaths of people. If we don't deal with this now, it will deal with us later and at far greater cost. That's what Mike's been trying to tell everyone for ten years. Re-localize. Grow food not lawns. And end our current economic system of fiat currency, fractional reserve banking and interest. Do that and Mike will be able to rest in peace.

Part 35: Bonding

"When I was about ten and had just moved to a new school, we had rope-climbing in gym. I'd never climbed a rope and I sucked. I became a champion rope-climber after that.

'Another time, also when I was ten, the kids were changing in the locker room at the pool. I was uncircumcised so I made my dad wait with me in the parking lot until the kids were done. He was furious. He spanked me. When I was twelve I got circumcised."

Then he told another story from his twelfth year — and not, as I'd incorrectly remembered, his teens — of his father's making him a screwdriver and Mike's airing dirty family laundry ("Then Dad beat the shit out of me,") while under the influence.

Exchanging stories of childhood scars had been for him, as it is for many people, a way of bonding with others. He remembered a former FTW intern, the son of a well-known actress, (FTW headquarters were in LA, after all) whose parents used to tie him to his crib until he was nine while they went out drinking.

I told him about a friend who left a career as a charismatic philosophy professor at a prestigious college on the eve of being offered tenure. The more popular and successful she became, the more anxious she felt.

"The impostor syndrome," Mike said.

Several years after leaving the college, she switched fields and earned her second Ph.D., this time in psychology, which she practiced, often pro bono, to the betterment of any who were lucky and perceptive enough to consult her.

Her understanding of the workings of both fields also led her down the path of self-analysis towards becoming a "mensch," a good human being, which didn't come easily because of her troubled upbringing which I described to Mike in greater detail than is possible here.

"I appreciate the story you told me about your friend," Mike says later.

Amy Goodman has signed a deal with King Features Syndicate and Hearst, publisher of Popular Mechanics, the infamous magazine that purported to destroy 9/11 "conspiracy theories." Mike is devastated.

"They couldn't have done this if I was still in the game," he says. "Maybe going to Venezuela wasn't such a bad idea. This shows the forces that were lined up against me.

'I'm Mozart; she's Salieri... I just had no idea it would be this hard."

"At least she's been outted."

He nods unhappily.

"And everyone watching that movie would rather be Mozart than Salieri," I add.

"But would Mozart rather have been Mozart?"

"He made that choice."

"I have the feeling they haven't finished with me yet."

I don't ask what he thinks "they" might still have up their sleeve. What's left but death?

He opens the door and looks both ways down the hall. "I thought I heard someone come in from the stairwell."

The door to the stairwell flaps open occasionally; when I first moved into the apartment, I also checked on the odd noises emanating from that quarter; Mike's behavior is edgy but not yet paranoid. Still, I'm reminded of the observation that one motive to become paranoid can be to feel important: Thinking "they" are after you is preferable to admitting that "they" don't give a shit anymore.

This is not to suggest Mike invented the persecution he alleged. But a natural side effect of government harassment is that the victim becomes wary, always looking over his shoulder and suspicious even in innocent circumstances, in the belief that it's when you let down your guard that they get you. When Mike finally did "get out of the game," it's understandable that his habit of hyper-vigilance lingered. And thinking "they" are about to get you is an honorable respite from your own drive to do yourself in.

"I have the feeling you're so mad because you'd like to respond but you can't; that's why you feel helpless again," I said.

"I castrated myself. The only way I could comment is if popular opinion wanted me to; otherwise it would just be perceived as sour grapes. Cynthia would understand this."

He still harbors a suppressed hope that, like Tinkerbell, he will return to his former way of life if the faceless public clap vigorously enough.

Later, as he takes a stab at planning his novel, I peruse the Sunday Times Book Review.

"Are you aware of the encroachment of nonfiction on the fiction market in the last thirty years?" I ask.

"No."

"People feel less of a need for fiction. I think Oprah has something to do with it. A hundred years ago, people went to fiction to find out the truth; society was so repressed. But now everyone shares their libido on TV."

He nods, seeing the plausibility of the notion.

"Great," he says drily.

In the end, he recognizes that his heart wasn't in the novel; his next book should be nonfiction.

After a breakfast of triple berry granola, he retires for his "favorite part of the day," a cup of coffee and a cigarette on the stairwell. We had planned to see the Ed Wilson/Ted Shackley movie but he's not up for it, opting, instead, to take a nap. Although he uses this as yet another reason for self-flagellation, he recognizes that he always feels better afterwards and gets things done.

"I don't want to just sit here like a bump on a log, dragging you down."

"You don't have the power to drag me down any more than I have the power to drag you up."

The prospect of Bellevue has crept one day closer.

"Maybe you're so afraid of being locked up because a part of you wants to be.

'You've been bouncing from a manic state — on the phone, smoking, taking a plane, lecturing for four hours — to this." I gesture towards him, dejection incarnate in his hooded sweatshirt, (he is always cold in Brooklyn, one more reason to hate it) hunched over with his elbows on his knees, chin in hands. "Each state is an escape from the other. Your last manic phase, you kept going 'til you hit a brick wall.

'Maybe you're looking to get locked up because all your life you took care of your mother; she didn't take care of you."

This is how Mike presented his early years, whether accurately or not. So it was a way of talking to him that he would accept.

"And God knows, your father also left you to take care of her. Getting locked up would be a way of saying, 'It's my turn to be taken care of, Goddammit."

He nods. "Yeah!" he says. "I don't want to face this mountain of crap."

It's a time-honored escape. My friend the clinical psychologist has said that people sometimes drive themselves truly nuts in order to do things they can't get away with when sane (an observation Mike has also made, but about people on drugs. Thus, although he believed it possible that some of his employees smashed his computers while high on crystal meth, he still didn't find the act excusable; in his view, the drug would only have freed impulses that were already in there.)

But why not take the vacation while saving yourself the trouble of going insane?

Because it's not allowed.

"I have a young kid to take care of," he asserts. "Maybe therapy would unleash something that would otherwise remain unconscious."

"That's the hope. But share with your shrink the dilemma that your fear of getting locked up will inhibit your honesty. [This would set the stage for his telling her of his suicidal impulses.]

'You could also ask her about biofeedback. It's sort of like what Dr. X was doing with you, visualizing peaceful scenes. It can be very effective."

As he takes off his shoes he says, "We may have to face the fact that I need to get locked up. It's not a matter of who or what or why anymore. I just feel like I want to die."

Part 36: Bellevue 2

This account is different from the previous post on Bellevue. I remember some of the scenes in both but not when they took place. I think there were two visits to Bellevue but it's possible that my notes were simply written at two different times.

December 31 2006 10:30 PM

Back from Bellevue, with the bag his psychiatrist told him to pack in case his assessment allowed it. (It didn't.)

We'd been lying down when he said, "I chose the location." He did not need to add, "to kill myself.'

"Are you going to tell [your outpatient psychiatrist]? Because this is the sort of thing I'd have to report."

He nodded. "I know."

"Which is why you told me," I realized.

He turned towards me, nodded again and smiled.

At 4:00 PM he woke up from a three-hour nap saying urgently, "Where's that sheet?"

He consulted the slip from the Effexor for side effects. He was suffering fourteen including anxiety, sleeplessness, loss of appetite, difficulty in urination, constipation, itchiness and loss of libido. The last symptom had nothing to do with me, he assured me, but I wasn't convinced. He had innumerable reasons to write me off.

"I woke up thinking, 'I have to read the insert,'" he said, ever the detective rising to the occasion. "Kelly O'Meara wrote about anti-depressants. Some of them can *cause* suicide."

He called Bellevue where the doctor on duty said that for suicidal thoughts or a rash, he should come into the emergency room.

"Where does it itch?" I asked.

He pulled down his pants and I noted a slightly raised red patch on his upper left buttock.

"As a mother," I said, "if they told me to bring the kid in if he had a rash, I'd probably bring him in with this and they'd probably say, 'It's nothing.'"

He called his outpatient psychiatrist, who called her friend at Bellevue. Five minutes later his outpatient psychiatrist called back to say that her friend would be going on duty at five. It was 4:15.

"We can leave now," I said. "But you haven't eaten anything since this morning, right?"

"Right. That'll take care of itself." And he set about packing with the efficient determination of the old Mike.

I emailed our two Peak Oil activist friends that our New Year's Day get-together tomorrow was probably off.

On the train Mike was silent.

"What are you thinking about?" I asked.

"Getting there."

"When you left for Venezuela, Carolyn wrote how you hugged and cried, then said, abruptly, 'We will not touch anymore.'" This was so he could go into "samurai mode." "Are you feeling that way now?"

He shook his head. "There will be hugs later."

He had once asked me not to hug him in public — like Alex when he was nine, saying in the park, "Don't call me 'darling' in public." But in Mike's case, maybe it was because he was afraid he would cry.

The waiting room was empty but for a patient who coughed and called out in his sleep, flailing his arm. I moved away from him.

"He's heavily medicated," Mike said.

An imposing female cop told the man, "Cover your mouth when you cough. You're coughing on these people. Here, move away; come sit here." Mike took my hand.

A man was wheeled out of the ward and disappeared down the hall.

"Great," said Mike. "That's me."

He promised to tell X [the Bellevue psychiatrist] the whole story: How he had "a location" and "a way."

"No offense," he said, "but there was something about being in that apartment on New Year's Eve that scared me to death."

His comment raised the unspoken question of how he'd feel about the apartment in three days' time, when he would probably be released.

"How would it be if I had a dog and a horse?"

"I don't know. But you don't."

My hunch was it wouldn't have made much difference. He looked at his watch.

"Seven thirty. Time for my valium but they told me not to take it."

A few minutes later he cried; quietly, because he was in public, but with abandon. I held him discreetly.

"This is my life," he cried. "This is what I have to look forward to."

The female cop at the desk absorbed this new data but had the grace not to stare.

The temporary catharsis subsided. Ten more minutes of limbo.

"Did crying help at all?" I asked.

"I don't know," he whined in his, "Stop interrogating me," voice.

I entertained a fantasy of walking out of the waiting room. Instead, I teared up.

"I'm sorry," he said. "Was I short with you just now?"

I nodded.

"I'm sorry." He hugged me. "I think the crying helps a little. Valium keeps me alive, breathing, but it doesn't make me feel better. Plus, it's Valium."

At eight thirty he said, "I'm taking the second Valium." He swiftly opened his suitcase before anyone could stop him and downed the pill.

That mini-drama over, we resumed our positions as bumps on the waiting-room chairs.

"I want to bolt. If I could get past the guard, I'd just go out there and kill myself," he said.

"That's why they have all these guards and those doors.

'I think this feeling is probably what you were running from when you fled to Venezuela."

He pondered this. "That's interesting. You think I was ready back then, in Ashland?" As though I had as much insight as he did.

"Depending on what one means by 'ready.'" One of our misunderstandings has resulted from the literal way he's interpreted my words. When I had used the term "manic" or "depressed," he took pains to explain the diagnosis wasn't certain. I told him it was shorthand; "manic" was the term I used to describe the state of mind in which he multi-tasked on the phone, at the computer, with a cigarette, ten hours a day. He was a quick study and adapted to the looser terminology.

"But I also wanted to consult for the government..." he said before returning to reflective mode. "That means I was thinking about suicide in July."

I mentally responded, "It probably goes back a lot further than that," but decided to keep that thought under wraps.

"I also think it's why you needed to leave Venezuela so urgently. You *had* to leave Saturday. Then when there was a flight Friday, you *had* to leave Friday." (I later learned that in the interim, he had been told of threats to his life.)

"Oh, well, in Venezuela, I *would* have killed myself. I know that...

'Always, 'Got to go; got to go...'" He lapsed back into reflection for a few moments.

'What a great place to spend New Year's Eve," he observed sarcastically, looking around.

"It's perfectly fine."

The staff were kind and wearing New Year's Eve hats. Granted, it gave them the air of characters in *Clockwork Orange* but if one could extricate oneself from that sinister turn of mind, there was much to appreciate.

"What you're complaining about is what's going on inside your head."

An EMT from the Fire Department brought in a drunk woman who tried to leave, complaining loudly, "I can't stay; I can't wait two or three hours."

"She has the right idea," I thought. She got much more prompt service than we did.

The nurse's cell phone rang and the drunk woman danced to it. The cop joined in. X, Mike's Bellevue psychiatrist, appeared at the door and discreetly asked the nurse, "Do you need a stretcher?"

"No, she'll come quietly."

132

The drunk woman was led into the ward where she carried on a loud, but now muffled, conversation.

"Did you see her left forearm?" Mike asked.

"Yes! Was that from heroin?"

Although the cut marks were on the outer part of her arm, I thought she'd run out of veins on the inner portion. I'd read about a play — by a 28-year-old woman who killed herself soon afterwards — in which a heroin addict out of options injects himself in the eyeball.

Mike winced. "Heroin is injected into the veins on the inner portion of the arm. Those cuts were self-mutilizations, mutilizations, mutilations." The Valium had scrambled his neurons. "They're usually self-inflicted by people who've been sexually abused."

A man was wheeled out of the ward with a strap around his chest tying him to the chair. He was followed by a beautiful young girl who changed into street shoes and left.

"I wonder if she was a patient or a visitor," I said. "She was wearing the no-slip slippers."

"Everyone has to wear those."

"I thought they were just so that patients couldn't kick."

"Shoelaces can be used for hanging," he said impatiently, "You can't bring them in."

He pulled a loose thread in his jeans (a pair Alex had never worn but which I'd kept around for five years. "You see the benefit of hoarding?" I had said triumphantly when three of the pairs I'd found fit Mike.) When he couldn't rush to the bathroom to pluck a noisome nose hair, a loose thread would do.

An inch long hole appeared in the jeans.

"The seams of my life," Mike said, voicing the observation I'd suppressed.

We watched some patients on the other side of the door wandering the hall of the ward; they did not inspire confidence.

"[My clinical psychologist friend] learned to speak 'schizophrenese,'" I told Mike. "They make sense if you speak their language.

'You know, 'idiom,' 'idiosyncrasy,' and 'idiot' all derive from the same word. It has to do with speaking a language which no one else understands."

"Great," said Mike. Then, attempting a posture of bravado: "I speak a language that many people understand.

'If anything dramatic happens," he instructed me, "tell [a FTW subscriber.] She's a sweet woman."

"Dramatic?"

"If I get committed long term."

His Bellevue psychiatrist called him in to the ward where someone was being strapped to a stretcher. The guy had a large, eclectic audience: Doctor, nurse, patients.

Back out in the waiting room, a nurse told a cop about her five-year-old son who already did single digit addition and subtraction.

"You're going to have a problem with him when he starts school," warned the cop. "He's going to be bored. They're going to be calling you in for teacher's meetings. He should skip a grade."

Mike returned from his interview with the Bellevue psychiatrist.

"Seventy-two hours," he said and began taking off his belt.

"The status you're under," said the nurse, "the only thing you can keep with you is your underwear."

"Oh, that's not what the doctor told me," said Mike. His outpatient psychiatrist had thought his status would be more stable but her information didn't have the depth or breadth of the Bellevue psychiatrist's.

"You can give her a hug," the nurse told him.

He hugged me but without conviction; his mind, elsewhere.

I turned to leave.

"Don't you want to watch him go in?" asked the nurse.

I stayed.

"You can wave, Mr. Ruppert," she told Mike.

He turned and waved, ever polite, obedient.

Part 37: New Year's Day in Bellevue

As a companion to this post, see Mike's article on fromthewilderness.com entitled, "New Year's at Bellevue."

January 1, 2007

Email to Ray with the heading "mike's phone number:"

xxx-xxxx

they're trying him on lithium today. i was going to visit him at 1 but he says he doesn't see much point. 'there isn't much to talk about here.' we may speak later about whether i should visit him at six.

in a couple of days they'll decide whether he can leave. they think maybe he should stay 'upstairs' (in the long term wing?) for a few more days to see how the lithium is working. they have the option of holding him if they think he's going to 'hurt' himself.

Ray calls to check in. He has not seen the email. I give him an update.

"If you look at Valium closely," he says, "it's in the alcohol family. I don't know what Mike told the doctors..."

"[His outpatient psychiatrist] knows he was in AA." She recommended a Bellevue therapist who was familiar with the organization but Mike said that wasn't a criterion; he wanted someone who was intelligent and who understood his situation.

"Certain points are non-negotiable," he elaborated. "I did write a book. I did have my computers smashed. I did find the government involved in some nasty activities."

"I'm not sure they made the connection," Ray says.

He wants to talk about setting up a regimen for Mike to get out for at least half an hour a day, preferably twice a day. This is a notorious time of year, no getting around it, and today is the bleakest of New Year's days.

I tell him about the email from the prospective buyer. The tone of it is friendly: Mike can quote from his own work but the buyer still wants the intellectual property rights.

"Do you know what he does?" Ray asks.

"For a living? No." Buying and selling companies?

"Snake oil salesman. He has a website, sells [an alternative form of medical treatment.]"

"My God, he really *is* a snake oil salesman." Of course, the alternative treatment might be effective.

"He wants the subscriber list."

"To sell the [treatment] to?"

"Yes. That's the intellectual property."

That doesn't sound like intellectual property, I think. Also, wasn't the subscriber list excluded from the contract?

"Also if there's a movie deal," I say.

"Ah yes," Ray agrees.

2:30 PM

Call from Mike. He's being subjected to fifteen hours of *Honeymooners* reruns.

"Jackie Gleason just doesn't do it for me anymore," he says.

"I always found it a depressing show," I say. "You said it was supposed to be."

He sounds livelier. I ask him if he wants me to come at six.

"I won't be able to do anything but say, 'I want to come home,' and cry."

"That would be a good thing. Nothing wrong with that."

"The other male patients just sit around talking about ways to commit suicide."

"Is that therapy?! Sounds like criminals going to jail and learning how to be better criminals."

"Right."

I tell him what Ray said about Valium being related to alcohol. He reminds me of how I've seen him drink in moderation and without getting drunk.

I say that isn't the point. I'm not sure how the dose of Valium that he's on relates to a drink.

"I've testified on alcohol many times," he says. "I don't need to lecture you on it but this is fine."

Although it's clear he doesn't care whether I visit or not, I go to see him at six. He's wearing hospital drab over his jeans and T-shirt. Having been taken off Effexor, he's antsy to leave and gossips about the other patients. Crying is not on the agenda.

The male patients are watching TV; the women, separated from the men by design, are on the other side of the doctors' Observation Room. Mike has a private corner, also on the other side, from which the doctors can observe his behavior.

The news is on. Mike wants to watch a report about cops who shot an innocent escapee from Katrina in the back seven times.

"See that guy behind me in the glasses? On the cell phone? He keeps saying, 'If I had a 38, I'd blow my brains out right now.'"

A small man in pajamas that are four sizes too big is wheeled out of the ward. As he passes, he shakes Mike's hand.

"So long, Michael," he says. "I made it to upstairs."

"Congratulations," Mike says. "That's what you wanted, right?" Upstairs is anathema to him but to each his own.

A report has come on about the season's second snowstorm in Colorado. Another patient says civilly, "I thought that was a hot state, an arid state." He has a Hispanic accent. Like the other patients, he treats Mike with respect.

"You're maybe thinking of Arizona," I say.

"Or parts of New Mexico," Mike adds.

A stout woman shouts in Spanish and rattles the exit door.

"When she first came, she cursed everyone out in the name of Jesus," Mike comments.

"You see that all the time on the subway," I say, wondering why this woman was brought in, of all the loonies New York is home to. Her shouts are coherent, if loud. "Perhaps she's not so much crazy as ill-mannered."

"She's been heavily medicated," Mike says. "I just want to go home. How's the apartment?"

He must really hate it here if he's homesick for my apartment which is dark, looks out on a construction site and lacks any vestige of nature. "I miss dental floss," he says wistfully.

"I can relate to that."

"This is worse than Venezuela. But the doctor who was here today thinks I might be able to leave tomorrow. What did you do today?"

"Remember how I told you this is the hub of the universe for Indian grocery stores?" Bellevue is on First Avenue and 27th. The Indian grocery stores are around 28th and Lexington. "On the way here I bought three kinds of curry paste. One is from Kashmir!" These days, of course, you can get the same products at the local supermarket.

He smiles indulgently. What kind of sustainability nut am I? A hypocritical one. Or maybe he's thinking about my food preferences which seem to him so alien.

"And I wrote. It's always a satisfying day when I do some writing. 'Have you seen a newspaper?"

"Someone had yesterday's Post. This is the first time the news has been on TV."

"There's a huge effort going on to interest children in what most people call 'classical music.' The Met did a kids' production of The Magic Flute. It's really successful. If there was going to be a world in a generation from now, this would be important."

"Yes!"

Sectarian violence has escalated in Iraq since the hanging of Saddam Hussein a few days ago.

"That was intended," Mike says. Of course. Divide and conquer, in addition to which, it gives the U.S. an excuse to "stay the course."

Since he's off the Effexor, he's able to go to the bathroom again.

"Is that my cue to leave?"

"Yes."

"OK. I understand these priorities. Call me if you want me to come tomorrow at one."

"I may be leaving," he reminds me like a kid who's afraid he'll be abandoned at school.

Part 38: Blowing That Joint

January 2, 2007 9:30 AM

Mike calls.

"Have you got [his outpatient psychiatrist's] number? Please tell me you have her number. I don't have it and they won't let me have a pen; this is a psych ward. But if I have a psychiatrist, they'll let me out today. Otherwise I have to stay here. I just want to get out of here."

I have the number. "Is there someone I can call with it so I don't have to sit here all day waiting for *them* to call?" (The reception on my cell phone is elusive.)

"Hold on a second." He goes off. In the distance I hear him tell everyone around, "Don't hang up the phone; don't hang up the phone."

He comes back. "Are you still there?"

"Yes."

"OK. Hold on."

Somehow he's gotten a hold of a pen with which he takes the number.

11:30 AM

"They're keeping me 'til tomorrow. They want to make sure the lithium is working. There's this woman who's been chanting for four hours and she's parked right outside my room. Oh God."

"What would happen if you just asked her nicely to stop?"

"No."

"Do you want me to come at one?"

"No, come at six like you did yesterday."

"I'm allowed to bring you food. Do you have any special requests?"

He thinks... "A Snickers bar."

8 PM

I've learned the hard way why they tell you to call half an hour before coming to visit; I wasn't allowed in as the ward was too crowded.

At least Officer A. took the Snickers bar, promising to give it to Mike.

Ray's going to call around 8:30, after I was supposed to have left. Mike can't call him because Ray's cell phone has an inaccessible exchange.

January 3, 2007 11:00 AM

"I'm getting out! They're letting me out at twelve fifteen, twelve thirty."

"Do you want me to come get you?"

"If you can, that would be great. Bring the knapsack so I can put this stuff in it.

'I've got to get out of here. I've seen things.... It's like a Freddy Krueger movie. I'm never coming back here...." I imagined he was alluding to people being put in restraints, his greatest fear.

"Last night a woman spread feces on the walls of my room."

I left for Bellevue where I headed for the Information desk. They called the Emergency Psych Ward who said that Mike had left.

"Damn," I thought. "He probably had had enough and went home, knowing I would figure it out." I went home too, stopping to shop on the way. If he was going to act on whim, so was I.

Three messages on my answering machine: "It's 12:15, I'm out front...." "It's 1:00; I'm going to wait 'til hell freezes over..." "It's 1:30; I've been sitting here two hours."

We sorted out the snafu — he'd waited so I could pay for his prescription (his inheritance still hadn't come in and we weren't sure it would) — and forty-five minutes later he showed up, bearing a shopping bag full of clothes that Bellevue provides to inmates when they leave.

"Are they usable?" I asked.

"Yes; these are keepers."

His cheek was covered in three days' stubble. He was tired, shaken.

"I guess if I've taken the subway in grungy sweats, no shave, carrying a brown paper bag, that makes me a New Yorker, huh?

'I saw things... You ate as quickly as possible; one man was doing his bulimic thing next to me as I had breakfast. Then there was the woman taking a dump on the stretcher. I don't know how people stand to work there.

'I'm never going back there. It's Skinnerian treatment, the way they do with dogs and it works. There were some people.... they ain't never comin' back. The nurse said to me, 'You never left.'

'And I had to listen to fifteen hours of *The Honeymooners*. You couldn't change the channel. They had hours of game shows, infotainment; one of the Olsen twins weighs eighty-five pounds.

'But I managed to help an eighteen-year-old black boy. I gave him hope.

'And this morning's rounds were cool. The head doctor — I forget her name — asked me, 'Would you mind giving us twenty minutes of your time? I want these people to understand what the government can do to journalists.'

'I said, 'If I can help someone.'

'All those doctors knew who I was. Some of them had looked me up on Google but they all knew how good a journalist I was.

'They knew about the sexual harassment stuff too. One guy said, 'Yeah, I saw that; it was bullshit.'

'And they understood when I said I wanted to go out in a Valkyrie blaze of glory."

I wondered what, exactly, they understood: Did the desire fit on one of their checklists for "danger to self or others?" For surely, their "understanding" did not merely indicate a sympathetic viewpoint. If it did, God help their patients.

"And they knew Gary Webb. They asked me if I knew him.

'I gave the eulogy at his funeral,'" he quoted himself telling them. He was crying. "I wish Gary could have known that."

"If it ever crosses your mind to kill yourself again, I want you to remember this."

"Yes.

'I told them the one difference between me and Gary was, Gary thought he was going to get back into the mainstream, get a Pulitzer. The [LA] Times hated him. I don't want back in that game.

'A lot of things became clear over the last three days. We have a lot to talk about. My priorities became clearer. My first priority is to take care of me. I deserve to live.... I deserve to live," he turned the phrase over in wonder, crying again. "I have to take care of myself even if the business suffers. I deserve to live a happy, Peak-Oil-ignorant life.

'The first priority is me, the second is the business. Only after those two things are taken care of can I address questions about Peak Oil.

'Gary," (he looked up, as though to Heaven) "I'm going to see you one day, but it isn't going to be for a while."

I joined his crying.

"When I left, the staff hugged me. They call you 'Honey.' 'How's Honey?'" Even some of the patients were cool.

'Oh, I need dental floss. I asked the nurse, 'Who do I have to bribe to get some dental floss?'

'She said, 'I've been working here ten years and ain't no one ever asked me for dental floss.'

"Can you hang yourself with it???"

"No." (One of my students later pointed out that you could use it to slit your wrists.)

"I wanted to bring you toothpicks the other day but they wouldn't have let me bring them in."

"No. They watched the way I brushed my teeth three times a day. All those things were points in my favor."

"What did you talk about with the eighteen-year-old boy?" I asked.

"We didn't have a lot of time; he wasn't a minor but there was something about his age that meant he couldn't stay. He had taken some marijuana and his behavior afterwards indicated he had something wrong. But it wasn't serious enough to keep him. I told him, 'Whatever it is, deal with it now. I've got stuff coming up now that I didn't deal with years ago because I didn't know it was there. Take care of it now.'

142

'When he left we did the knock-fist handshake." He demonstrated.

"He said, 'Take care, Bro.' I could tell that something I said got through to him; somebody he met in the Psych Ward cared.

'There was another girl, beautiful, fair-haired girl, C –, with cuts all the way up her forearm, worse than the woman the other night. That's text book self-mutilation and it almost always comes from sexual abuse."

"Suicide is here," I agreed, indicating the inside of my wrist.

"Do you remember how they did it in Apocalypto?"

I shook my head.

"Here." He drew an imaginary line up his forearm rather than across it.

"Veins run lengthwise. Tendons go across. I learned that as a policeman.

'There was no privacy. You took a shower, the men's and women's bathrooms were the same, with no lock on the door."

"That's more problematic for the women than for the men. You mean the toilets also had no locks?"

"They had no *doors*. I guess they didn't want anyone to get too comfortable in there."

"No one gets that comfortable in there."

"You'd be surprised."

After dinner he said, "I was thinking, if I want to establish roots here, I'd like to pick out a picture to put on the wall so I can think, 'This is mine.' And we have to clear some space in the closets. I could clear out half that closet over there."

"You probably want to throw out that lampshade, which is fine."

"And matching sheets. The sheets there didn't match. I'll pay for them."

"No problem."

We talked about the news.

"The Iranian oil bourse is a joke," I said. The ever-looming, now-you-see-it-not-you-don't bourse which was going to follow in the footsteps of Saddam Hussein and accept non-dollar currencies for oil. The exchange was an omnipresent threat which was about to open any day; then experienced delays, then disappeared for months, then popped up again, keeping the United States on tenterhooks for years.

"And notice how they're playing it. Russia's also playing that game.

'Now, say you were France…" He warmed to the scenario. "If you saw the way the dollar was going, you'd buy more euros and you'd only change back into dollars at the last minute when you wanted to buy oil. Because when the time came to buy oil, you'd be able to buy more."

"Say you were China. To what extent does it matter that you want the U.S. to be there to buy your plastic toys?"

"That market will become saturated. That's why there's something called the Shanghai Cooperation Council that's building up Malaysian, Cambodian and other markets."

Part 39: Dinner with Friends

When I came home at four, Mike was edgy with hunger.

"I forgot to eat lunch," he explained.

"I think that's because you wanted to be served," I said.

"I think it's because I didn't want to eat alone."

That rang true, as well as endearing, but by way of admission that I also had a point, he's been volunteering more to help cook and clean up.

I loaded the dishwasher with pots and pans.

"You're such a girl," he said.

"I chose the location," Mike said, coming in from his morning cigarette, which suggested that the location involved the stairwell. Did he envision climbing over the rail and just letting go, falling to his death? That sounded too passive and feminine an m.o. for him. Had he gone up to the roof? (Later, following a reference in an email to a prospective webmaster, I wondered if he meant the Brooklyn Bridge.)

"Not here," he promised. Carlos has no idea how close he came to finding Mike hanging from the shower head. "I'm wondering how I managed to get this far. I went for fifty-five years..."

"It's like a racing car that goes faster and faster until it crashes. That's the only thing that'll stop it.

'The odd thing is, they let Rubicon go by. You went as far as a person can go in that. It's not as though the Tillman series was any bolder."

"But Rubicon would have brought down the whole machine, including the Democrats. The Tillman series focused on Donald Rumsfeld. That's an important distinction."

"Did you think about that when you were writing it?"

"I thought about it. Did it stop me? No."

Even if it's "time to leave New York," Mike's decided not to go yet. "I don't trust myself to build a lifeboat until I've got some therapy under my belt," he says, reasonably.

And I'm not ready to leave until I sense it's the last possible moment. For me to leave New York is tantamount to Mike's leap to Venezuela only in that case, he was looking forward to being received with open arms. I don't expect Portland, Oregon to welcome me. What do I have to offer them? And I would be leaving behind everyone and everything I've known most of my life: My trench buddies from the 9/11 environmental movement; family, friends... My son must come too. Only to come up for air from a tsunami would I leave him.

Having embarked on therapy, Mike's bought a book on bi-polar disorder. Like anyone cracking his first book in psychology, particularly one about an illness with which he's been diagnosed, he bestows on the book too much power. If the book said, "Such-and-such % of people suffering manic depression commit suicide," he'd think he was doomed; as though suicide were a mortality rate and he had no say in the matter.

Last night we went out with BBC producer Marian Lewinsky who was in town briefly. She gave Mike a St. Michael medal with a prayer card and me, an Our Lady of Guadalupe medal.

With her was a friend who had information on a power struggle at the newspaper slated to publish the profile of Mike in February. The journalist hasn't gotten a kill fee but the likelihood of the article's seeing the light of day seems remote.

Marian said there's speculation on the net about what's happened to Mike. "Inquiring minds" have a tendency to fill the void with malice. ("Hmm... Maybe those rumors are true that he smashed his own computers. Maybe he's lying low because he's in hiding from the law.") She suggested asking Sander Hicks to snuff out those fires by letting people know Mike's in New York. Mike said, "Good idea" so long as he's not dragged into a conversation about 9/11.

Today's been rough; partly, Mike thinks, as a result of having had two beers last night as well as two cups of coffee; and coming down from the high of hanging out with Marian as in the good old days when he'd fly home business class and there was money in the bank. His book on bi-polar disorder recommends keeping regular habits and avoiding alcohol.

Then at 5:30, Marian called to ask if we'd be interested in getting together for dinner again with Sander before she flew back to London; she'd pay for a cab to bring us to Flatbush. It was too much too soon for Mike. He understood his limits but the hint of a return to his old lifestyle shook him. His "irritability" which, according to his book on bi-polar disorder, is a harbinger of a manic episode, seems to be a kind of grasping-at-straws to control his environment.

But also, his state of mind is a response to the state of the world. The news that the U.S. raided the Iranian consulate in Iraq (claiming that the facility had not yet achieved diplomatic status) is a bad sign; the decision to add 21,000 more troops, a worse one. "Bush is in disgrace," Mike says and Congress seems to agree. "Even I'm surprised at the level of hostility."

In addition, the military are going to ratchet up domestic spying, particularly into financial records. He hasn't explicitly said so but Mike seems to fear they're going to go after him again, asserting fraud. His honor is his most valued asset.

60 Minutes — to which Mike has been drawn back after becoming disenchanted with them for using his information as background without granting him air time or even acknowledging him — does a report about the three accused rapists at Duke University who were recently exonerated by the news, until now suppressed, that their DNA had not been found on the rape victim's underwear.

The report focuses on the parents of the accused who believe their sons' lives will forever be haunted by the event.

"In these days where everyone googles everyone else..." says one father and Mike looks at me, smiling warily. If someone googles him after the anticipated newspaper hatchet job, what will be the first hit to come up?

"Google needs to change its algorithm," I say, "to reflect innocence. If someone's been exculpated that should come up before the accusation."

"How would they do that?" he says. (The prospect of asking

Google to erase one's history is not yet in the cards. But of course, if the media paid equivalent attention to exoneration as to accusation, Google would automatically follow.)

On the psychology front, he is learning fast. From an attitude of morbid fascination a few days ago, nodding along with the checklist of symptoms in his book on bi-polar disorder, ("Yup, uh huh, oh yeah,") he's graduated to adolescent rebellion. A few minutes before dinner he closed the book decisively, saying, "Enough of that."

Part 40: Dangerous Books

January 15, 2007

"I'm going to need help today," Mike said this morning at breakfast. I already knew that, from his silence and the resoluteness with which he chewed his toast, revealing no pleasure, just grim determination.

A couple of hours later he couldn't take it anymore and called his outpatient psychiatrist.

"She said what I already knew. I'm only on 600 mg of Lithium. I can take another one!"

This simple knowledge so cheered him, he didn't even seem to need the pill anymore. But he took it just in case and remained sanguine until this afternoon when he cracked his *Nutrition for Bi-Polar* book, read a page and threw the book down in disgust.

I read the passage, which described a man escorting the single casket containing the bodies of his late wife and their seven-year-old son.

"I didn't need to read that," Mike said, crying. "Damn it!"

He paced the floor. "That's not uplifting. I wanted to read about what foods to eat to avoid depression.

"What it is, is... I'd been holding out the thought of suicide as a possibility. But this makes it impossible. There are too many people who love me. They'd be left with questions. For the rest of their lives, they'd wonder if there was something they could have done.

'You'd understand and forgive me but...'"

The book had thrown him off balance. But if he was so quickly able to dispense with me as an obstacle, he'd probably be able to talk himself out of the others too.

Another piece of unpleasant news arrived via email: Barry Silverthorn has checked the inventory FTW sent him; 260 items are missing.

"Out of how many?" I asked.

"I don't know!" Mike wailed. It's always a gamble asking him anything. He takes the question as an assault, just as he took the anecdote in the nutrition book. I've told him he has porous boundaries.

"I think a lot of the problem is honor," I said.

"No kidding! My honor's been compromised and I have no control. The Japanese call it..." I can't remember the name, which sounds like "Hoboken."

"I thought it was harikiri."

"That's the act. And sepuku."

"It's as though you'd be saying, 'Look, I'm suffering too. Forgive me. You've lost some money but just to show you I'm honorable, I'll give up my life.'"

He dealt with the email, the only immediate task on his agenda, and turned to the subject of his novel. Why was he finding it so hard?

"Traditionally in fiction, a writer's first book is a loosely disguised memoir of his or her youth," I said. "What does she do for an encore? It's sometimes hard to decide on a subject.

'Rubicon was the product of the first thirty years of your adult life. You're now facing that same 'blank slate' problem."

He seems more chipper now but it's known that suicidal people may become more lighthearted just before killing themselves; they've planned their exit.

"Libby's wife is a real lefty," I remark, reading an article about the jury-selection process in the Scooter Libby trial.

"If you read his background about his anti-Vietnam protests," answers Mike, "it reads like he was CIA spying on the left."

That makes sense. But then, is he spying on his wife or is she a spy too? I don't ask.

Mike's outpatient psychiatrist is not sure about his diagnosis: Apart from the fact that the onset of his "illness" wasn't until age fifty-five, he's suffered so much trauma this year that all his symptoms may be attributable to PTSD.

Mike's thrilled and has metaphorically thrown out the two books he was assiduously, if with macabre interest, engrossed in for the past two days: One called something like *Manic Depression and You*; the other, which was supposed to be about nutritional antidotes, depressed him even more because it grew out of the author's family history.

"There was a horse, Baron. Maybe if I'd groomed him more, I'd have been more balanced and none of this would have happened. But it played the way it played.

'I only went to see him three times. The bond was so close, it was scary."

We watched CNN.

"They're going to impeach Bush," Mike said. "That could mean Cheney too. That's why the Libby trial is important. Maybe this is why it was delayed. This is some kind of step in setting up a new world order. Who's in line after Bush and Cheney?"

"Pelosi."

"Right." He looked at me in disbelief at the notion. "This could be a step in setting up a military dictatorship."

Jay Rockefeller came on, the Chairman of the Senate Intelligence Committee.

"I wonder how much the Intelligence Committee is told," I said.

"A lot. They sign an agreement not to disclose anything about what they hear to anyone, with draconian measures if they don't adhere. They can go to jail for the rest of their lives with no pension."

The New Yorker cover features a cartoon of Bush fiddling while Rome burns.

Mike observes, "I'm having the thought – and if I have it two more times when sober, it could become a reality – that if this goes on, my time may not be over, I could be back in the game."

"You'd only do that if you had hope it could do some good."

"If I thought it would be worth the risk."

Part 41: Perfect Cup of Coffee

January 21, 2007

Last night we had our first argument. Mike wanted me to put the hosting fees for the archived website on my credit card. I wanted to know what responsibilities I was signing up for if it came to getting sued. I've always maintained that FTW's treatment of T-17's could land them in copyright trouble.

T-17's, or Title 17's, were a critical wing of FTW in which Mike or occasionally, one of the rest of us, commented on a mainstream news item. This was where the research Rice Farmer and I did ended up. We both sent links, sometimes pointing out significant quotes from the article.

Copyright law, especially on the internet, is in constant flux with inconsistencies about what per cent of an original article can be quoted or what per cent of the resulting article the quote can take up. Sometimes it's not a question of quantity but of quality. For instance, prior to publication, a memoir by President Gerald Ford was quoted in a review which highlighted Ford's pardon of Richard Nixon over Watergate. The quote was small but the court found that it was virtually the only interesting part of the book. This redounded to the disadvantage of the reviewer. You can't cut out the heart of a work, even if it's proportionately minute.

I was aware of the "fair use" exception to copyright law — the freedom granted in the case of educational intent — and sympathized with FTW's stand that readers were at least as interested in the commentary they found at the website as in the original article. If they only wanted mainstream news, after all, it was readily available. Even when FTW didn't comment, its readers wanted to know what, of the deluge of mainstream information available, FTW considered significant.

But I didn't want to have to make that argument in court.

Mike called my worries "irrational" and said "Fuck" several times. The word "fuck" itself doesn't faze me; I use it many times a day but not to someone's face about what they themselves are doing.

152

"We've never had that problem," he said, in the venerable tradition of, "We never thought a plane would fly into a building."

Sure, but the enemy is inventive when it comes to new forms of victimization. History doesn't repeat itself verbatim.

The next morning was when he awoke from the dream about guys in jackboots breaking down the door. This was followed by the dream of his leaving for a trip, the way his father used to, while his kids were in the bath. (For anyone who missed the earlier post relaying this dream, his wife in it was the young female employee who sued him for sexual harassment.)

He sent an email to his psychiatrist about the dreams and the argument last night. She responded that his behavior in the argument was the sort that had probably gotten him into trouble with his employees in Ashland.

In the bath, he cried with regret for the people he'd pushed away.

"You heard me apologize, didn't you?"

I said yes, inferring that if he died, I should convey the apology to them.

"You can tell them yourself," I added, thinking it would be therapeutic for him.

"I don't know how to reach them."

Later he said, "I know everything you've done for me." Another final-sounding comment.

January 22, 2007

This evening we went to a meditation class led by a young woman in Buddhist robes with a shaved head. She had a sweet, soothing voice and masterly command of her subject.

"We need to become interested in other people," she said, "more open to people who may not be like us or interested in the same things."

This was perfectly timed for Mike, I thought.

She was from Seattle. "In Seattle we take coffee seriously," she said, by way of illustrating a point. "People come into a coffee shop and rattle off two paragraphs about the coffee they want. Then they get it and if one thing is off, it's, 'But that's not what I ordered. Ach!'"

The next morning, as he was rushing out to an appointment with his psychiatrist, Mike couldn't find his pen, the ultrafine tip ballpoint, or his hat. This, as he stomped around with one boot on.

"It's not funny," he grumbled.

"Remember the story last night about the coffee?"

He saw the point. And found the pen and the hat.

Later he said that the young woman's advice was familiar to him from AA but he still found it hard to apply it. He stared unhappily at the floor.

"Why don't you take an interest in me, now? Ask me something about myself."

"OK. What experience have you had with horses?"

It was a start even if it was along the lines of the virtuoso violinist who said, "But I've talked enough about myself. Now you talk about me."

January 23, 2007

We were watching the State of the Union address, Cheney on camera throughout, which unsettled Mike.

"I read him too well," he said.

Part 42: Boys' Night Out

[T]he Rosetta Stone in the movie Collapse is a throw-away line where Mike is talking about how early in his career, people would ask him why he didn't give up his crusade and get a more balanced life. He answers to the effect that he tried but looking around, he saw that there was, in fact, nothing else in his life. So he had no choice but to go on with his investigative work.[11]

I love humanity but I hate people. — Edna St. Vincent Millay

January 25, 2007

He is in deep shit. Not with the government but with me.

Ever since Marian suggested that he see Sander Hicks, it's been on the agenda. That's been fine with me. A "boys' night out," as he described it. Mike flexing his independence muscles in NYC.

This morning Sander called to arrange to meet tonight. I heard Mike's end of the conversation, which concluded: "Great. So you and your wife'll be by here with the car at seven."

"That's an odd configuration," I said when he got off.

No more, "boys' night out." Now it's, "Everyone can come but you." And it wasn't Sander who put up the objection.

"You've been out, what, ten times on your own since I've been here, to events you couldn't bring me to, to your mother's... And I haven't said a word, right?"

He wanted to come to my mother's? Give me a break. As for the event I wasn't allowed to bring him to, he threatened to kill himself.

"I brought you to everything I could."

"Barry and his wife each go out on their own. Do you think we should just stay home every night doing nothing?"

"What do we normally talk about?"

"My stuff," he conceded. "I need to get out of here. Remember, 'Absence makes the heart grow fonder?'"

---

[11] http://mikeruppert.blogspot.com/search?updated-min=2009-01-01T00:00:00-08:00&updated-max=2009-11-27T19:48:00-08:00&max-results=50&start=16&by-date=false

"That's the principle I'm operating under.

'Don't worry; I won't throw you out. You can eat the food."

"I'm going for a walk," he said, changing tack when he realized he wasn't getting anywhere. "I'll do the shopping." You could see the middle-aged cylinders turning: *"Girls like it when you offer to do the shopping."*

"I already bought dishwashing powder."

"I guess I'll just go for a walk, then."

He came back with a bouquet of African daisies. What cliché are we living in — 1955?

"Do we have anything to put these in?" he asked, since I hadn't acknowledged the peace offering.

"In the kitchen, on the right. Not there. The other corner, that's your bête noire." Like many New York City apartments, this one came with some ingrained grime between the floor tiles which made Mike recoil in horror.

On the way to the gym, I thought about how cramped he felt in my apartment and how he subconsciously blamed me for cramping him. He was treating me like a good mother, nurturing when he needed it, then kicked aside as soon as the fledgling grew strong enough to venture out on his own.

But I'd already raised an adolescent. I didn't need another one, especially one with a graying mustache.

Since absence makes the heart grow fonder, or at least less hostile, for the rest of the day I absented myself.

11:30 PM

He got back at 9:30.

"Would you have had a less good time if I'd been there?"

He thought a moment: "Maybe. We talked as two peers, authors and publishers in the same genre. If you'd been there, we might have had to stop and explain things."

Despite having written for FTW at Mike's request — not to mention other publications — and found many of the articles on which he built his analysis, apparently I was not a peer, much less an "Author." Did he know how strenuously some renowned writers avoided that designation as pretentious?

"What did you talk about?"

"Mike Vreeland and Brad Ayres."

"I remember Mike Vreeland." An entire chapter of *Crossing the Rubicon* addresses the problematic US Naval Intelligence officer whom Mike interviewed in a Toronto jail. While not wanting to get involved with the "gigantic wriggling can of worms," Mike couldn't avoid the fact that Vreeland had forewarned of the attacks of September 11 in a sealed statement written the previous month.

"Brad Ayres was in the book too but you wouldn't remember him."

True. He takes up less than one page of the 600-page work and as an honorable guy, makes less of an impression.

"I thought you didn't want to talk about any of that stuff."

"Sander turned out to be very mature, very spiritual."

The word made me puke. [Sander, if you're out there somewhere, I'm sure you realize that the reaction is not personal.] So I was good when he needed something but when the conversation got interesting, it was above my head?

"Wouldn't you have *wanted* to explain it to me?"

How pathetic. No, of course not.

He did get credit for trying to hash it out but disputed the notion I was a mother figure or that he was acting like an adolescent.

"Look," he said, "I went out without you. I had a great time and I'm not apologizing for it. You go out without me and have a good time, don't you?"

"Yes, but I don't exclude you by choice." I might have added, "or because you're too dim to follow the conversation."

"It's part of a healthy relationship that men have a boys' night out, women have a girls' night out. I feel less cramped here because I went out and had a great time. And I don't love you any the less. Do you believe that I love you?"

"I don't think you know me."

He mock-collapsed on the floor in surrender.

"This is what I told you was going to happen," he said. "I'm getting stronger and more independent and you don't like it. I think you *want* me to be dependent."

Maybe that's true if independence means he comes back when he needs something then goes off with the cool crowd for the interesting times.

January 26, 2007

He still hasn't acknowledged anything and stalwartly maintains his right to "independence." But something must have snuck in because he's more solicitous and doesn't automatically assume I want to talk about his problems whenever he needs me to.

Part 43: Ten Grand

January 28, 2007

It's 8:15 PM and Mike's gone to bed, partly because he wants to get up early since the water's going to be off tomorrow for six hours; partly because he's wiped out by the loss of the book sale — $10,000. It helped to get the rage off his chest, first expressed to Ray as "disappointment," then vented fully in a longer email:

From Mike to Ray, Ken, (his agent and general factotum) with Jenna bcc'ed:

The fact that we have been unable to connect with Mr. X [the prospective buyer of the surplus copies of Crossing the Rubicon] is very upsetting. For weeks I have stressed to all concerned that I did not want to lose touch with this kind man or his offer. Unfortunately, it appears that we have let too much time lapse since we haven't gotten any response from him. But I am praying that this message might get through.   There have been two developments which change the picture. The good outweighs the bad.   New Society has done a second printing of Rubicon recently. It's the same book and looks the same. It just poses a problem for bookstores if there are returns now. That's no big deal.   The much better news is that we have as close to a full confirmation rom the [newspaper] that a cover story on me, FTW and Rubicon is going to appear in their Sunday magazine "XX", on either Feb 4, 11, or 18. It's written and "in the can".   My problem is very simple. These books are owned by me and they are stored in a warehouse under my name. They represent $24,000 of my money. But what's worse is that the storage fees are eating me alive. I have only a few thousand dollars to eat, live and get medical treatment -- critical medical treatment. Right now the books are sucking the life out of me. No one else's credit or finances are getting hurt.   The books are a black hole sitting where they are and they are threatening my ability to survive in the medium term.   X, if there's any hope of rekindling your offer I beg you to reach out to me, xxx-xxx-xxxx, or Ray Kohlman xxx-xxx-xxxx. You wrote the kindest emails and I swear I was reminding Ray Kohlman like three times a week to close the deal with you and not lose touch. He had court and I apologize if we let it go too long. The [newspaper] story is going to create a whole new picture for the book. I'd keep

*them myself but I have no way to sell individual copies or even cases and ship them.
I don't have any account and the books are in LA while I'm in NY. If you're out
there X, please respond and accept my apology if we have offended you. Thanks,
Mike Ruppert*

February 12, 2007

"We have bad news," said Mike when I came home at 6:45.
"What?!"
"Take off your coat first."
He was eating a bowl of cereal.
"Is that a late lunch? Are you going to have dinner after you go to
meditation?"
"This is dinner. I'm not going. Ray's going to call at eight."
A first, that he hadn't waited for me to come home and cook. We
hadn't eaten together since he imitated the way I chewed a roast beef
sandwich, supposedly with the repulsive smacking noise of his mother,
but I cooked enough for each of us to eat when we wished at our
respective stations; mine, in "my" room which was also the living-
room; his, at my grandmother's card table which he'd set up next to
the TV in the bedroom. My plan was to stop providing his food when
his inheritance came through but for the moment, he needed to
conserve every cent he could.
"Y did send the ten thousand. He has the return receipt, signed.
We never got it. The government intercepted it, forged the signature.
Also the [newspaper] piece is dead."
"[The journalist] told you?"
"Kenny. The advertisers would have been calling by now about
the book. There's been nothing."
"Dumb question: How do you know Y's not just saying he has the
signed receipt?"
"This is the guy who sent me two grand to go to Venezuela.
'Promise me you won't call [my psychiatrist] or 911 or do anything
that might get me locked up in Bellevue again."
I screamed at the ceiling. "What do you mean? If you're here
unconscious, I'm going to do what I have to do. They won't come

160

lock you up. They'll say, 'Has he threatened suicide before?' 'Yes.' 'Is he under the care of a psychiatrist?' 'Yes.'"

"You have to let me have the option of dying with some dignity. The government won't leave me alone. Maybe it's something you said on the phone: 'He's planning to get back in the game.' Or I said it, although I don't think I said it on the phone."

"I didn't say that on the phone. The only thing I say to you on the phone these days is, 'I'll be home around seven.'"

"Or in an email. What difference does it make? They could have this place bugged. The point is, they won't let up."

"I know," I cried. "I've always known that they won't stop at anything. That's their secret...

'But I don't see how all this jives with Victor Thorn." Thorn, Mike's nemesis while FTW was going strong, packed his "bags," i.e. his website, as soon as FTW closed up shop. If he'd been called off the case because Mike had surrendered, why would the government still be harassing Mike through other means?

"Victor Thorn was FBI," Mike shouted. "He was a middle to low level employee. They could have gotten rid of him because they didn't need him anymore. He didn't make decisions. Someone higher up did."

I had taken at face value Mike's conclusion that "the heat was off." I didn't talk about Mike's affairs but I did keep notes of our conversations and it would have been possible for an interested party to read them, if said interested party was the government with its overweening powers of surveillance.

"I'm a broken man, humiliated."

I shook my head emphatically.

"Don't tell me how much I can take!" Mike shouted.

"I'm not telling you how much you can take. I'm shaking my head because you haven't been humiliated. Your work is out there. It's still there. You said it all. People can find it."

Mike called Ray.

"Should I get on the other extension?" I asked.

"Stay here."

Mike's end of the conversation was terse. I could glean only that at Ray's house were a landlady and someone's mother-in-law and Ray had asked only one of them about the package which had been signed for February 5. Also, the fact that 10K was involved meant that filing a complaint could raise flags about money-laundering and "terrorist financing."

"Oh, for a gun right now," Mike said. "I used to have guns. There's one I could still get."

"If you had it sent here, I wouldn't give you the package."

"You can't send firearms through the mail."

"You can't send ten thousand dollars cash through the mail either; what do I know?"

"I'm going downstairs to smoke a cigarette, that's all."

"I know."

He got his coat; I followed him out.

"Is it OK if I call Ray? I want him to talk to you."

"I just talked to him."

"I want him to talk to you again."

"OK."

Ray picked up his phone which was about a 1/50 chance.

"This is really bad," I told him.

When Mike came back up, Ray told him he'd trace the package. This made no difference to Mike's state of mind.

"Remember [V] on my computer," he said, naming the password for the archives. "Because right now the website is in the hands of you and someone called [the current webmaster, whom Mike barely knew.]"

"No! No! No!"

Part 44: The Importance of Being Ernest
Missing Ten Grand, Continued

February 13, 2007

"Dumb question: How do we know it wasn't just some employee who scribbled a signature, said, 'Sorry, my dad's taken ill,' and quit the next day?"

Mike nodded. "You have enough bills, the Mylar can be scanned. You don't know what Mylar is? It's a code like RF fucking ID." He took out a fifty-dollar bill and held it up to the light. Towards one of the short edges a lead line was visible. I knew about that line but didn't know its name.

"A postal worker would have scanned it and taken it to an Inspector," he went on. "They don't just take packages like this. It could be being tracked by Karl Rove. They know the CIA sends packages; some are decoys. That's how some of the [I didn't catch the word] got caught in LAPD."

If Ray asks questions, he could get the sender in trouble: Ten thousand dollars is the threshold for an investigation into money-laundering and terrorist financing.

Mike looked at me as we faced the insolubility of the problem. "It isn't you. You couldn't be more kind, more loving."

"I could be smarter about who the enemy is. I may have been the one who tipped them off."

"That's just fate. Don't blame yourself."

When Mike got out of the shower, I showed him a video that had been sent of an interview between him and an FTW reader.

"That man is dead. He's gone," Mike said flatly. "What's left is this shell."

"And the people who loved you before love you even more now." I was thinking of a Peak Oil activist in New York who'd been helping with the books as well as of the people who'd written from everywhere from Thailand to South Africa to Norway.

"That's probably true."

We sat in silence while he ate lunch. Pressing on my mind was the urge to tell him that his thinking wasn't straight. If money was the problem, I could help. If the problem was that the government would pounce if he spoke, well, he'd often maintained that he had said everything he had to say anyway.

"I keep thinking about that judo principle," I said. "Use the enemy's weight against him."

"I know judo and I don't understand what you mean by that."

"The enemy is using you against yourself. They're using you as a weapon against yourself."

"Ten thousand dollars gone. Are you suggesting I do a jig about that?"

"No, but anger is not the same thing as what you're talking about doing."

"What do I have? There's nothing."

"There's me."

"No offense darling," he said, making an effort to keep the sarcasm out of his voice, "but you're not the universe."

"Not me personally; the resources I'm offering. What kind of asshole do you think I am?"

"Resources... I don't need resources. I need a miracle.

'How can they be so cruel?" he asked rhetorically.

"Probably it's like the people flying airplanes who dropped bombs on civilians; they couldn't see the damage they were doing.

'Or for that matter, all of us who live well while other people are starving. It would be morally reprehensible to eat gelato if a starving person was sitting here. Why is it OK if they're far away so you can't see them?"

"You're not a murderer for eating gelato."

"It's not illegal but it may still be immoral." Morals are mores; ethics in the ether. By that reasoning, anything is OK if everyone around is also doing it.

"Nah."

As he got ready to go to his psychiatrist's he said, "I don't have anything in my pockets."

164

Like a gun? What did he mean? But I didn't ask as I didn't want to imply a belief that he was at imminent risk of suicide; perhaps the mere comment itself could exert influence of the wrong kind.

Meanwhile the New York Times published a front page story about how Cesar Borja, the latest Ground Zero worker to die of his exposure to World Trade Center dust, did not, as previously stated in the Daily News, rush downtown on 9/11, but had worked as a traffic cop in nearby streets, his formal shift not starting until December. The implication was that therefore his illness was not related to the disaster.

This revelation was intended to undermine claims linking terminal illnesses to the air quality following the attacks, not to mention questioning the heroism of some of those filing for compensation. The irony is that it hadn't been Borja's family who put out the "myth." On the contrary, they were the ones who brought attention to the inaccuracies. But such details tend to get lost in the ensuing brouhaha.

This imbroglio was one of a string of such sordid efforts which would come to include allegations that James Zadroga, for whom the 9/11 Health and Compensation Act was ultimately named, was a drug addict. He did require painkillers at the end of his thirty-five year life but was not capable of administering them himself; that tragic task fell to his parents since his wife had died, partly, the family believed, from the stress of tending to his illness. (Zadroga's father, Joseph, said privately that when James Zadroga died, his daughter told her grandparents, "I knew he was sick; I just didn't know it would be so fast." She was four years old.)

The media furor functioned as an obstacle along the road to securing health care by Senator Hillary Clinton and Congresswoman Carolyn Maloney who'd invited Borja's 21-year-old son to the State of the Union address. (Borja Sr. died on the eve of the event.) In addition, it distracted readers from recognizing an inconvenient truth: If Borja had died of his exposure *without* working on the pile, the implications were even more dire for residents, students and office workers.

Great news. The package was signed for by someone called "Ernest" (not his real name) at Ray's house. The money might be gone but at least not due to government interference.

Mike said if that money didn't come through, he "didn't know what [he] might do."

"This is going to make you mad but I have to say it again," I said. "If it's the money, that can be replaced." That seems sappy of me now but he was truly suicidal, I was acutely aware this was a once-in-a-lifetime event and I didn't want to look back some day and think, "If only I'd offered..."

"As a man, I can't accept what you're saying."

"You take donations all the time, including from me. Is it easier when you're not living with the person?"

"But I'm in love with you...." He stopped. "That's all the more reason I should take it, isn't it?"

For the rest of the evening, he was calmer which was further enhanced by a Scotch and a beer.

Part 45: Lucy Does Some 'Splainin'

Recently, some readers have become riled by my account of living with Mike. (Others have been riled all along but have given up arguing.) "Don't speak ill of the dead," is the gist of their viewpoint. The irony is that the posts these people are responding to are not, to my mind, particularly negative. The last one that raised hackles was about a deal for $10,000, which got lost in transit. Mike was disturbed enough to return to active suicidal agitation, not that he'd ever left, but it had briefly been set to snooze mode. Although in the case of the waylaid $10,000, the government seemed not to be the culprit, Mike believed, correctly, that they had a vendetta against him to which they had devoted enough resources to do him in professionally. And they would not have hesitated to go further if necessary.

FTW was his baby, even Mike himself. It represented all that was best, most insightful, most humanity-saving and heroic about him and it was dead. The movie *Collapse* was not yet a glimmer in even director Chris Smith's eye and Mike believed that he had fallen from a position of high productivity and honor to that of a wandering obsolete prophet, dependent on the kindness of strangers. (Apparently, some readers have also been offended that I've depicted him as "couch-surfing." He made no secret of that and it is not offensive. There's a fine tradition, from Socrates on, of itinerant teachers. Those of us who were privileged to host Mike did so only for so long as we wished. He'd given more than we could repay.) He had no family and although he thought he should love me, and made a heroic effort to say the right words, he didn't and couldn't. At times, he hated me.

The events of that year should be told, I believe, for the sake of anyone who might learn something from them. This is what his work was made of; this is what it cost him.

Somebody said that a poet describes how beautiful a flower is while a scientist shows you how it works. Does the scientist find the flower less beautiful? Probably not. Not, I hasten to add, that I'm the scientist here. I present some facts from his life during a particular period; you're the scientist.

As anyone reading this knows, Mike's work was as controversial as it gets. Also, as important. This is why he transcends the, "Don't speak ill of the dead" rubric. The topics he investigated are still in play, big time. Telling those parts of his story that we know is a way to keep his work alive.

Part of the controversy over Mike has stemmed from that dichotomy which insists on casting people into mythic roles: Hero, villain and so forth. Those who've been involved with him over the years have witnessed oceans of cyber-ink spilled describing him as a white knight on the one hand; on the other, a nut.

Mike himself professed sympathy for Carl Jung, Sigmund Freud's contemporary and sometime colleague, who wrote of the tendency of the unconscious to think in universal archetypes. It's not a big leap from there to Hollywood stereotypes and Mike was, after all, a product of Los Angeles in more ways than one. Staying in that mode of thinking may be hazardous to your health. Several of Mike's closest associates have remarked on how it may have ultimately contributed to his suicide.

Of course, it had also inspired him. The Jungian/Hollywood wish to be a hero (a noble wish in itself) motivated him to do the work to make that a real possibility (a heroic act in itself.) But secretly and not so secretly, he was aware of a darker side to his personality as well. No one hated that side more than he did as will become apparent in future posts. Remember what he said: "There is a deep flaw in me which is the source of everything I've done."

Mike's lasting legacy is his work at FTW, in *Crossing the Rubicon*, the movie *Collapse*, etc. In order for this work to be taken seriously in a larger arena, it might be helpful to break out of the clichés and accept the real guy.

Part 46: Paradigms

February 14, 2007

I wished Mike a Happy Valentine's Day and he returned the wish sincerely, without bitterness at his situation. But we didn't go out to dinner as planned because Ray was supposed to call in the evening with news of "Ernest," the guy at his house who had signed for the package.

While Ray was busy tracking down the missing $10,000, his landlady asked him, "Where's last month's rent?"

"That was it!" he exclaimed, which galvanized her into becoming a diligent aide de camp.

Fortunately X, the guy who sent the package, has given a green light to pursue the money via the postal inspector. Also, the subscriber lists have arrived so our new webmaster can send out a "blast" of Mike's article, *From Me to You* and attract more donations.

Yet this good news doesn't counterbalance the bad. Depression looks for reasons to feed on; it spits out positive signs as irrelevant.

Mike scrolled through the subscriber list with its inventive usernames and sighed, "The members of Congress..." The long-awaited treasure only revived memories of what he'd lost.

As he went out for his afternoon cigarette, he looked across the street at the old Board of Ed building now being converted to condos, an especially bleak sight on a sleet-driven mid-February day.

He scanned the window, taking its measure, and said to himself, "Don't let them know when or how." It had the ominous ring of Vreeland's pre-9/11 warning: "Let the first one through; stop the rest."

Later, I found an occasion to talk about the reasons people have to be depressed, yet how few of them throw themselves out the window.

"It occurred to me," Mike said, "that *From Me to You* may have been what killed the [newspaper] piece. The tone didn't conform with the tone of whatever they had. Wouldn't that just be the final fuckup?"

"There are more things in Heaven and earth..." I answered. "People have all kinds of reasons for doing things that we know nothing about."

"Every day, all day, the thought in the back of my mind is, 'I want to die.' That's the background music. It's a miracle to me I'm still alive."

"Because a part of you wants to be. That's the part that acts."

"What act?" he said bitterly.

"The acts of living, going out for a cigarette, going out for milk, whatever you do instead of killing yourself."

"With a gun it would be so easy. In Ashland I had guns, beautiful guns. I never misused one.

'I don't see how things can ever be right again."

"That's what the trust is for. You earned it."

That evening, CNN did a report about the border patrol controversy, for which chunks of information were missing.

"CIA," Mike remarked.

This was followed by the Paula Zahn hour which Mike took as his cue to leave for another cigarette, explaining, "Infotainment."

Indeed, Soledad O'Brien spoke of Obama's candidacy only in terms of his being black with zero mention of his stand on a single issue.

"This borders on insulting," Congressman Charlie Rangel accurately pronounced.

A minute after Mike went to bed, a call came from Nick Levis. We'd given up on hearing from him weeks before.

When Mike got off the phone, I used the call as a "teachable moment:"

"People have other stuff going on; it doesn't mean they don't care about you." Code to his subconscious not to get depressed about the promised calls from other friends that remained as yet unmade.

February 15, 2007

Ray says there's an 80% chance the package is gone.

"I'm going to shower and shop," Mike said after the call. "Then I don't know what I'll do."

"But suppose you don't get back in the game, maybe they'll leave you alone," I argued.

"You're missing the point. Did I take any overt action to get back in the game?"

I thought about his response to the journalist assigned to write the now obsolete article: "Let me talk to my lawyer and my agent." "The fact that you wanted to talk to your lawyer shows you had misgivings," I had said at the time.

"This is punishment. They won't let up. I must have hurt someone real bad for them to keep at it like this."

Mike's right-hand man didn't want to give X the books. No money, no books. But X had been such a great friend, Mike argued.

"This drives a wedge between friends," he continued now. "People will say, 'Don't get involved with Mike Ruppert; look what happened to Kenny and Ray...

'Well, I won't kill myself for at least a few days, 'til I see how this turns out."

"I wish I was Scheherazade."

"Who?"

"Every night I'd start a story and you'd have to live to the next day to see how it ended."

Then Mike went to Keyfood and I went to the gym, knowing he'd come back.

"The thing is," he said later, "has anyone besides me noticed that these things keep happening?"

"Yes."

"You never know when. You think things are going OK, the enemy's gone away and then... Ten thousand dollars."

"Your enemies will retire and die or get put on other assignments," I said.

"Nice try," Mike said thoughtfully, without sarcasm. "Good argument."

"Would someone please stop talking about me as though I got 'depression' like a cold and acknowledge that I've had some real trauma in the last year?"

"Yes. It sounds to you like minimizing; we're just trying to say that traumatic as it is, you shouldn't kill yourself over it."

"Gary Webb did."

"And there are plenty of people who have good reason to kill themselves but don't do it."

"That's true... You can write some piece for the New Yorker that somebody'll read while they're taking a dump and the world goes to shit, no pun intended."

"Charles Simmons [author of Wrinkles, which I'd given Mike to read] knew what a great book he'd written. Yet he once said it was no compensation for the prospect of dying."

I'd discussed this with Simmons. A literary, as opposed to a commercial, writer doesn't go into the field for the money; it's a vocation. Simmons remarked, "You know what they say about academia: The reason the fighting is so fierce is that the stakes are so low." Materially speaking, of course, that's true. But artists and many academics, like investigative journalists, believe in what they're doing; it engages the soul. So it wasn't far-fetched to think it might be worth dying for.

"It isn't. That's why I won't finish that book."

"Why?"

"Because I know how it'll end: With how he'll be remembered."

"I don't remember how it ends but it's definitely not that."

"When I think of all the things I had in Ashland, the couch, the silver, the beautiful glassware... And the hole in my heart that you're now filling. It more than compensates."

Over dinner he talked about the people he could trust.

"I have to trust you," he said.

"The main reason I could never be an agent," I mused, "is that they have to keep things under wraps all the time. Since I was very small, my goal has been self-expression; it's the opposite of what an agent does."

"Don't make excuses," he said angrily. "It just raises suspicion."

Raises suspicion? He of all people should have known that I had none of the attributes required of an agent. Forget about my primary purpose in life which is to write; that is, to reveal rather than to cover up. Agents are savvy about technology whereas any twelve-year-old is more adept with a smartphone than I am; I can't even see the screen.

"I'm not making excuses; I was using that conversation as a jumping off point to tell you something about myself."

"You were making excuses."

"No, I wasn't. You're operating from a different paradigm. Your life would become easier if you understood that other people operated from other paradigms."

He didn't get it but dropped the argument.

Part 47: Reaching Out

Mike reflected on a former friend from LAPD:

"I thought he might not get Rubicon. I let him go. Such a good friend!" he cried.

He googled the man, remembering the street where he lived, and found him, but no email address.

With Mike in such a heightened state of distress, I contacted all of his old friends I could think of to whom he might listen.

February 16, 2007 From Jenna to Peter Dale Scott:

hi -

below is an email i sent last night to [former congresswoman] cynthia mckinney. this morning i suggested that mcr call you (peter; this email will also go to [Narco News founder] al giordano when i find the address). mcr got the number from information but i said, 'it's early in california.' (it was 10:30 here.) mcr said: "oh yeah. 4:30 in the morning." I said, 'he's in california.'

this is an indication of some ways in which his mind isn't working clearly although mostly, it's working all too clearly.

while he was having breakfast i said, 'why don't i send the same email to peter dale scott that i sent to cynthia?' he said ok.

he's v close to suicide. much discussion of gary webb...

I'd asked Mike: "If you'd been able to talk to Gary before he killed himself, what would you have said?"

Mike said, "I would have said, 'Come work for me at FTW.

'But that's before all this happened to me. Now I'd just say, 'I understand. Point the gun up towards your brain, not down into your jaw.'"

For anyone unfamiliar with Webb's suicide, some controversy was generated by the fact that there were two shots. How could that be, went the argument, if it wasn't murder? But Mike saw the evidence and said the first shot had failed because of the angle.

Jenna to Peter Dale Scott, cont'd:

...this morning he looked up hunter thompson on wikipedia to see the circumstances of his suicide.

over breakfast he said, 'i made one mistake they didn't. they didn't give away their guns.'

he went on. 'i know how to take away guns. i wouldn't take one from a cop, though.'

"No!" i said.

he looked at me a little cross-eyed.

"They need their guns," i explained.

his eyes crossed further.

"I'm not following you at all, am i?"

"No. i was lapd. it's honor among cops. i could take a gun from a security guard, though. i saw one who had one.'

he stared fixedly at the lamp as though he was figuring out where he'd seen the guy and how to get back to him.

enough detail for now. the point is, he reads the gvt interference with his book deal as a message: Anything you do to get your head above water will be snuffed out. he says he's broken. either he'll kill himself or they'll kill him.

to boost his spirits, a friend sent a link to a website where someone had nominated mike as an alternative attorney general.

mike said, "the person who did that put me back in the crosshairs. i don't care what sort of obscure website that is, this means my name's still out there and it will be as long as i'm alive."

i said, "even more if you're dead." (he's always answered the query, "why haven't they assassinated you?" by saying, "because the next day, my book would sell 2 million copies.")

his biggest fear is of guys in jackboots breaking down the door to come get him. he says if i call 911, they'll put him in four point restraints and that'll be the worst humiliation of all.

i said, "my inclination would be to call [his shrink.]"

he said, "she has a legal obligation to call 911."

i said, "then i probably do too, or at least a moral obligation."

he said if i do that he'll never speak to me again. i could say, "what difference would it make? at least you'd be alive," but you'll see why it's not an option...

Throughout that conversation, he had walked around picking up bits of black fluff that had come off my socks and stuck to the carpet where they looked like tics and drove him crazy. This is one of the ways in which he "makes himself useful;" to whom, I'm not sure. I've told him many times that his "usefulness" to me lies not in the household tasks he performs but in his presence. But the notion is so alien, it doesn't take.

He asked about my vacuum cleaner (courtesy of FEMA, to shut up New Yorkers who complained of the "toxic air" after 9/11.)

I told him, accurately, that you can only pull, rather than push it. "It only works backwards."

He repeated the phrase to himself in astonishment.

Jenna to Peter Dale Scott cont'd:

last night's email to cynthia:

hi cynthia - just tried your cell. no dice. mcr wants to know if u have a new number.

btw i asked mcr's permission to contact you; it wasn't his idea. i'm trying to keep him from killing himself.

v bad thing happened. the books had been sold to a subscriber for ten grand. the subscriber sent the money, certified return receipt requested to ray, mike's lawyer. the return receipt was signed 'ernest' something, a guy who lives in ray's building. ernest says 'that's not my signature. i never saw any package.'

mike's interpretation: the gvt intercepted the package under some pretext the bush admin has put into place. they will never let him get his head above water ie out of debt. he says this is not to stop him from getting back in the game in the future. he says it's punishment. he gave me permission to tell u any fukkin thing i want, including by email.

sorry, cynthia. i don't know what any of us can do. am just grasping at straws.

just now mike suggested sending this email also to al Giordano, "a great historian." i need to find that address.

he says he won't kill himself today because nick levis is coming over later, or tomorrow because we're going out with two other friends. does this mean if we

*maintain an active social calendar, he'll keep going one day at a time, as they say in
AA?*

*his argument is that i'd be doing him some sort of favor by letting him die with
some dignity, some control and that to try to keep him alive the way he's feeling now
is cruel.*

*he equates money of his own with pride. not to have it is to be stripped of pride.
it's that simple since even without money of his own, he's not starving here.*

he also says that the last thing he wants now is a pep talk.

sorry to lay this at your doorstep. trying everything. THANKS!

Peter Dale Scott sent a kind, helpful email in response. He made
sure it was prompt as well, saying, "He who gives quickly gives twice."

Part 48: SHTF

February 17, 2007 From Mike to his psychiatrist:

*1. I have not gone for the blood levels yet. I will go Monday after fasting from 9
PM Sunday. Thursday night I was so upset over the stolen $10,000 I woke up at
3 AM and chugged about a pint of OJ and then realized what I had done. I didn't
start the fast again on Friday because we had a late dinner engagegment. So I'll fast
Sunday and have the levels drawn Monday AM. Sorry.*

*2. But more, I put myself and Jenna thru hell on Tursday night. I was overwhelmed
with the belief that anything I ever tried to do again would be cursed. It's pretty
clear that the gov't intercepted the package. Fortunately, on Friday, (though we
didn't know this Thursday night) the man who sent the money released the books
back to us and said he was sorry he didn't beter protect the money. That essentially
left us back where we started, with 4,000 books in an LA warehouse with $1,700
in overdue fees. I have since turned it all over to X who might be able to scrape
something together out of a patchwork of contacts. I don't know if I'll ever see a
penny. He deserately needs a hernia operation and since he's there with the books
I'll let him have his shot.   But on Thursday night and Friday AM (before the
message) I was suicidial again. I made sure that Jenna wouldn't make any calls
that would get me back to Bellevue. It was very hard on her. I selfishly shared
different ways that I could do it. I see that I was just tryng to get her (someone) to
understand my pain now and have let her know how sorry I am for that. I was
torturing her. I was just so sick of the cold, the isolation and the powerlessness. I
read the emails she sent out desperately to close friends of mine the next day. I
couldn't help it. I just felt so helpless and hopeless. Late Friday AM is when the
message came in that at last we could still sell the books if we could find a buyer at
this late date. (Legally, the guy who sent the $10,000 could have taken the books
and the law would have supported him.)*

*3. BETTER NEWS -- Last night we reunited with an old 9-11 activist who I
had met in 2002, Nick Levis, who I had worked with both here and in Germany.
He's a brilliant guy and was right on the money the whole way... it was because the
9-11 moement had been so successfully sidetracked and subverted by the
governement that it is now just a comical, ludicrous joke and a self-serving cottage*

178

industry. There is a syndrome here. Nick and I are going to stay close and talk frequently. It is so obvious we need each other...

4. Tonight Jenna and I are going out with two friends from the Peak Oil movement for more socializing. I definitely do better when I interact with people. Sorry for the length. But I knew I needed to let you know how bad I was Thursday night. I swore I would never go back to Bellevue. Not like before. That's as honest as I can be and I know that if I am to benefit from your generosity and care I owe you complete honesty. Mike

Mike wonders if his psychiatrist has an obligation to act on what he told her. But he couldn't stop himself; it's not in his nature to withhold information.

Also this evening he got an email from Ray, forwarding an email from the LAPD cop whose lost friendship he'd been lamenting.

He repeated the name of his friend over and over, marveling. "You know that if he wants to see me out in LA, I'm going."

But his excitement was short-lived, for reasons relayed in the email below to Larry Chin and Sander Hicks, with Ray cc'ed:

Hi all –

The government campaign against Mike marches on. The latest front is Wikipedia where the article on Mike says:

"On December 4, 2006, as reported by the Ashland Daily Tidings, Mike Ruppert/From the Wilderness was sued by their landlord, Aro Partners, for back rent owed on the Ashland office space. In the same article it was confirmed that Ruppert is, in fact, an official suspect in the burglary of said office space back in July of '06. [28]" http://en.wikipedia.org/wiki/Michael_Ruppert

It is the last sentence in that passage which is patently false and which we need to refute. If you google Michael Ruppert, the Wikipedia article on him comes up second. Someone has seen to it that it gets a high google ranking by putting links to it in other Wikipedia articles, for instance on "Scholars for Truth" and "Loose Change."

Mike's lawyer, Ray Kohlman, who is cc'ed on this email, has confirmed with the Ashland Police Department that Mike is not, and never has been, a suspect in the burglary of his own offices. Ray's phone number is xxx-xxx-xxxx. The Ashland Police Department is: xxx-xxx-xxxx. The Case Number is xx-xxxx.

We were wondering if you two would be interested in writing a short article on this. Ray: Sandor [sic] and Larry are two great journalists and friends of Mike. (Btw, as you undoubtedly realize, I would do this article myself but for possible allegations of conflict of interest.)

As you will see from my correspondence with Wikipedia below, they are refusing to change the article on Mike without other journalistic evidence to refute the allegations of the Ashland Tidings and its progeny. This is why we're asking you if you could write a brief one.

MANY THANKS FOR ANY HELP YOU CAN GIVE!!

Jenna

Correspondence with Wikipedia:

Dear Jennakilt@aol.com, Thank you for your mail. Jennakilt@aol.com écrit [wrote]: Dear Wikipedia: The current article about Mike Ruppert on your website contains a grossly incorrect, libellous statement that Ruppert has been "confirmed" as a suspect in the burglary of the offices of his own company, Fromthewilderness.com. In fact the Ashland Police Department has confirmed to Ruppert's lawyer, Ray Kohlman who is cc'ed on this email, that Ruppert has never been a suspect; his status is, and always has been, solely that of victim. The current Wikipedia article grossly interferes with Ruppert's ability to get a job or accomplish other eminently worthy endeavors which he is currently pursuing. Please correct this inaccurate, injurious statement immediately. Thank you greatly for your consideration of this matter. Jenna Orkin, Former Researcher and current Blog Administrator, etc. Fromthewilderness.com.

[Wikipedia's response, obviously from a French speaker:]

I've made some research, and found out some newspapers saying that Michael Ruppert has been considered as a potential suspect. Do you have sources to give me saying Michael Ruppert has never been a suspect, it's the only way we have to change that he is suspect into he is the victim. Yours sincerely, XXX-- Wikipedia - http://en.wikipedia.org---Disclaimer: all mail to this address is answered by volunteers, and responses are not to be considered an official statement of the Wikimedia Foundation. For official correspondence, you may contact the site operators at http://www.wikimediafoundation.org.

February 18, 2007 From Jenna to Peter Dale Scott:

Thank you so much for your expansive, generous and wise response re mike a couple of days ago. At his request, I read it aloud to him.

Thank God he's now told his shrink about his state of mind so the weight of that knowledge doesn't rest entirely on my shoulders. But I still need to be careful not to get sucked into the vortex of his thinking which can lead to the conclusion that interfering with his suicide would be to deprive him of the opportunity to die with honor. Surely between that and shackles at Bellevue lies some acceptable third option.

His frustration is reasonable: The latest front of the gvt campaign against him is Wikipedia which has so far refused to remove the entirely false allegation that he is or was a suspect in the burglary of his own office. That allegation has been refuted by the Ashland Police Department.

He greatly appreciated your email. The connection to you and other friends is what's getting him through this precarious time.

"I can't kill myself today," Mike said; "it's too cold."

Another sympathetic email from Peter Dale Scott, underscoring the ways in which Mike's situation diverges from that of Gary Webb at the time of Webb's suicide. Uppermost among them is that Mike's social support system is wider and stronger.

From Jenna to Peter Dale Scott:

I've shared your email with Mike who understands and appreciates the depth of thought and effort that went into it and also thanks you. I said, "As in those old movies where one guy slaps another and the other says, 'Thanks, I needed that?'" He said yes.

It was especially important for him to hear the distinctions you drew between his situation and Gary Webb's. He has a tendency to look at Gary and a few others as predecessors which would make suicide his destiny as though he had no say in the matter.

At the moment, destiny is indeed conspiring with Mike to paint him into a corner. It's cold out and his medical conditions or medication make him even colder. This keeps him indoors and isolated.

But he wants to get a job or volunteer work which is why it's important to correct the wikipedia business as Mike's lawyer is trying to do.

Meanwhile I get the Aristotelian pleasure of exercising a hefty per cent of my faculties.

A reply from Peter Dale Scott offers generous words about my role in Mike's welfare.

From Jenna to Peter Dale Scott:

gulp. that's one perception i'm keeping under wraps. i try to emphasize to mike how many people care about him which they do; they write to the blog or to me or ray (his lawyer.)

today he had another setback when his shrink 'fired' him. i think she got scared, understandably. so now we have to find another.

This turned out to be entirely false. Shrinks can't back out of a case because they're afraid the patient might kill himself; on the contrary, their commitment becomes all the stronger. The reason for Mike's having to leave his shrink was logistical; if my memory is correct, she was simply moving her practice out of the city.

also ray's gotten busy with a new client.
so one can understand why he feels things are closing in.

Part 49: Furies

February 20, 2007 From Mike to Ray:

I really want to talk to them [this probably referred to the Ashland Police Department] *as the victim also. I have nothing to hide and I wouldn't mind if they asked me questions.No 5th amendment issues.You tell me.*

From: "Mike Ruppert" stgeorge119@gmail.com To: "Ray Kohlman" Subject: Ashland PD Date: Tue, 20 Feb 2007 14:43:21 - 0500

Can we get a letter from Ashland PD stating that I am not a suspect n the burglary? I still kind of want to let them know about [two employees.]

February 21 2007

Two days after I tell Peter Dale Scott that Mike is suffering from the cold, the heat goes off in the apartment. Mike thinks the government would know of his susceptibility to cold. He doesn't know that I emailed Peter about it and I see no point in telling him; it would only add heft to his sense that TPTB (the powers that be) are behind the confluence of events conspiring against him.

Today we went to Sovereign Bank to set up a joint checking account but as they're going to do a credit check, it's unlikely he'll be okayed.

Also he's punishing himself for having been so honest with his psychiatrist and gotten himself kicked out. He thought back to the turning point: when she asked him, "What would you have done if I'd said you should go back to Bellevue?" He said, "I'm not going back there."

He now believes that that was when the line was drawn in the sand. She had no choice but to hand him over to someone who could deal with him.

He's still in shock over my assertion that the vacuum cleaner only works backwards.

"So how do you vacuum?" he asked.

I showed him, miming pulling the vacuum backwards, doing a U turn, then resuming pulling it backwards. I've even tried turning around so it's behind me.

He sank back on the pillow in amazement.

February 22, 2007

His psychiatrist called. Our interpretation of her defection is 100% wrong. She isn't trained in what Mike needs: experience with survivors of [the sort of childhood trauma he'd suffered, to be discussed.] As for suicide, it's when he's suicidal that she's least likely to jump ship; her obligation to him is strongest. Anyway, she's found him another shrink.

Also today we learned he's been accepted for Medicaid so he can get checked out for why he's so weak, not to mention cold.

"In California this would've taken a year," Mike said, the only compliment, indirect or otherwise, that he's given New York.

A FTW subscriber is in town who wants to take us to lunch but Mike says it would be downright stupid of him (Mike) to meet a stranger.

Since the weather has relented, he's in a more upbeat mood and has found a stable nearby where he may go Saturday to offer his services as a volunteer.

"I'm going to wear my Tony Llama boots," he said. "That'll speak volumes to the people there: the stirrup marks."

But the big question remains, will Sovereign Bank allow me to add Mike to my checking account? He's steeling himself for another blow.

February 24, 2007

We just got back from *Breach*, the movie about Robert Hanssen, the biggest spy in FBI history. It depressed Mike, especially when the legend came on at the end about how the real Hanssen is currently spending twenty-three hours a day in solitary.

"What did you think?" Mike said.

"I couldn't believe that Hanssen, who supposedly had a great BS detector, didn't catch on with Eric [his assistant, who turned out to be an FBI agent.] If I'd been in his place, I'd have been paranoid, particularly of someone placed the way Eric was.

'And I bet that the porn that the real Hanssen watched wasn't hetero but homo."

Maybe I'm unfairly biased in relation to Jesuits (which Hanssen was) vis a vis homosexuality, but I didn't buy the assertion of the film that his downfall had only to do with his sharing videos of himself with his wife. However, Wikipedia supports the claim, for whatever that's worth.

"I wonder if he had a thing for Eric which blinded him to the clues."

"It's possible," Mike said.

Meanwhile someone on Portland Indymedia linked to a fromthewilderness.com article in reference to government techniques for psychological torture. This rallied his spirits a tad but it was insignificant against the weight of his gloom.

"According to Hesiod's Theogony, when the Titan Cronus castrated his father Uranus and threw his genitalia into the sea, the Erinyes as well as the Meliae emerged from the drops of blood when it fell on the earth (Gaia),[10] while Aphrodite was born from the crests of sea foam."[12]
http://en.wikipedia.org/wiki/Erinyes

The Erinyes, or "Furies," spent their days tormenting what George Bush might call "evil-doers" and the Catholic church in earlier times, "sinners." For his sins, as he believed them to be, although he certainly didn't use the word, Mike's furies pursued him relentlessly.

"Will I have to go to bed every night for the rest of my life thinking about this?" He was referring to his three supposedly treacherous employees. His latest coulda shoulda woulda scenario is that in the last days of their employment, he should have stopped them from erasing all the files. Those were his computers, after all.

---

[12] http://en.wikipedia.org/wiki/Erinyes

For a guy who's been in the sort of work he's been involved in, he's awfully trusting. I guess there has to be someone with whom you let down your guard. And the enemy just waits for that moment.

Part 50: Shaking

February 25, 2007

For whatever reason, Mike overcame his misgivings about meeting a stranger so we got together with L, a lean Vermonter, who treated us to lunch at a Midtown hotel with a panoramic view.

He'd heard a lecture by one of Mike's former colleagues who is now peddling investment services to poor dairy farmers. Then he pulled out his phone (unless it was another electronic gadget in 2007) and showed us pictures of his beautifully appointed house, set up to have a fighting chance of surviving global collapse. We were invited to come whenever we wished.

Later, Ray came by bearing cash from donations and dropping a tidbit about the same former colleague teaming up with an eccentric guy who writes 50-page emails.

The upshot: Rather than leaving him feeling more connected (the Vermonter was a devoted follower; Ray, a true friend in the most vital ways,) these conversations reminded Mike of the trail of betrayals which had led him to this place of rage and helplessness.

But eventually, he got around to reading the notes that arrived with the donations and be left weak and tearful.

"A waitress sent tip money..." He shook his head at the miracle.

February 26, 2007

These have been the hardest three days so far, in spite of blips of triumph, like his acceptance by Medicaid.

Partly, it's the news that Zbigniew Brzezinski testified that the White House might instigate an attack in the U.S. and blame it on Iran. Partly, it's the wrenching move away from his psychiatrist.

"I'm so scared, so scared," he said as he shook on the bed, causing it to shake as though in sympathy. "I'm scared if I call Ashland PD and tell them about [two employees] missing in the files, that [those two employees] will come after me."

"I don't know enough about their proximity to the powers that be to be able to answer that," I said. "On their own, they don't have the resources."

"They weren't the ones working with X," Mike said.

"I know."

The last shaking bout followed a flare-up at dinner between us. Mike said something hopeful, then added, "Knock wood" and knocked my forehead.

I do that all the time but with a difference: I knock my own forehead, not someone else's. Making fun of yourself doesn't give other people license to make fun of you.

"There are times when your head is more wooden than mine," Mike said. By way of example, he quoted my line when he first arrived: "I don't know how to work the dishwasher."

"I never bothered to learn," I exclaimed in exasperation. "I didn't want or intend to use the dishwasher so I never put my glasses on to read the instructions."

Mike's IQ, he had let drop shortly after we became friends, was 169, one point away from genius on that particular test.

"Sometimes when I can't figure something out, I say to myself, 'If only I had that one more point!'"

The message was clear: One point is inconsequential; IQ, like everything else, fluctuates within a range so at times, he was a genius.

I don't know what my IQ is, thank God. And although there's no question that someone who does well on the test is intelligent, it doesn't follow that someone who does badly is stupid. I used to tutor a five-year-old Russian girl. When she felt like paying attention, she got everything right; otherwise, she got zero. There are legions of people like that who do badly on a test because they don't give a damn. When they put their mind to a task that interests them, they're top notch.

Not only that, but one IQ test was developed specifically in the context of world war, to differentiate between officer material and cannon fodder. The sort of intelligence desired in the army may not coincide with what's necessary to do well in civilian life and even that may vary from one society to another. If you were lost in the Kalahari desert, would you rather have Shakespeare as your companion or any average Bushman?

My friend the clinical psychologist also says that when the IQ test was in the planning stages, they tested some trial questions on a sampling of the general public. To their surprise, women performed better than men. Since without question this indicated a flaw in the test, it was back to the drawing board until they achieved the desired results.

I didn't say any of this to Mike and as it wasn't yet 2012, women hadn't yet out-performed men so I didn't say that either.

Instead, I launched into a righteous exposition about how irrelevant IQ is going to be post-Peak, when all anyone will care about is building sustainable houses and growing food, while virtually no one knows how to make shoes anymore. Not that I know how to do any of these things either, of course, but nor did he.

Then I decided it was time to share some insights:

"When you're helpless, you're 'Mom.' You feel inferior to the rest of the world that's busy getting and spending, earning a living, doing whatever people do, however misguided it may be, or likely to send civilization over a cliff.

'When you get out of your depression, you turn into 'Dad' who feels superior to whoever is around.

'Your dad first took care of your mom, then of [his second wife,]" I said.

"He didn't take care of Mom; I took care of Mom," Mike corrected.

"Yes but you told me yourself that he'd patronize her and tell her pseudo-patiently how things worked. I bet he chose helpless women so he could feel superior to them."

"Yes."

"Helpless" seems an odd description for Mike's mother, a cryptanalyst at the forerunner of the NSA during World War II. And at one point, Mike had remarked that his father probably felt inferior to his mother because in some ways, she was better educated. Nevertheless, that mentor/acolyte relationship seems to have been a critical part of the dynamic between them.

"Anyway, what you never learned from your parents was how to deal with people who are equals. You either feel inferior to them or superior, with your IQ of 169," I said dismissively. "The IQ test is a necessary evil, OK for predicting how kids will react to school but much abused, as its inventor warned it would be.

'Your Dad didn't raise a kid he treated as an equal or intended to turn into an equal. He didn't explain things; he just got mad when you didn't already know."

"Except when he died, but then he was my child."

"It was all in the can by then anyway.

'What you never learned was give and take, the osmosis of a relationship between equals."

"That's brilliant but for the last ten minutes I've been craving dental floss."

"Be my guest."

Then he stumbled to the bed and shook and cried and I thought, "Did I go too far?"

"I can't go through another day like this," Mike said. When he got through shaking on the bed, he dropped to his knees and shook on the floor. "Watch me carefully tomorrow."

I nodded.

"I don't mean I'll kill myself. I just mean if I have to shake like this, stay with me.

'If anything happens, please tell [his LAPD colleague] he was my best friend."

"You can tell him yourself. I'm not going to make it any easier for you to kill yourself."

"I can't call him when I'm like this; what would I say?"

"It's not a performance; you'd just call him to be with him on the phone."

Our conversation brought a reprieve; he felt well enough to call the LAPD cop.

The cop and his wife had almost died in an accident caused by a homeless man who tried to commit suicide by jumping in front of their motorcycle. Swerving to avoid him, they ended up with broken arms and ribs. When they recovered enough to function, they hired a detective to find out what had become of the homeless man but never could.

The conversation soothed Mike but soon his anxiety returned.

I mentioned going back to Al Anon to help with the isolation but Mike says he and his psychiatrist are adamantly against it; it triggered unwanted emotions. Anyway, he's beyond Al Anon, he said; they reproach him for having fallen off the wagon even though he's able to drink in moderation which defies their archetype.

He's itching to go to LA, see Kenny and the LAPD friend as well as the old AA crowd even though he got mad at them in the end.

"But I wouldn't have you," he said. What that mostly means is, he wouldn't have anywhere to stay long term. If someone offered to host him, he'd be gone in a heartbeat.

"We have to ask Ray what would happen to the trust if I died," he said as he got ready for bed.

"Since you'd be intestate it would probably go to [your aunt]," I said. "The assumption is you'd want it to go to the nearest blood relative.

"Great," he said, his trademark sarcastic response. "That's exciting."

It always feels nasty when he goes into "tying up loose ends" mode.

February 27, 2007

Day four in the worst bout so far (except for the Effexor episode.) Legs buckling, leading to helpless crying.

"I wouldn't wish this on [a former colleague!]" he said, "or on X or Y or anyone else I've been mentally torturing."

"Does it make you question your faith in God?"

"No. I know there's some force but I don't understand why it's allowing me to suffer like this. *I* wouldn't allow me to suffer like this.

'But I've seen too many times when I should've died but I didn't."

"You've been acting as though you're in jail. You speak in those terms: 'I've got to get out of here. I'm climbing the walls. I'm trapped.'

"I *am* in jail. I can't leave Brooklyn. You're here; Ray's here; [his psychiatrist]'s here."

"Venezuela was jail; Brooklyn is jail. Your jail is here." I tapped my head.

He lay back on the pillow, thoughtful.

"I'm going to sleep now," he said.

He sent a bleak email to his psychiatrist who's decided that tomorrow he should switch from Lithium to Zoloft.

"It's an antidepressant," Mike explained. "Lithium is a mood stabilizer."

"Hmmm..."

"I know. But if Lithium slows down sexual response, Zoloft kills it."

(That issue had not been on my mind.)

He went out for his after-dinner cigarette.

"I left AA in order to write the War Games chapter of Rubicon," he observed. "The two hardest chapters of the book. Without alcohol, I wouldn't have had the courage to write those two chapters. But if I'd stayed in AA, I wouldn't have had the break-in in Ashland. Was it worth it?"

"That's for you to say. You also might be dead."

"I have to remember that."

Part 51: The Enemy in My Bed

February 27, 2007 From Mike to his psychiatrist:

For several days now I have had less and less energy. Each day I have spent as much as an hour vibrating and shaking with rage on the bed as Jenna comforts me. I have been afraid to shower or shave. I did both after 2 PM today. I don't want to go out. We went out to shop a while ago and Jenna had a number of options (DVD, new sweater, health food, see a movie). I nixed the local movies and felt so weak I just came home after we bought some liqueur for Jenna and Scotch for me. [No, that wasn't what I'd meant by health food.] *My scotch use is still very moderate. One, one to one and a half oz drink maybe five nights per week now between 5 and 6 PM. That's it.. I begged Jenna to stay close to me to today, which she did willingly. The depression is so heavy it feels like I am swimming through molasses. I wondered if my lighter AM lithium dose might be causing this. Nothing excites me. All I want to do is sleep, especially after the violent shaking fits on the bed which wear me out. They start right after breakfast. There have been a lot of unplesant revelations since the 10k went missing. We have no new news on the LA books. Now, even the thought of seeing the horses someday is losing appeal. It's scaring me because I don't know where or when it will stop. Still the letters of love and priase come in over the net. Last night I talked to my oldest friend in the world, from 32 years ago, a retired LAPD detective, [X]. It was great to hear his voice and we were both moved. But afterwards I was so homesick and so full of remorse. He's going to be 65 soon but he's happily retired and very comfortable, living a happy stable life with a good wife, grandkids in a nice home. Me, I'm a broken and broke, depressed writer who's not happy to be in Brooklyn and who is terrified of waking up every morning. The Wikipedia folks aren't letting up, so there I sit falsely accused on Google of being a criminal when I was the victim. Please, if you've got any magic words, throw them at me. I have not had an episode like the last one where I was so unfair to J enna. I am actually just scared now. The last four or five days have been almost the worst since I got here excetp for the Effexor, It hit me last night, right between the eyes, full and unavoidable, that I have a mental disorder and that it's not going away. My situation is not just the product of lot of tragic circumstances. The First Step, as they say. I recalled your words about a good prognosis but that seems so incredibly distant. And my lack of energy and drive just seems to be getting worse. Until I get to Beth Israel I feel lost. And even*

*then Dr. Y said the first two sessions were to evaluate me to see if I would be
accepted. So that means maybe three weeks before getting real help? Sorry if this is
long. Winston Chrchill called depression his "black dog". Well my black dog is
chewing on me like a T-Bone steak. This was what we used to call a "dump" in
AA. But I really needed to, and with someone other than dear Jenna who's heard it
all anyway. Thanks for reading and you can forward to anyone you want.   best,
Mike*

February 27, 2007 From Mike to Ray with the subject line: *I need a will*

    *Just in case. I'd like to do thi soon please. What does the Power of Attorney
leave you with with if I die intestate?Issues to deal with:- Trust- Personal library-
Seeing to it that Barry Silverthorn receives the balance of the inventory he paid for
that is still in Ashland waiting for money to ship them to him. What;s owed
toBarry must be made right.- My laptop- My personal belongings stored in
Ashland- Personal belongings in NY- Residual income from Rubicon and rights to
same- Copyrights to FTW Mike*

February 28, 2007

    A break in the weather. Mike took a walk, got milk — the kind
I drink — had a bowl of chicken soup and a bagel and tried to use his
Medicaid card to get reimbursed for the Zoloft. (Not covered.) Came
back exhausted.

    "You've seen me fight the good fight, haven't you?"

    I nodded. Maybe I should have protested. Maybe I was
acquiescing that suicide at this point would be understandable.

    Apart from his walk which was more extensive than usual, he spent
the day shaking or, when worn out from that, sleeping. The blog is
down because Blogspot's been bought by Google so apparently we're
all supposed to switch to Google accounts to get in although if I access
it via Internet Explorer it looks as though anybody can edit anybody
else's blog.

    "I want to die," he said.

    "Part of you wants to die, part of you doesn't."

    "Which part doesn't?"

"The part that's still here, that hasn't killed yourself yet."

"The part of me that wants to die is winning.

'They'll never let me get independence, be a human being again."

"I have the feeling if Ken was suddenly able to sell the books and you had ten thousand dollars, it wouldn't make any difference."

"Getting the checking account would."

I called Sovereign Bank. Mike has been confirmed on the account.

Indeed, it makes no difference. He shook while I pursued the blog snags, then lay down for another nap.

I thought back to Venezuela when I was afraid that he would die by letting himself succumb to illness.

"I have to make a will," he said. "I talked to Ray. If I died now, everything would be up in the air. The Power of Attorney ends with my death. The trust would be up in the air."

"That's what I thought; your possessions would go to your aunt."

February 28, 2007 9:39:31 PM EST From Jenna to [Mike's psychiatrist], Mike and Ray:

Subj: check-up for mike

hi [Mike's psychiatrist]

mike can't face an emergency ward but once we go through the medicaid forms, perhaps we can just pick a physician and go to his/her office. there again, it might smoothe the way if you could tell said physician that mike's story of gvt persecution is not psychotic.

what we're leading up to is that we'd like to get mike tested for metals poisoning as well as other possible forms of toxicity. as you know, such tests are more than justified in his case.

i'm cc'ing mike's lawyer on this email because he's aware of precedents for such a potential diagnosis and needs to be kept up to date on mike's medical situation.

thanks so much for all your work.

hi ray

the reason i wrote that email to [Mike's psychiatrist] a few minutes ago is that since saturday mike's been spending more and more time just shaking.

sometimes when he walks to the kitchen his legs buckle so he lies down and shakes til he's exhausted and goes to sleep. apart from a half hour walk today plus another reprieve after he had a bit of scotch this evening, that's how he spent the entire day. no lou dobbs, no conversation, i don't even think he read the paper.

if this continues, any thought of going to a movie much less the stable is beyond the realm of possibility. he musters energy for five minute phone conversations, that's it.

the symptoms don't match up impressively with those of heavy metal poisoning and we know that whatever might be in his system didn't get there in the last three months since i'd undoubtedly have it too. but it's possible someone gave him something with a delayed reaction; you know far more about these things than i do.

on the phone [his psychiatrist] said she'd like to see him get checked out physically. since he doesn't have a regular dr she recommended an er but he can't face that.

so that's where things are right now...

February 28, 2007 11:30 PM From Jenna to Ray:

i also told [his psychiatrist] that when mike lies down shaking he also ends up complaining of feeling cold; fear and cold seem to go hand in hand, the one inducing the other.

March 1, 2007

Another month, another emergency room, this time at Beth Israel, to see why Mike shakes all day.

After six hours, he was seen in the Drug Induced Sexual Assault examining room where, dressed in a floral hospital gown, (what a sport!) he put his feet in the stirrups, lay back and stared at the cherry blossoms on the ceiling.

"Any surgery?" asked the nurse.

Mike told her about the peritonitis, the several eye surgeries as a child and the gunshot wounds.

Gunshot wounds?

After the nurse left, he showed me where the bullet from a faulty gun in his holster had gone off, pierced his arm, gone into his left ear and out next to his temple.

"This is one of the times when I know God intervened," he said.

"You could have sued the manufacturer."

"Except that I got the gun at K-Mart, my uncle was on the board and I was a security guard there. Officially, we weren't allowed to wear guns but it was tacitly encouraged. It would have been complicated, legally."

"What is that guy holding?" I asked about a young man in another examining room.

"Some sort of foreign currency. Don't stare," Mike said.

Our fellow patients this time included several elderly parents with long-suffering children; a heroin addict who'd taken a double dose; the ubiquitous young woman with two roommates.

The muscle spasms are tied to rage, Mike thinks. But the experience of the Emergency Room, frustrating as it was, was a lesson that when the source of rage is outside him, he handles it reasonably.

March 2, 2007

Mike's stepmother is dead. Ray called. The LA lawyer for the trust found out two days ago. For all we know, she could have died six months ago but at least the papers have been filed so now it's confirmed.

This opens up more questions for the other side. Mike and Ray will be going to California in a few weeks, then up to Ashland. I wish I could figure out a way to be useful to justify tagging along but I can't.

Ken's been told. "He needs good news as much as anyone," Mike said.

This development makes some difference to Mike's mood. He didn't cry tonight but he did still take a nap. That won't change as long as he's on all these pills. I've told him to factor that variable in to his calculations about his trip west. It's not as though he'll be able to operate on his old schedule of one meeting at nine, another at ten and so on.

March 6, 2007

He raised the subject of Effexor, how suicidal it had made him.

"But you have such grit, such determination," I said. "You got straight to the hospital."

"Don't say that. I'm just breathing in and out, OK?"

For the last week, he's spent every day either shaking on the bed or sleeping. A couple of days ago, we had this conversation:

MR (shaking helplessly:) I'm so scared, I'm so scared.

JO: When you were going strong, you were like one of those cartoon characters who run off a cliff and keep going. When the computers got smashed is when you were forced to look down; then you fell. But since this is a cartoon, you've just gone 'splat' and gotten up again; you're not dead.

MR: I just want to die.

I reminded him about a woman who'd once been interviewed on Sally Jessy Raphael. She'd jumped out the window but been blown back by the wind onto someone's balcony. Sally asked her, "What did you think while you were falling?"

The woman answered, "I thought, 'I've made a big mistake.'"

March 7, 2007

Two Google alerts blaming climate change on China and India.

No question their environmental standards leave something to be desired but it's hypocritical of us to point fingers; like the person who eats all but one chocolate in the box then whines about the person who eats the last one.

Tomorrow it's supposed to be nine degrees, the very prospect of which makes Mike shudder.

"It won't stop," he says.

"That's where I can assure you you're wrong."

We've had this conversation before, about his tendency to live so vividly in the moment that he thinks it'll last forever.

198

But on Saturday, the clocks will leap ahead, three weeks earlier than usual, which should brighten his outlook.

March 10, 2007

"Ray won't write a will for me because he's afraid... you know. But in case anything happens, I want someone to know that I want the debts liquidated. Whatever is left I want to be divided between Cynthia McKinney, for political purposes, and you."

"The debts won't be a problem; those people have a claim. Cynthia and I have no claim. Your aunt has a claim. And all her nine children."

"She won't do anything.... There may even be something in the trust about that. Of course, I haven't seen the trust."

He was scared all day today, dreading writing to his stepmother's niece (at Ray's suggestion) to propose that they not drag out the process which would bleed the trust away over the next year in lawyers' fees. "Last time we spoke, I was a man of substance."

"We have to work on your self-image so that 'substance' is not determined entirely by how much money you have. You still wrote that book. You still ran that website. If I measured my self-worth by how much money I'd made, I'd be far more miserable than you."

"You don't have my credit report. I know what [his stepmother's niece] is like."

"The point is to have your own criteria of self-worth so you're not so vulnerable to other people's."

March 11, 2007

Once again he awoke shivering with fear and cold only today it is 51 degrees out.

The cause of dread is the looming letter to his stepmother's niece; not because he's afraid of rejection but because, as he puts it: "What'll I do when I get the money?"

He has a deep sense of not deserving it.

"Perhaps the cold is a metaphor for feeling isolated, left out of the common stream of mankind."

"That makes sense." He paused. "But I'm still cold."

"Are you afraid that getting the money could trigger a hypomanic phase?"

"Partly, yes. But I think I have enough self-awareness now to deal with that." *(I won't squander it, God, I promise. Please let me get the money.)* "I just want a hand to lift me out of this."

"Deus ex machina."

Another thought also occurred to me: "It doesn't work that way; you have to go step by step." But that would come off as priggish. We had to put the admonition into practice.

"It would be good if you could think of it not in terms of superego," I said, and gave an example:

"'I shouldn't indulge myself; I mustn't.' Because that'll just make your Id want to rebel."

"So what do I think?"

"Instead of 'should,' you could think, 'I *want* to hold onto this money long term. That's more important to me than a momentary feeling that I'm a man of substance.' If you could remember that…"

"This is working. This is sinking in. All right. Much as I'm afraid of this pattern, I'm going to take a nap now."

When he got up, he channel-surfed, a normal activity he hasn't engaged in in months.

Dichotomy permeates his entire way of being: Superego vs. Id, male vs. female, superior/mania vs. inferior/depression. This is why he lives in the moment, unable, when he's in one mood, to bear in mind what it felt like to be in its opposite.

But I can't just spill all this; it must wait for the right moment.

March 12, 2007

This morning I felt amorous. It's been a while, maybe a month and the last time was inconclusive, though enjoyable; on both sides, or so I thought.

We didn't get far. Mike apologized for being "the iceman."

An odd metaphor, as I pointed out: "But the iceman cometh."

I started to nuzzle his arm but he leapt up, wild-eyed and bolted to the bathroom.

"I could do it right now," he said in a matter-of-fact monotone as he got back into bed.

"Because you can't carry this through?"

"You mean have an orgasm? Give me a break."

"There's something about your approach that's freaking me out. You're a woman, a pretty woman. But your touch is so light, you're like a fourteen-year-old. It's almost as though it's insincere."

"It *is* like that. You're not the first person to say that."

"It's as though you have some desire but not for flames."

"That's quite true. The fire is contained."

"But when there's passion, there are flames."

Later he said, "I'm glad you told me that, that I'm not the only one. I've been suppressing these thoughts and it's been adding to the depression."

Poor guy, feeling obligated and partnered to a person who makes him sick. I, who am supposedly saving him from his own craziness, may be crazier than he is. Perhaps the sense I'd gotten over New Year's wasn't so far off: That he had himself admitted to Bellevue not so much to avoid killing himself as to avoid killing me. One can see why jumping out the window might have seemed the only honorable solution.

Part 52: Rosebud

Citizen Kane is the story of a newspaper magnate who, while publishing a rag that was the diametric antithesis of FTW, bore some superficial resemblance to Mike. The film's director, the legendary Orson Welles, said, "Kane was selfish and selfless, an idealist, a scoundrel, a very big man and a very little one. It depends on who's talking about him."

Kane dies uttering the mysterious word, "Rosebud." In the belief that uncovering the meaning of the word will provide an "open sesame" to the man's life, the editor of a news digest sets out to interview former associates of the newspaper giant to see what light they can shed.

He never learns the significance of the word, but the audience does, by means of a zoom in to a close-up in the last minute of the film: It was the brand name of Kane's sled when he was a child and taken from his mother to be "adopted" by a bank and groomed for his career. "Rosebud," then, symbolizes the last time in Kane's life that he was simply happy.

There is a situation in Mike's life which may perform the same service as Rosebud, but it is not a happy memory.

When I asked Mike about his mother's good qualities, he said something I neglected to include before.

"She dressed well."

But that one "good quality," towards which Mike clearly felt ambivalent, (the implication, "frivolous woman" lay not far beneath the surface,) fast devolved into a horrifying one. "She had tons of clothes, I mean *tons* of clothes. When she died, it was like a horror movie. The hangers were hooking onto the furniture, onto plants as though they wouldn't let go. I said, 'Mom, it's OK; you don't need them now. You're dead!'"

Later came this:

"When I was nine, she seduced me. She was in the middle of a breakdown and she molested me. I suppressed that memory for a long time."

"How did you recover it?"

"It came up in an AA meeting. X, [Mike's AA sponsor] said, 'Listen to what you say.' I was at the podium talking about how I always stayed one achievement short of perfection but also one achievement ahead of the devil.

'I was talking and I said, '... and when I was nine my mother had sex with me.'

'I went to a hypnotist to recover the whole memory." This was probably the man Mike met while on his UPS route.

He didn't describe in any detail what the incest consisted of apart from the influence of her purported breakdown.

Mike used the word "breakdown" loosely. Certainly — and with good reason — he viewed his own state of mind after the burglary almost until he moved back to California as a breakdown. But also, when he described his break-up with a former girlfriend who was under pressure to finish her thesis, he said she was having a breakdown. His employee who sued him for sexual harassment was, in his lexicon, going through a breakdown. And one evening when the prospect of preparing dinner made me physically ill, I went to bed instead; Mike later described that as, "when you had your breakdown."

So it's impossible to know what condition his mother was in when she "had sex with" her nine-year-old son. But it did resurrect my clinical psychologist friend's observation that people may go "crazy" in order to do what they want to do anyway but which the sane mind will not allow.

There are also clues that some sort of molestation may have occurred earlier. Mike's dream, relayed in previous posts, of leaving for a business trip while his two children were in the bath, bore the suggestion that he was abandoning them naked and helpless to the predations of their mother, (the former employee who was suing him for sexual harassment and whom he viewed as a predator and government agent. It's worth remembering that both his parents worked for or with government agencies which he pursued his entire adult career and which paid him back in kind. And once, while referring to the women in his life who'd abused him, he listed his mother, Teddy and the young female employee. I've wondered if he leapt out of bed when I touched him lightly, saying my approach

seemed "insincere," because he suspected me of being an
agent. Agents and young women, as I'd seemed at that moment —
fourteen years old, to be exact — were intertwined in his experience
and therefore, his mind.)

He once said, "My mother was destined to be crazy, with all the
incest in her family. That stuff about West Virginia is true.

'I don't know why I think so, but I think she was once pregnant by
her father."

The reader may remember earlier in this account where Mike said
his mother was crushed by his father's betrayal because he'd saved her
from her own father. Perhaps her pregnancy by her father, if Mike's
intuition was correct, was responsible for the two stillbirths she
endured after marriage.

One morning a groan emanated from the bathtub. "I remember I
was eight or nine. [An older boy] sodomized me. But I don't
remember if it really happened or not.

'When I was five, we were living at [he gave the address] in
Pikesville. A neighbor boy, X — I remember his name — and I... We
were about five. We had our pants down. You know those hammer
and tool sets? I had an anvil and I touched his rectum with it but I
remember thinking, 'You can't put that in there; that hurts.' How did I
know that?"

In his dream of leaving for a business trip, the ages of his two
daughters are five and nine.

Deadly Nightgown

My main nocturnal garb that winter was a standard issue flannel
nightgown with blue flowers on it, placed at delicate intervals. A more
innocent garment could hardly be imagined.

But Mike was terrified of it.

"There's something about the way we made love that reminded me
of [a teenage crush.] When I was nine, we went to visit [his mother's
friends.] They had a son, A, who was a year older than I was and B
was eight. 'A' called me upstairs. There was B with her legs spread

204

and her vagina lubricated. Her mother walked by while this was going on. C was there too, about three. She wanted to play too.

'Their father called me in that night and said, 'Do you know how to play [a kind of] poker?'" (I didn't catch the name.)

"He brushed all the cards onto the floor. 'That's what happens when you touch something that isn't yours.'

'When B was twenty-one, she visited me. She wore a nightgown like the one you had on. She pulled it up; she had nothing on underneath. We made love. We had a torrid affair after that."

My nightgown also reminded him of the grandmother in that household where he had spent a portion of his youth.

"You know, teenagers sometimes get so tired in the afternoon, they just fall asleep on the floor.

'One day I fell asleep by the fire. When I woke up [the grandmother] was standing over me in a nightgown like that. I could see right up to her [obscenity.]"

I've never been entirely sure the grandmother was aware of what Mike could see. His hallmark question, "Cui bono?" or, "Who benefits?" helps trace corruption to its source. But like any valuable way of looking at events, it can be taken too far. Those who followed Mike closely at FTW or later, Facebook, witnessed how he could lash out against a comment he took to be disinformation generated by an enemy whereas it was more often a guileless observation from a newcomer not versed in Mike's perceptions.

Anyway, perhaps now the reader has a greater understanding of the implications when I did something, such as worrying or not having pictures on the wall, that reminded Mike of his mother.

Part 53: Klutz

Today was a more normal day — we went to the bank, ordered joint checks, talked, joked, watched part of *Command — The Far Side of the World*, with Russell Crowe. Another he-man's movie about male bonding during hardship; a stalwart leader.

I pointed out what progress this represented but Mike assured me he felt as depressed as ever.

"I want you to know I don't think I'm going to make it," he said.

I never know if his occasional cheerfulness stems from the knowledge that he's holding onto suicide as a way out. Psychologists have observed that people don't commit suicide while in the depths of depression; it's when they start to come out of it and have more energy that they act.

But this evening he said, "I'm glad we had that talk this morning."

He was referring to the conversation about how any romantic overtures from me make him want to throw up or kill himself. "We need to talk some more about that because it has implications for both of us."

"Meaning I should go to the shrink too and grow up, finally. Been there, done that. No dice."

But even though my shortcomings in this arena are a real obstacle to us, at least he's thinking long term about the future.

March 13, 2007

He's back to shaking, possibly because he's withdrawn from Lithium. A while ago it looked like another Ativan alarm but instead he took a nap from which he just rose and called me into the bedroom to say, "I've given myself unreserved permission to stay in bed all day." He was in a, "Fuck you, gods" mood which is a damn sight better than where he was pre-nap, shaking and saying, "I'm so cold."

"Partly it's you and me," he explained, which was a new slant.

"You mean, 'How can I be stuck with this person? How can I make love to her, she's so weird?'"

"Give me a break. The sexual problems are way down on the totem pole.

'I'm wondering — you're so good to me — if you're not making me more dependent."

"I try not to do things for you that you can do for yourself." I refrained from adding that apart from the effect on him of such enabling, performing supererogatory tasks would only fuel resentment and fury on my end. Did he think I enjoyed hanging out at the bank?

"I know. I'm also wondering whether that relationship isn't also playing out in bed. But don't ask me how that works; I'm just throwing it out.

'I was having a fantasy before of putting out a barn fire. You had inadvertently knocked over a lantern."

He laughed hollowly at how he'd made me the perp.

(Klutz: "A person who is never without a scrape or bruise. Always finds a way to trip, bump into things and
people." www.urbandictionary.com/define.php?term=klutz)

"Lantern? What century are we in?" I asked.

"A kerosene lamp, or oil or gas, after the electric grid went down."

I have a fantasy too — far more immediate — of his going to the roof to throw himself off. I chase him up, arguing why he should live. He jumps.

The police accuse me of pushing him.

I remember my clinical psychologist friend's admonition that a fear of something can be "reaction formation," a defense against one's own wish.

He talked about making a will, leaving half of whatever is left after the debts are paid to me and half to Cynthia.

"You'll be OK. You'll see the signs and get yourself to a lifeboat. They'll take you in. And you won't have to drag me along."

"Try to get it through your supposedly brilliant mind that I might *want* to drag you along."

"That's where I really think you're crazy."

"I can't have these conversations with anybody else."

"They are great conversations."

Ken says if Mike went back to LA now, he'd be hot shit; all his predictions of three years ago are coming true.

He looks agonized.

"You told them everything they need to know," I said to mollify him. "They just have to read FTW and move."

"My work is done," he said. "There's nothing left for me to do."

"The only job anyone has to do now is build a lifeboat and go there with a few close friends."

"I'm in no position to build a lifeboat. You'd have to drag me along."

"You have to stop looking at yourself in terms of that world that's falling apart. Stop using their criteria. The people who you're afraid look down on you now are going to be in exactly your position in a few years. You're judging yourself according to the standards of a system that you yourself have argued is corrupt at the core. 'Man of substance' and all that shit."

"Might as well get out now, then."

"Whatever rationalizations you come up with, whether you live or not comes down to whether or not you want to."

The morning headlines included one about terminally ill newborns.

"I couldn't even look at that one," Mike said.

It was newborns who got to him in a movie a few weeks ago, too. No wonder he avoided being a father. The unconscious memory of his own newborn self, declared dead on arrival, still exerts power.

From Jenna to Ray:

"he's having a really rough time all day every day. it's a good day when he gets out at all. there were many days which consisted literally of just shaking on the bed then lapsing into a nap which could last two hours. on those days he barely ate two

meals and observed — accurately, i think — that he wouldn't have eaten anything if i hadn't made it. (he does make his own breakfast and might eat lunch if i made it but i don't and won't.)

yesterday we went to the bank, — tada! — which i attribute largely to the intervention of the holistic guy last week who gave him supplements and acupuncture.

last night he finished the scotch and isn't going to buy another bottle so that may improve his energy level.

today he took up shaking again, possibly because he's now off lithium. but he's resisting taking ativan as it usually knocks him out.

i'm not sure i see a general vector in a good direction but depression can last a year, a fact i don't remind him of too often. at least he's been talking for the last couple of days. before the holistic guy, conversation had been spiraling down to a cypher. and he does do better when we have a positive project like watching part of a movie, which we did last night and which would have been unthinkable a week ago. so what this indicates is that the reasons for his paralysis or whatever you want to call it are not systemic but can be treated.

i keep an intermittent journal of some of our conversations. i mentioned this a few months ago when he raised the subject of a history of ftw, but by now he may have forgotten. i didn't want to keep this project a secret but i also know that he doesn't want it to be in his face.

right now he seems to be waking up from a nap and is making bad-dream noises.

Sent at Mike's request to Ray, Mike's psychiatrist; X (a colleague) and the "holistic guy," an acupuncturist/FTW subscriber who treated Mike for free. (The needles which are supposed to relate to particular organs, in Mike's case had tapped into memories, arousing profound grief:)

mike asked me to talk to you "out of school" and give you an update.

he's now out smoking a cigarette.

...his self-report that he's sinking and becoming more agoraphobic and bedridden is accurate.

as he sat on the edge of the bed a few minutes ago, he said he was scared even to stand up.

X, i know he just spoke to you and sounded sort of normal, though downbeat. you should know that i used that call as an example to him of how he's able to muster attention and stop shaking when he's talking to someone he feels comfortable with. that call was the closest he's gotten to normal life all day.

What I did not say in this email is that Mike explained the reason for his comfort zone with X this way: "We used to hang out after an event and have a Guinness. Now we've both lost everything." X has a serious illness and while Mike was filing for Medicaid, X was filing for the equivalent program in his state.

Update email to Ray a few minutes later:

Subj: "he let slip that he's planning a trip to the hardware store"

...this must be to buy rope or something. it was clear that the trip had to do with suicide. he didn't deny this.
    so now what am i supposed to do? i don't think he'll do anything before a will is made out.

To Ray, Ken, the holistic practitioner and Mike's psychiatrist:

a few minutes ago he said, "i don't have the balls to make a will. i don't have the balls to fill out the medicaid form."
    i said, "you do realize those goals are in conflict."
    he said, "i do."
    right now he's eating one of the holistic practitioner's nutrition bars and says he's going to take another ativan.

210

Part 54: Q and A

A couple of emails came in from a colleague of Mike's who's versed in his work going back to the nineties. They raise valid points which force me to articulate the thinking behind this account, a useful exercise in itself.

Email 1:

On Rosebud, I wonder if you go too far. Although I suppose at this point, it's all or nothing, but I wonder.

Much of this detail is known only by you.

I think the comparison with Citizen Kane is inappropriate. Kane was a fraud, morally ambivalent, miserable, pathetic, a liar. He was only a mess and nothing else. He did none of the genuinely courageous and heroic things that Mike did. I wish you hadn't used it.

Email 2:

There are moments reading your series that I wonder if you unintention-ally make the strongest case that Mike was so psychologically compromised from childhood that he was unfit to be a whistleblower. Vulnerable. Easy to manipulate and strongarm. Easy to destroy.

We know that he accomplished great things in spite of the tidal wave of personal traumas.

But does this case need to be made at all?

How much, before it begins to tarnish the work?

Comment: Much of this detail is known only by you.

Response: Sure; we all know stuff that no one else knows which is what those of us who write tend to write about. There are other people who know about Mike's memories of childhood sexual abuse, which is what I assume you're referring to. About the shaking, fear and consequent self-loathing, I may be the only person outside the medical profession who knew the details of that. And there are probably people out there in cyberland who will blame Mike for it. But one can't tutor one's actions to accommodate such warped thinking.

Comment: Is there any detail that you would refrain from revealing?

Response: Yes. I've refrained from revealing certain scenes on the grounds that they're petty. The point is not to smear Mike; the point is to reveal what I know that might help other people understand him better.

I don't know if I'd refrain from revealing something significant. There's one more skeleton in the closet that will come out in some form; I haven't yet figured out how to deal with it. But let me assure you right now that as skeletons go, it's not so terrible, I think. Others will not agree and I'm betting you'll be among them. Please remember when we get to that one that at no time did he do anything illegal and that's a tremendously important line not to cross. That sin was more in the realm of "thought crime."

Comment: I think the comparison with Citizen Kane is inappropriate. Kane was a fraud, morally ambivalent, miserable, pathetic, a liar. He was only a mess and nothing else. He did none of the genuinely courageous and heroic things that Mike did.

Response: OK. You've given me pause. I've forgotten the bulk of that movie. For a long time, I'd thought of the incest as Mike's Rosebud. It explains much about him: his ambivalence about women, particularly those of the age that his mother was when he was growing up and his father abandoned him to her for long stretches. This, I think, is another reason, in addition to the constant moves throughout his childhood, that male companionship was so important to him, the band of brothers which was the LAPD.

So it was only Rosebud that I had in mind, rather than Citizen Kane himself. But then I thought, there's a whole generation out there who don't know who Citizen Kane was, so I googled for a synopsis. This led to Orson Welles' description of Kane himself as such a controversial character. I thought the quote intriguing since Mike was also a newspaperman and also aroused great loyalty and its evil twin, twisted disinformation. I did say that Kane's rag was diametrically opposed to FTW but maybe that distinction got lost in the over-all impression. Kane ended his life enormously wealthy (as he'd also begun it, at least, after his "adoption" by the bank) but empty. Mike had no money but thousands of grateful followers. Obviously, though, he felt something to be missing. Since, as several people have observed, he was making it in the mainstream and had a place to live as well as a wonderful woman in his life, the missing link was probably within him.

Comment: There are moments reading your series that I wonder if you unintentionally make the strongest case that Mike was so psychology-ically compromised from childhood that he was unfit to be a whistleblower. Vulnerable. Easy to manipulate and strongarm. Easy to destroy.

Response: They strong-armed him by seizing his bank account and destroyed him by taking a sledgehammer to his computers. If the female employee who sued him was indeed a honeypot, then he succumbed to the time-honored trap which has worked with virtually every man whom TPTB have wanted to take down; he was no more susceptible to it than the average guy in this CEO-rock star/groupie society of ours.

He couldn't be manipulated in relation to the final skeleton which we haven't come to yet because, as I said, he didn't do anything illegal. He did think the government was aware of it.

Of course he was vulnerable; who isn't? This is why torture works. On everyone, Mike said. So that wouldn't render someone unfit to be a whistleblower.

Comment: We know that he accomplished great things in spite of the tidal wave of personal traumas. But does this case need to be made at all?

Response: This is a variation on a theme. Each variation shows the theme in a new light.

Comment: How much, before it begins to tarnish the work?

Response: "Anything you say may be used against you." If we praise Mike, even in the form, "He could be difficult but..." we'll be vilified as blind members of a sort of cult. If we point out a flaw, the enemy, if they're so inclined, may run with it. If we do nothing, it'll all be forgotten which is what they'd *really* like.

There's no question that I've provided fuel to anyone who wants to belittle Mike. But again, if we live according to the rules of misguided or malicious people and what they might do, information remains unshared and those who might benefit from it won't.

Part 55: Hegel

My email correspondent in yesterday's post had more observations worth discussing:

1. As Mike himself said to you (at the time), he thought that the MCR of pre-Venezuela was gone. But to give a complete picture, you would have also [to] go back to that MCR to balance the brutal freefall you are writing about. The MCR of the CIA-Drugs era not only functioned through all of his problems, but provided support and counsel to other whistleblowers who were in far worse shape. Guys like Cele Castillo. How can you do that if you're beset with seemingly every psych malady on earth? This would require that you find these guys and interview them, which I know is beyond the scope.

Reading your series without knowledge about the "old MCR", the image is heavily negative. Which leads to...

2. Propaganda. My worry throughout all this is the Powers That Be. Anything that the PTB can use to weaken collective hope. Their contempt, their laughter. You are being honest showing MCR's humanity, but are you giving the PTB a lot of ammunition to giggle over? Those on the other side are never portrayed as less than gods. Dick Cheney is invincible. That is how they win. While our side has no one to believe in.

Comment: As Mike himself said to you (at the time), he thought that the MCR of pre-Venezuela was gone.

Response: That's a double-edged sword. It meant that the fight had been knocked out of him; he no longer had what it took to do the investigative journalism that had forged his career. Also, he knew that if he did, his unwritten "deal" with the government — "You keep quiet and we'll allow you to live in peace" — would be off.

But after saying that, as everyone now knows, he did get back in the game. With a difference, though. Nowhere in the movie *Collapse* will you hear 9/11 mentioned.

The flip side of "the MCR of pre-Venezuela is gone" is the private demon which he attempted to exorcise by fleeing the country. He said that it worked and at least for as long as he stayed in my apartment, that seemed to be true.

Please note the symbiotic relationship between the demon and the avenging angel here. You can't have one without the other. This is why he said, "There is a deep flaw in me and it's responsible for everything I've accomplished."

Comment: The MCR of the CIA-Drugs era not only functioned through all of his problems, but provided support and counsel to other whistleblowers who were in far worse shape. Guys like Cele Castillo.

Response: Thank you for raising that! Yes! I hope someone writes about it but if they don't, thank you for adding it to this record.

Comment: How can you do that if you're beset with seemingly every psych malady on earth?

Response: Actually, just speaking anecdotally from personal experience, I've found that it's the people with stable backgrounds who are least able to understand those of us who are screwed up in some way.

He wasn't beset by every psych malady on earth. The provisional diagnosis was bi-polar but the manic side was supremely functional, as it often is. As soon as he received the diagnosis, he googled it and was gratified to read the list of his fellow sufferers which included Hemingway. He never hallucinated so all of those diagnoses are irrelevant. He was narcissistic in a way that is pandemic in our society and also worked to his, and his readers', advantage. I used to wonder why his various mental health professionals never mentioned that, at least not that he passed on to me. Maybe they thought he'd take it the wrong way and only needed the other diagnosis for prescription purposes anyway. That's pure speculation.

Note that in psychology, "narcissism" does not have the same meaning that it does out in layman land. The average person thinks a narcissist is someone who thinks he's hot stuff in some way. To professional psychologists, however, a narcissist is someone who doesn't have a solid sense of "self" and so seeks approval from outside. This is why narcissists are attracted to the performing professions — from acting to teaching; they like to be watched or listened to with some form of applause as reward. Probably, the same may be said of writers. In modern society, virtually everyone has narcissism of one kind or another. We find it hard to take when people don't like us, or our work. And we reward narcissism by holding movie and rock stars in highest esteem. The late transvestite wit Quentin Crisp observed that while his youth was marked by beatings from thugs who objected to his dress, his later life was marked by reverence from those same populations because they'd seen him on television. Television, he maintained, was the medium through which he regained his "virginity." Hence the title of one of his books: *How to Become a Virgin.*

Comment: Reading your series without knowledge about the "old MCR", the image is heavily negative.

Response: In your previous email, there was a suggestion that even revealing the sexual abuse when he was a child could serve to discredit him and undoubtedly this is true. People use every tool they can. So I googled what percent of men have been the victim of this sort of abuse and found:

About 3% of American men — or 1 in 33 — have experienced an attempted or completed rape in their lifetime...[1]

- *2.78 million men in the U.S. have been victims of sexual assault or rape.*[1] https://www.rainn.org/get-information/statistics/sexual-assault-victims

Mike didn't say his mother attempted to rape him; it was more of a seduction so we'll have to expand that 3% to include the less violent category. (There was also his flashback to the older boy sodomizing him. But he wasn't sure if it was real or not.)

For women, of course, the statistics are considerably worse:

1 out of every 6 American women has been the victim of an attempted or completed rape in her lifetime (14.8% completed rape; 2.8% attempted rape).[1] *https://www.rainn.org/get-information/statistics/sexual-assault-victims*

Again, add in those who were simply abused without completed or attempted rape. Then add to that those who've been traumatized by violence and the number mushrooms. In the end, how many people are left whom we can "trust" because they weren't scarred by some horrific event in childhood? Speaking of that: Isn't it ironic how shocked we are by his mother's alleged sexual abuse whereas no one bats an eye at Mike's nonchalantly mentioning memories like, "And then Dad beat the shit out of me."

Comment: Propaganda. My worry throughout all this is the Powers That Be. Anything that the PTB can use to weaken collective hope. Their contempt, their laughter. You are being honest showing MCR's humanity, but are you giving the PTB a lot of ammunition to giggle over?

Response: Ah, but that's the point. The opposition does not write; they are not in search of the truth. Quite the reverse; they're engaged in covering up the truth. That's what propaganda is for.

Propaganda is descended from ancient Greek Sophistry, which has come to mean "false reasoning." It uses whatever tactics are at hand to manipulate people, usually by way of their emotions, appeals to "pathos."

So if this is a war of propaganda, yes, I'm a turncoat for the other side. But what we're doing here is the opposite.

We are of the Socratic school who engage in a dialectic of opposing views (in Hegelian terms, thesis, antithesis, synthesis) to arrive at a multi-faceted truth by way of "logos" or appeals to reason.

Comment: Those on the other side are never portrayed as less than gods. Dick Cheney is invincible. That is how they win. While our side has no one to believe in.

Response: We have plenty of people to believe in! I grant you, none of them are gods or invincible. Do they need to be, in order for us to believe in them? Glwt (Good luck with that.)

Mike's traditionally been portrayed as a seer on the one hand and a kook on the other. Of course, he was neither. He was not clairvoyant. He was extremely smart and well-informed. He was the right man in the right place at the right time. Having been raised in a CIA-family, he had the right mindset and background to understand what was happening. He worked to uncover government malfeasance with a great deal of help from whistle-blowers and researchers, most of whose work will never be divulged. He published and sang out his findings from the rooftops for anyone who wished to listen.

There's a friend of Mike's whose email signatures are inscribed above a quote from Emile Zola: "I have come to live out loud." Mike did that. If you were close to him, he let you know what was on his mind (except when he felt like killing you in which case he decently kept the thought under wraps and transferred that animus to planning his own death.) What a loss it would be not to tell people what was really going on with him, which had nothing to do with a propaganda war.

And re: *"This is how they win."* It's only a small part. They win because they own the government and the media. They win because the public likes the status quo; they just wish they had a bigger piece of it.

We'll never win as long as we engage in the same game. To tell the truth about Mike or anything else is simply to change the paradigm.

Part 56: Burning

Kellia Ramares-Watson commented on the last post, "Hegel:"

You could have written nothing and TPTB would be laughing. They laughed as soon as they got word that MCR had pulled the trigger. I heard that Raw Story laughed and while I deliberately did not read their story on MCR, I saw the first two words in my emails. Conspiracy theorist...

If Cheney seems like a god, it is because he is still alive, rich, and listened to, while Mike, Cele Castillo and Gary Webb, etc are gone. Son of a bitch survived 5 heart attacks. That looks godly to a lot of people.

I had some thoughts about Mike's dream where he's putting out a barn fire because I'd knocked over a lantern. For anyone who missed that post, he "gave a hollow laugh at how he'd made me the perp."

I'm going to do something that would be heresy in the field of psychology if he were still alive. But first, a word about dreams.

Sometimes I ask my students how they figure out what their dreams mean. Usually, someone says, "I google it." Then someone else will point out that there are books that can tell you what your dreams mean. A third person will say that in their culture, dreaming of someone means they're thinking of you; in another culture, a certain dream situation means the dream figure is going to die.

Then we do an exercise where we take, say, three words such as "dog," "ocean," and "green" and they write down whatever the word makes them think of, "free-associating;" following the train of thought.

With any luck, we end up with a variety of responses. Not everyone goes from "ocean," to "relaxing, beach, happy" though at their age, most do. Some people associate the word "ocean" with a frightening experience or climate change.

And not everyone thinks of dogs as faithful, playful friends. Arab culture, for instance, forbids dogs as pets on the grounds that they're unclean; and a few students may be afraid of dogs.

So then, I ask them, if one person dreams of a dog or an ocean, does it have the same meaning as when someone else dreams of it? No. Then who is in the best position to tell you what your dream means? You are.

This is analogous to the approach many psychologists take to dreams. They'll ask, "What does that make you think of?" and watch where the train of thought takes you. Or, "How did that feel?" and ask you to relate that feeling to something going on in your life now.

Mike's not here to answer any of those questions on his lantern dream so what I'm going to do is speculate which is something one normally avoids.

The dream took place in a barn. What was in there? For sure, something important; our vision of the future contained no room for frivolities. Perhaps the barn even housed a horse since Mike yearned to have one when we finally moved. In fact, the stupidest argument we ever had concerned that horse.

The lantern was a kerosene lamp, he said. So we were using a valuable resource — kerosene — the supply of which was diminishing at an alarming rate in his acutely informed view, to provide light to this place which contained vital necessities.

And I knocked it over. Not only that, but in doing so, I was burning down the whole edifice.

There's a general theory that when you dream of a house, it represents you. (My first therapist said *everything* in your dream represents some aspect of yourself; you created the dream, after all.) In Mike's dream, the "self" is burning; he has to put out the fire.

What fire was it that I started in him which he so desperately needed to put out? Rage, for sure. And whatever complicated reaction he had when I made an amorous move one day and he bolted for the bathroom, returning panting with fear.

It was not just a question of his being turned off by me. Had that been the case, he could have simply said, "No thanks, honey," or made some excuse about what his medication was doing to his libido.

But his reaction was primal. I'd reminded him of a fourteen-year-old, he said, and possibly, a honey-pot. He needed to escape the feelings which that sparked; to put out the fire within before it destroyed him completely.

Now, our argument about the horse.

He was emphatic that we would have one when we moved to a sustainable community. A horse was next on the list after a dog. Then, in Mike's fantasy, when he went off on a "business trip," I'd remain home to feed the horse.

Horses are beautiful animals and I've had a good time, when staying with equestrian-minded friends, riding them. But I have no wish to get up close and personal with a horse and take care of him. I'll throw him some hay over the door but if that's not good enough... I'm still not going in there alone; there has to be some barrier between me and the horse.

"So... what???" Mike exclaimed. "You'll just let him starve?"

That was the argument: Already, in the fantasy, Mike has his horse, goes off by himself for the interesting adventures, the ones I wanted most to be part of, and I'm left to do the dirty work. And here we are arguing about my neglect of his non-existent horse at a non-existent house in a hazy future about which we both had serious doubts.

Part 57: The Social Ladder of Psychiatric Asylums

March 13, 2007 2:44:24 PM From Jenna to Ray:

Subj: he wants to know the likelihood of your being named administrator

[email text] if he died intestate. he's rattled bcs the will requires three witnesses. he knows i wouldn't help out there. nor should i, if i'm named in it.
i think he could probably get the three witnesses at the stationery store [a central source of materials required by the legal profession and located on the accurately named "Court Street" in Brooklyn, the store could have summoned five witnesses at a snap simply from among their employees] but i haven't suggested it.

I report Mike's recent actions and conversation to his psychiatrist who strongly recommends hospitalization. It doesn't have to be Bellevue but the subtext was, if we don't do something, she'll have to call an ambulance.

This is Mike's worst nightmare which is probably why she didn't just go ahead and do it outright. So when he wakes up, we'll have a three-way conversation. Best would be if he'd go inpatient voluntarily, a possibility he's brought up himself. I suggest he try Payne Whitney, the crème de la crème of loony bins, since if he's to be there long term, it might be advisable for him to focus on therapy rather than on, "Who do I have to screw to get out of here?"

[A colleague] has to have his dog put down. She's only seven but has spinal cancer.

9 PM

Mike's psychiatrist is obviously scared. She said, "We've always operated on trust so I need to be able to trust you tonight. Because as your psychiatrist I have the authority to call 911 and Jenna, you can too, if you think it's necessary. So Mike, do I have your word?"

She seems to understand that honor counts more than anything with him.

"Yes."

He's still stymied by needing three witnesses for the will, or two with a notary seal. I'm not helping out there, not with suggestions or in any other way.

March 14, 2007 From Jenna to Peter Dale Scott:

...he's in the inpatient ward of payne whitney, the ritz of nyc mental asylums. it's better than bellevue, he says - tomorrow he can wear his own clothes - but he was freaked out to run into a fellow inmate from his previous incarceration. so the asylum circuit is taking the place of 9/11 and peak oil conferences.

it was indeed rope that he had been intending to buy at the hardware store. the most ominous specter in all this is, i think, his mother's history of depression from the time she was about 56, mike's current age, til she died in her eighties.

March 15, 2007 5 PM

Visiting hours at Payne Whitney. I gave Mike a package of chocolate chip cookies which he took gratefully; he's down to 174 pounds and wants to gain weight.

Being a man of simple tastes, he also longs for dental floss but they don't allow anything in the rope family. Why they let him keep his sweatshirt whose hood closes with a cord is a mystery.

We hung out with his friend X who, earlier today and much to the relief of her fellow inmates, organized a storming of the closed library. (For thirty years she was a labor leader in England, as well as a journalist.) Perhaps she was energized by her medication.

This evening her brother Y visited her. He's an actor I'd met years ago at the beach house of Marty Bregman, a movie producer.

It was a scene out of Woody Allen, this social reunion in New York's hottest loony bin.

"Did we date?" Y asked.

"No, but you taught me Gershwin's *C Sharp Minor Prelude* on the piano."

Mike said Marty Bregman had, around the same time, been interested in an option on Mike's LAPD story. Apparently, he made *Serpico* instead.

224

Being originally from New York and a long time Bi-Polar 2 (one of Mike's possible diagnoses,) X knew the skinny on the various programs in the city. Payne Whitney is the most well-appointed — each room has a view of the Upper East Side and *its own bathroom.*

But all day, no one knew what was going on. Mike didn't see a doctor 'til close to five. He and X speculated that the powers that be were seeing how far they could push the inmates before they snapped.

X's husband, Z, once stayed for three weeks at Beth Israel where a whole team of doctors saw him every day.

Z had also been suicidal, getting to the point of writing suicide notes to everyone in his family and renting a room at a hotel on 34th Street — first checking that the windows opened — where he ordered his last meal (shrimp, wine) to the tune of $660. Then he opened the window only to find that there was a terrace on the floor below.

He climbed out anyway, lit on the terrace, climbed over the half-wall and dangled, waiting for the foot traffic on 34th street to ease up so he wouldn't land on anybody. For anyone unfamiliar with New York, 34th Street is the heart of Midtown, with Macy's and Madison Square Garden on the West Side and the Empire State Building two blocks away. If you're looking for a street that's light on foot traffic, you've come to the wrong place.

After remaining suspended for twenty minutes, he pulled himself back up to the balcony. By this time, however, the inhabitants of the room had returned from their evening out. He waited for them to go to bed, then slid along the floor and out the door to Beth Israel where he recovered.

X gave Mike a pep talk, the sort he usually brushes off but in her case it's hard as she has had breast cancer for twenty years and it's now at stage four.

We were also joined by a woman whose five or six children (she's lost count) were taken from her by Judge Judy. Not one to admit defeat, she says she's pregnant again.

After our companions drifted off to the pay phone or to play Scrabble, I told Mike about Venezuela's new Oil Intelligence Bureau in, of all places, Vienna. He didn't know what to make of it.

I also told him about how Khalid Sheikh Mohammed, or someone professing to be he, has "confessed" to every terrorist crime of the last thirteen years, especially 9/11. Case closed.

"Lee Harvey Oswald did it," he said.

Then there was a weird spoof that just came out called *VP Cheney Thanks AIPAC for Staging 9/11.*

Payne Whitney isn't letting him go 'til the end of next week. How they can know in advance how he'll be by then is another mystery. Meanwhile, I'm watching his email.

March 18, 2007 From Jenna to Peter Dale Scott, Cynthia McKinney, Ken Levine, Barry Silverthorn:

Hi all

He's having a tough morning, worried about being helpless to file taxes. Went to a jazzercise class where they played Barry Manilow which for Mike evoked the Teddy era.

Yesterday morning he left three messages on my machine:

A, a bi-polar football player who must weigh 250 pounds, was banging on the piano. (By evening he was under control and asked me for a lesson, which I gave him.) Mike's friend, X, was distraught that someone had stolen the fruit leather I'd brought her. The weekend staff were capos even though "Nurse Ratchet" was off. We had a funky time talking to W, a physicist with Asperger's.

Visitors aren't allowed in the rooms but I was told that the showerheads are small so patients can't hang themselves from them and that the stream is intermittent so they can't drown themselves. If you bring a gift, you have to give the plastic bag to a nurse. Mike's allowed to have his cell phone but not the charger, because of the cord.

The numbers for the pay phones are XXX.

They're answered by whoever's around which is usually a patient. One phone is almost always being used by B, a blind musician who talks, probably to dial tones, about copyrights from 1927.

If you'd rather communicate by email, I'll bring him the message.

Thanks, all.

Part 58: Emerging From the Winter of His Discontent

To Mike's psychiatrist:

...we discovered that there's a fire exit to the ward which warns that if u open it, an alarm goes off. i understand why a fire exit shouldn't be locked but still, it seems to me (and no doubt also seemed to mike) that it would be v easy for a determined patient to flee out to that stairwell and throw themselves down the shaft before anyone could stop them, alarm or no alarm.

he's on zoloft and depacote and feels no better.

March 25, 2007 To Cynthia McKinney:

when i proposed that he call you he said, 'what would i say?'

he wanted to see you but imagining how a phone conversation would probably go seemed to depress him. would he say, "i'll be up and running again soon?" no. he meant it when he said he was out of the game.

but payne-whitney has definitely improved his mood. instead of sleeping all afternoon, he's playing long scrabble games and, much as he hates nyc on principle, is forming attachments which i hope will make it harder for him just to write the place off.

great luck as you resume globetrotting. we look forward to hooking up with you next time 'round.

March 25, 2007

I arrived at the hospital at five twenty-five, in time to hand over a pack of Marlboro lights, as ordered, before Mike and the other patients who'd earned the privilege were taken for a walk.

As we got out of the elevator downstairs, he pointed to the portrait of Hank and Corinne Greenberg.

"Know who he is?"

The name sounded familiar but no, I didn't know.

"Head of AIG whom I investigated. There's a great deal of irony in my being here."

"Well, isn't it a good thing he did something for your benefit with all his millions!"

(Four years later, I would pass that portrait again on the way to visit my mother in a different wing of the same hospital, as she embarked on her own descent into hell, an experience recounted in *Against the Dying of the Light* at the end of this book.)

We went around the corner since you're not allowed to smoke in front of the hospital. L, who had on a new secondhand sweater donated by the ward, made a B-line for a planter in front of the courthouse. She collected cigarette butts, Mike explained.

"How does she get away with smoking them inside?" I asked.

"Ssh, don't bust her." Yesterday he said she was a scam artist and had told other patients about the spiritual line she used to con the people at her church. When not in the hospital, she is homeless. "Probably stands on the toilet and blows into the vent."

A., the 250-pound college football player who'd been admitted to Payne-Whitney because when he was in a manic episode, he threatened a diminutive female family member, is now under control. Two security guards stand outside his room in case the medication wears off but recently, he's been docile and taking piano lessons from the blind musician.

This evening, however, they had a disagreement and the blind musician told A he wouldn't teach him anymore. The musician, who's slight in stature, chewed A out, jabbing his finger towards A's solar plexus and I wondered if he had any idea of A's true size. If so, he was one courageous slight blind pianist. A. looked sheepish.

March 29, 2007

Mike to the journalist of the proposed newspaper article, which has not yet been shelved:

Hope this finds you well. The correspondence below is with Stan Goff who wrote our Tillman series. The burglary occurred as wer were publishing Part V. Pls note that what went to congress (all overongress) was taken directly from that series... As for me, I just spent 11 days inpatient for depresssion. I'd prefer to keep that confidential. Still alive and battling. best, Mike

April 3, 2007

I forget what we were talking about but Mike used a phrase that stuck in my mind: "...He was from the 'rubber gun' brigade."

I looked blank.

"That's what we used to call it in LAPD when someone went crazy; you gave them a rubber gun."

He added something about how you could still get hurt.

"An actress I knew once said you could even get hurt with blanks," I said.

"Yes. There was an actor who killed himself ten years ago by shooting himself in the head with a blank."

"You can't really blame him; the word 'blank' implies there's nothing in it."

"You have to put something in it so you don't have a huge cloud of smoke.

'That's what they used with Sirhan Sirhan. The guy who really shot Robert Kennedy was a security guard: Thane Eugene Cesar." Further details of that assassination are revealed in his article, *Bobby, I Didn't Know!* as well as in an article by Lisa Pease in Salon. "He had a 38 [he named the gun] which left little smoke and made very little noise."

Then Michael Kane called which made Mike's day. He's been leading a normal life, he says, Mom and apple pie. Some of Mike's former associates have had disconcerting experiences which mirror Mike's and which they have interpreted as a warning to back off.

"And yet they've never messed with Stan Goff," I said.

"No one would ever mess with Stan Goff," Mike said. "Special Forces Delta Group... *No* one messes with Stan Goff."

April 17, 2007

I told Mike about Gordon Brown, the Chancellor of the Exchequer, in deep shit for dumping two billion pounds' worth of gold when it was at its lowest.

"That was through BIS," he said, "the Bank of International Settlements. It was done with the blessing of the Queen."

We watched a program about the world's top ten guns, rated on the basis not of how many people they could kill but of durability, accuracy, etc. (Last night we watched a show about American's cutest puppies.)

Somehow, (from the program on guns, not puppies) Mike was reminded of his great-great-uncle.

"He spent twelve years in jail for setting John Wilkes' Booth's leg after he shot Lincoln."

The good doctor, apparently, hadn't known who his patient was or what he'd just done.

"He's the origin of the phrase, 'Or my name is Mudd.' His name was Mudd."

April 26, 2007

Tonight we were given complimentary tickets to a fundraiser for a publication Mike's worked with but which I won't mention unless I can find the publisher's email address and ask for permission.

Someone asked Mike whether or not he'd ever killed anyone when he was a cop.

"Two great Danes," he said. (It's an odd coincidence that another of my former partners also killed two dogs simultaneously, in a driving accident.) And once he shot at someone who'd tried to run him down but the bullet was defective and bounced off the windshield.

Since I'm not allowed to ask him about the subjects that used to be his hallmark, I ask him instead about other subjects that engage his interest; among them, aerodynamics. This afternoon, which was windless, we watched a sparrow zooming through the sky, wings

230

tucked against its streamlined body so I asked Mike what propels it. Was it the sparrow equivalent of jet fuel?

"No," he said, decisively. "It's not farting its way through the air."

He explained about lift but that accounts for why a body goes up, not why it goes forward.

He says when he dies, he wants to be buried naked so his body can be absorbed directly into the earth and nourish it. I said, "Without a casket?" He thinks for a moment, then says no, with one.

May 2, 2007

We just finished watching *Borat* from the video store. Perhaps it was a pirated version, since it was even more gross than I remembered, the over-the-top nasty, guest-insulting Groucho Marx's evil twin. Mike thought Borat was ridiculing Jews but I said on the contrary, he was ridiculing anti-Semites; I resisted the impulse to say that you have to be a closet anti-Semite to see it the way he did. No one else would take the depiction seriously.

He's started volunteering at a Brooklyn stable I had taken him to in January so he could check it out.

(At the time, I'd noted the sign in front: "NO INSURANCE" but Mike was unfazed.)

Now that spring has arrived, he strides off in his $300 cowboy boots.

When he returns he says, "I loaded sixty bushels of hay, groomed three horses. Look at that." He flexes his biceps.

Part 59: Reward

Now that we're coming out of the depression phase, the heart of this account, I should relay a scene which got overlooked early on.

One night after Mike had settled in at my apartment and we were still eating dinner together, I showed him a story I'd written (it appears in *Writer Wannabe Seeks Brush with Death*,) about a quirky kid with oddball parents. It's not a children's story although it's written in a deceptively naif style.

One of the mother's eccentricities is that if she has a snack at night after she's taken out the garbage, she puts any ensuing detritus in a bag in the refrigerator so as not to attract roaches.

Mike said flatly, "If I lived with that woman, I'd kill her."

There was an awkward silence as we both faced the fact the woman was me.

"I'm sorry." The image was too close to home, he elaborated. "Have you ever seen a head in a refrigerator?"

At that stage, I attributed his gruffness to the trauma he'd lived through and held out for an improvement once his mood lifted. But it was not for nothing that Mike had said, "I think you *want* me to be dependent." With the advent of spring, the deft calibration of medication at Payne Whitney and the receipt of his inheritance, he was growing more able to function on his own and his neediness was transforming into a drive to get away. "I'm not going through another winter here," he announced. I thought, "Don't knock me over on your way out."

He deposited the money into our joint account and I made sure never to go near that account again. I stopped buying his food and he cooked for himself with gusto (usually steak or some other hearty, traditional fare) once saying, only partly in jest, "You can't have any." He said that when we moved and had a properly equipped kitchen, he'd cook for me but my kitchen wasn't up to that standard. I don't doubt it.

He still needed me for his Paypal account, as a result of which my relationship with Paypal may remain forever in limbo since I've lost track of the password and his driver's license number.

Then there was the laundry episode.

He did laundry once a week, since he didn't have many clothes; I had enough to last for several weeks. Often he'd ask me to accompany him and help fold "the" laundry, meaning his laundry, since there's little of my own which requires folding. But I didn't mind as the conversation was absorbing.

One time, however, he was putting his laundry into the wagon and carefully, with a grimace, removing anything of mine.

"Why don't you just take it all?" I asked, genuinely mystified. To this day, I can't figure out the advantage of doing only his own laundry. It wasn't cheaper as you paid for the machine anyway. It didn't take less time; in fact, it took more. And if you're disgusted by the other person's laundry, surely it's more disgusting to handle before it's laundered than after.

So he took it all.

Probably the point was just to ensure I understood my laundry was barely touchable.

One morning I woke up and was so busy with something, I didn't brush my hair first.

Mike made a face. "Don't you want to do something about your hair?" he asked. "Meryl Streep would…"

"Would what?" I challenged him.

"Would gag."

Give him credit for making me twist his arm.

"Well, it's better than being bald," I shot back. His hair was short then so its sparseness on top was more noticeable. He looked injured and I wasn't sorry.

But the flip side was no better. When we were getting ready to go out with some friends, he made a mincing face as he imitated the carefulness with which I put on make-up.

Once I told him about one of my students who was from Burkina Faso. (He found my students' stories interesting, often asking for more.)

"Burkina Faso?" Mike exclaimed. "Where's that?!"

"Africa," I answered. "I don't know what it used to be called."

Burkina Faso is one of a cluster of African countries that changed their names when they claimed independence from the colonists. I've since learned it used to be Upper Volta.

"I'm not going to lose any sleep over it," he responded, becoming absorbed in a backgammon game.

Note to self: Next time, stop with "Africa." God forbid you should offer an iota more information than what was requested.

But it was precisely that curiosity for its own sake, even if the knowledge didn't seem immediately "useful," which had propelled the research he'd so depended on when I'd done it for FTW.

This underscored a basic difference in the way our minds worked. He always had a project, an agenda, whether it was to investigate a government cover-up or find someone who could help him feel better or even just to make dinner or play backgammon. Any subject not immediately related to the goal was "in the way," an annoyance. I, on the other hand, was curious about subjects which seemed unrelated to each other; that curiosity which is usually called "idle" but often has a deeper goal of understanding what makes something tick. He didn't see the point and therefore thought this a waste of time. He would not have known what to make of those artists who practice their art regardless of how small the audience may be.

When he first came, I took him on a walk to show him the landmark buildings of Brooklyn Heights. He never glanced at any of them. At the time, I chalked this up to his shellshock but when he recovered, his attitude didn't change. This was New York, which he loathed and was therefore determined to keep at arm's length. If he took a walk, it was only to find someplace to work out and build up his upper body strength.

We did once go rowing in Central Park, an outing he later described as, "I took Jenna rowing." I reminded him I'd also rowed. I'd taken us towards shore when Mike cried, "No! We're going the wrong way!"

"I want to go to the shade," I explained.

We explored the lake under the trees and he understood that the destination hadn't been a "mistake." But this was a prototype scene: I was stupid until proven otherwise.

That attitude led to one of the greatest compliments he ever gave me.

We'd grown up in the era of the same TV shows: *I Love Lucy*, *Huckleberry Hound*... If you're of the baby-boomer generation, you can fill in the others and if you're not, the list doesn't mean anything to you anyway.

Mike preferred the more hyperactive, boy-oriented cartoons like *Adam Ant* whereas I went for the leisurely *Yogi Bear*. And I have no idea why he hated *Car 54, Where Are You?* which was about two goofy cops.

(Tangential to this discussion is one of the ironic disparities in our upbringings which had to do with our father's army careers. His father was a hero pilot in two wars; mine, a writer on the Emmy-award winning *Sergeant Bilko* series which was a comedy about the absurdities of the army.)

The compliment arose when Mike, referring to another comedy series, *Gilligan's Island*, said, "If we were all stranded on some island somewhere, you'd be the ditz who figured out the solution that saved everybody."

It's lines like that that make the insults dissolve into a dew.

Part 60: Gold

Anyone who was following Mike back in the FTW days knows that as soon as he got his inheritance, he would buy some gold.

He did — $20,000 worth, and arranged to have it shipped to the apartment.

Precious metals dealers are not fools — nowhere in their return address will you find the word "gold," "silver," or the chemical symbols thereof or anything else that might give the mailman ideas.

The gold didn't arrive.

I checked downstairs. There was a cabinet where packages too large for the mailbox were placed to await pickup by the intended tenant. The doorman wrote the appropriate apartment numbers on a whiteboard on the door of the cabinet and when a tenant retrieved his or her package, he or she erased the apartment number. Nice, clean, simple... as long as everyone was honest.

The system had always worked; no one was interested in anyone else's package. I did once lose some dry-cleaning (from a different cabinet) but I placed a MISSING ad with a hand-drawn picture of the pants (which was no help) and got them back.

Fortunately, however, it turned out there was more to the system than we tenants knew.

The doorman also kept a book of which apartments had received packages on which day so the day Mike's gold arrived, the building knew which other tenants were likely to have gone to the cabinet. I believe that when possible, the doorman also noted what time we picked up our packages.

Mike called the police to open an investigation.

A couple of mornings later, he was at the computer when the doorbell rang.

I answered it.

A scrawny man stood holding a large package, the size that might be used for a shirt.

He spoke rapidly, saying his name (which I remember) and mumbling a convoluted story about not realizing he had the wrong package. He handed me the unopened package, then turned and dashed up the stairwell immediately to the right rather than walking to the elevator.

I took the package and closed the door.

Mike leapt up. "You didn't ask him why he kept it for so many days! You didn't ask him anything!" he cried.

"I didn't want to let on that we were suspicious," I answered. "So go ask him yourself."

"No — you have to ask at the time. It's too late."

When he described the incident to a friend by email he wrote, "Jenna didn't think to ask." This, despite my having explained that quite the contrary, I'd thought but decided against it. Anyway, he was sitting less than ten feet away; why didn't he get up and ask? I'm not the one who was valedictorian for three classes at the LAPD.

But once again, he more than compensated.

I was working on an investigation of the White House Council on Environmental Quality in relation to the environmental catastrophe which followed in the wake of 9/11. My fellow activists and I, in occasional coordination with the offices of Congressman Jerrold Nadler or Senator Hillary Clinton, (we were looser cannons than some Congressional offices might have liked) had focused our attentions on the EPA which had lied, dragged their heels, tested with antiquated equipment that found 1/9 the asbestos revealed by independent contractors and engaged in a host of other obfuscatory tactics covered in *The Moron's Guide to Global Collapse* and elsewhere.

It was acknowledged that the White House Council on Environmental Quality had edited at least one of EPA's press releases, turning cautionary statements about asbestos into reassurances. And Hillary Clinton duly called to account the Chairman of the Council, James Connaughton (later collaborating with him to create the World Trade Center Expert Technical Review Panel which met for over a year, with nothing to show for it in the end) but the Council had otherwise been given a pass.

But who were they? How did their mandate differ from that of the EPA? etc.

In the course of answering these questions, I stumbled on an article (which no longer appeaers on the net) about Sidley Austin,

Connaughton's former law firm, and their actions on 9/11. It seemed that the law firm had its offices in the World Trade Center. They also had a number of partners who'd served in the Bush White House; in fact there was something of a revolving door between the two institutions. And on September 1, 2001, they had doubled their insurance.

I'd been careful in the article, *Conflict of Interest, a 9/11 Windfall and the White House Council on Environmental Quality*, (which was inexplicably later removed from the FTW homepage,) as I was in speeches, not to go overboard so as to avoid that tedious term, "hysterical mother," which had first been hurled in my direction in relation to the air quality downtown; later in relation to Peak Oil.

Mike read the article excitedly. But when he reached the revelation about the insurance he cried, "You've buried the lead!"

That was useful — to know that in toning down the excitement of the find, I'd gone too far.

He finished the article. Then, as he got up to go watch a TV show in the bedroom he said, "I would have been proud to have done that article myself."

Part 61: Thumb

A call: Mike's broken his thumb. He was assisting the guide of a tour group in Prospect Park. His horse, Mack Truck (not really, but the name was similar,) the biggest, baddest horse at the stable, had been acting up; he didn't "get along with" another horse on the ride.

As they crossed the intersection, Mack Truck "must have gotten stung by a bee" (not impossible, but unlikely at Grand Army Plaza) because he bucked. Mike landed on his thumb. The bone got pushed back into his wrist.

His body is still in shock so his mood remains upbeat. But after surgery which installs six brightly colored pins into his hand that come out the other side, he sleeps through the next three months. Each prescription for painkillers lasts thirty days. If he can't stand it and takes a little more one day, he pays at the end of the month.

This happens in August. Mike goes to the drugstore to throw himself on their mercy, showing them his cellphone picture of what lies beneath his bandages. The drugstore sees the light.

The following month, he appeals to a doctor he doesn't know but who's available on Sunday. As he is required to do, the doctor refuses to give him a prescription for extra painkillers. But after seeing the picture he says, "Do you want morphine? I can get you morphine."

The picture garners gratifying horror in every venue he tries. Medical pros are speechless; waitresses, aghast.

The cast is scheduled to come off on October 9th. Two days later, Mike wants us to fly to Los Angeles, so he can take me down memory lane; and Oregon, where I've never been but where we're planning to move. However the main reason for my presence, although I don't realize it at the time, is so that I can be a witness to his meeting with the Ashland Police Department about the break-in.

I'm not sure the removal of the cast is going to signal the end of his pain, nor that this is the right time for our reconnaissance trip. But when Mike looks forward to something, he cannot be gainsaid, particularly when one's only argument is uncertainty.

"I need to get back as soon as possible," I tell him. I will not get paid for any work missed while I'm away.

To do everything on our agenda, he's mapped out a schedule that will take three weeks.

"This is something you could never do," he says.

"What?"

"Organize this, think of everything."

"Why do you say that?"

"The way you planned to remodel your kitchen, not taking into account that the floor tiles need to come up when you install new cabinets."

"I know nothing about remodeling or construction; that's why I consult professionals. But that's not the same thing as being disorganized. I organized that whole Petrocollapse conference on seven weeks' notice and we got through it with everyone getting a stipend and on speaking terms." I didn't add the protests I instigated and co-organized over the air quality following 9/11.

"Good for you." Having had his say, he is already focused on the next project, a backgammon game.

No matter what happens, we always revert to his image of me as an empty-headed woman, a stereotype he picked up from TV five decades ago; certainly not from his mother, the NSA cryptanalyst, although I embody the worst aspects of her as well.

After the cast is removed, I pick him up at the hospital. He hands me a slip of paper. I don't have my glasses on so don't see what it is.

"Guard this with your life." I put it in my wallet.

We walk home. At the door, he hands me another slip of paper.

"Go fill this at Duane Reade."

He's in pain or I would tell him to do it himself.

Instead, I oblige.

When the prescription is ready, I pick it up and give it to him.

"This isn't Keflex!" he shouts. "They gave me a painkiller!"

I go back to Duane Reade but the pharmacist is gone for the day.

I don't remember the details now but I was at fault on this one. And he was certainly in great pain as well as worried because the future flexibility of his hand was at stake (which he didn't explain until later.) But that didn't stop me from feeling fed up. I'd fallen down on the job but it wasn't a job I'd applied for. What about Mike himself, opting for the meanest horse in the stable? Did it cross his mind to question that choice?

I will kill him. I will strangle him. I will bend back his thumb.

If Mike's employees were indeed patsy/hatchet men of the government, I understood how they could have smashed his computers. I would have fantasized something along the same lines and I'm not a twenty-something male with a tattoo.

Part 62: Lessons from Los Angeles

October 11, 2007
On the plane to LA

"See out there on the back of the wing?" Mike said. "Those are the flaps and the helions. When the plane takes off, they're down. You have more air passing over the plane than under it to increase lift on takeoff."

I had a flashback-by-proxy to a talk that must have once taken place between Mike and his father. Only now Mike himself was Dad and I was little Mike.

"See that jet of water?" A stream arced from the front of the wing. "That's the [I missed the term.] I'm talking a lot because my thumb is hurting again. I don't want to take another pill yet."

He closed his eyes and concentrated on breathing, like a student in a Lamaze class.

A couple of hours later

"Those look like the Rockies. My father had a memorable way of explaining things. Once I asked him, 'Daddy, what's the Continental Divide?' He took out his penis and started peeing. 'If I pee on one side of the Continental Divide, it goes into the Pacific. On the other side, it goes into the Atlantic.'"

We did whatever people do to pass the time in the air until we reached California.

"We're probably approaching from the south," Mike said, looking out the window.

"I thought planes that went from New York to L.A. went in a straight line."

"There are thousands of flights at any given moment. Remember in my book, on 9/11 they had to ground thirteen thousand flights? Pilots have check points. They have to report when they get to each one."

"Oh. I thought it was like a highway; they just left a certain space between. Anyway, if there are thousands of flights and we're looking out for dozens of miles, how come we can't see any planes?"

"No; they track them. They go like this." He made little crooked motions with his hand.

"This is what cops and body guards learn and people who have to drive defensively: Make sure you can see the wheels of the car in front of you when you stop. That way you can get out without having to back up."

A great teacher, so long as the subject was not related to his investigative reporting. For that, you had to glean whatever you could from FTW itself. Rice Farmer and I understood that which was one reason why we'd lasted as the main behind-the-scenes researchers.

But even without that most coveted information, there were still Things You Could Only Learn from Mike Ruppert, such as, How to Mess Up a Polygraph: "Every time you answer a question yes or no, clench your asshole." Perhaps the ploy also works for Computer Voice Stress Analyzer tests because his own in the sexual harassment lawsuit came back "inconclusive."

Los Angeles

We drove to the home of Mike's best friend from LAPD and his wife. After all the travel, as soon as I tumbled out of the car, I threw up on the lawn. Fortunately, I hadn't eaten anything so the result was invisible. If Mike's friend noticed the indelicacy as he came out of the house, he was too polite to mention it even when I greeted him from a nearly prone position on the grass.

"He's a cop," said Michael Kane when I described the scene to him later. "He's seen people toss their cookies."

Day Two

We were about to have the grand tour of LA but not the usual rubber-necking of movie star estates; this was Mike's memory lane.

There was not enough time for brunch so we headed for Sunset Boulevard, doing a detour to Rodeo Drive, the 57th Street/Champs

Elysees of Los Angeles, featuring the same names: Tiffany's, Armani, Hermes. The main difference was there were no pedestrians; no delivery guys, secretaries or commuters heading somewhere else. The few people we saw looked as though they belonged there; that was where they'd gotten their $1000 sandals.

In a Bentley directly ahead of us, the profile of an expressionless woman with a platinum blonde ponytail looked to the right. She could have been played by, or playing, Grace Kelly.

"Probably married to an executive," said Mike.

The light changed and she drove out of frame. Cut.

That's another thing: No one there, at least none of the women, was over fifty. By that time, they're probably divorced or staying home like Arab wives, not daring to show their faces — at least, not unless they've "had some work done."

At Malibu Beach, two thousand crosses stood in the sand, symbolizing the American casualties in Iraq. An explanatory sign added the number of Iraqi dead: 655,000 to date. If they had placed a cross for each Iraqi as well, the exhibit would have taken up the entire beach.

From there to the Gump Shrimp Company, named for Forrest Gump who "founded it with his Vietnam buddy...

'This is the boathouse where I sang after I left LAPD."

At Venice Beach he said, "Ah! Now you see why we didn't have brunch? I've been holding out for a cheeseburger at Hinano's.

'This is where I got your T-Shirt." He had gotten me three on a previous trip: One said, "Ashland;" another, with an embroidered shark, "Bite me;" but the one to which he was referring read: "What part of [fearsome passage of piano music] don't you understand?"

We visited a freak show in front of which a hawker stood on the boardwalk holding a live two-headed turtle that craned out of its shell in both directions like some sort of Hindu god. Inside were jars containing the preserved remains of a six-legged pig, a similarly afflicted squirrel, a two-headed fox and pictures of the miserably exploited sideshow exhibits of P.T. Barnum.

Back outside, I bought bird- and tongue whistles for our hosts as well as my nieces and took a picture of Mike with a man in a suit who had painted his skin silver.

244

The passing overhead of a putter of helicopters (if there's a term for a group of helicopters, Wiki-answers doesn't have it) prompted the next chapter in my aerospace education:

"Lumination is measured in candle strength. The search lights on those helicopters are a million candles. If they were on the ground pointing at you and you were fifteen feet away, they'd set your pants on fire."

Thence, to the original FTW headquarters.

"This is where it all began. I wrote FTW here for the first six years. I moved my mother across the street so I could take care of her three times a month. Then when she died, I moved into her apartment."

His mother's apartment was in the old Oliver Hardy estate, he said, which now housed retired actors. I envisioned forgotten movie stars — the victims of scurrilous accountants — mingling with down and out actors who'd never made it above U-5 (under five lines, which allowed them to be paid at a lower rate.)

"After taking care of my mother and then my father, I got tired of all the old people."

As he drove on, he expounded on the sights: "All this used to be wetlands but Steven Spielberg built it up...

'We're in the heart of the airline industry." He nodded towards the headquarters of Lockheed Martin, Howard Hughes' former estate, after which we drove on Military Intelligence Memorial Highway.

"I didn't know it had died," I said.

He said that Sepulveda is the longest street in the US — thirty miles long — and mentioned a town which was at the exact midpoint between San Francisco and Seattle. He pointed out where the Pacific Rim meets the Continental US fault line — ("That's why there are hot springs.")

My notes continue with unrelated conversation fragments as I remembered them later:

"I can kiss my own ass." He had gotten a skin graft from his butt to his arm because of second and third degree burns. "They peel it off like a cheese."

He said Lincoln may have been assassinated because he had pissed off the Seward banking family.

Ahead, Mt. Shasta was sticking up through the clouds. We'd just emerged from the San Joaquin Valley which was completely flat. It used to be a lake bed, Mike said, continuing that California and Florida together supply half the country's citrus fruit. The implications of water shortages here were intensifying exponentially by the minute. I resolved to reread Joan Didion's *Holy Water* and watch *Chinatown* again.

He said he wanted to call his sustainable house Out of the Way as in: When the shit hits the fan, you get out of the way.

What a different person he was when in his element: expansive, generous with information, not interested in putting down the other guy even when that other guy was at her most abjectly ignorant.

And surely, somewhere he was conscious of telling me all this because he knew that one day I'd be writing about it.

The last item on the LA agenda was to meet up with old friends.

The first friend was working on a project about a nightclub at the end of the world. This fused together two of Mike's abiding passions in life: Music and the end of petroleum-dependent civilization. When he lost contact with that friend, he adopted the notion of such a nightclub, referring to it often on Facebook and in his radio show, The Lifeboat Hour.

We met the guy at his studio where he'd turned out scores for scenes from recent blockbuster movies, sometimes on forty-five minutes notice. Most of the evening was spent discussing the proposed project but during the course of the conversation, the guy observed that Mike and I were like Hepburn and Tracy in a film where she plays a nun who turns out to be the one with real balls. Mike didn't seem to notice the comment but I appreciated it.

The other friend was one I'd had email and phone contact with. On the way to the guy's house I asked, "What's his wife like?"

"Typical Jewish wife," Mike answered. "Everything's money." And he rubbed his thumb and forefinger together in a gesture I remembered from a British woman in Saudi Arabia who had also used it to describe Jews.

The wife turned out to be an overworked teacher whose main preoccupation in life was her children. The family faced not only the expenses of approaching college fees but also of the husband's health problems as well as the dog's — a far cry from the concerns of a "Jewish American Princess" that Mike had implied.

Part 63: Oregon

I came across the complete account of the time Mike was bitten on the testicle.

He and at least one other cop had been summoned by a sergeant, 6'5". When they arrived, they found him cornered by a small, wiry man holding a 35" TV above his head. The guy had a glazed look in his eye and a thin sheen of perspiration all over, telltale signs of PCBs. The cops wrestled him onto a gurney with Mike at the head. They managed to get plastic handcuffs on him and canvas restraints on his legs. The guy broke the restraints but not without consequence; his shin bone now hung out. In a rage, he bit Mike on the testicle upon which Mike lashed out, breaking the guy's skull.

Oregon

After arriving at the hotel in Ashland, we watched CNN until it was time to go out in search of dinner. California was burning and for reasons I no longer remember, the report showed an actual burn center.

"That might be the one where I went," Mike commented.

"When they grafted your ass onto your arm?"

"Yeah."

As I'd anticipated, the residual pain from the fall on his thumb was more intense than he'd hoped and that evening he stayed in bed while I settled in at the local internet café.

October 30, 2007

Ashland Police Department Detective Randy Snow says that Mike's former female employee, now the plaintiff in the sexual harassment lawsuit against him, finally took her CVSA (Computer Voice Stress Analyzer test, reputed to be more accurate than a polygraph) after having her baby and against the advice of everyone including her lawyer. She has passed with flying colors. This means the other employee whom Mike suspects of having executed the burglary would have acted alone. That doesn't comport with his original scenario in which the perps were a meth ring.[13]

We went to Mike's interview with the detectives where, to his surprise and gratification, they allowed me to sit in on the entire proceedings. (This was what he'd brought me to Oregon to witness.) Mike came away with a positive sense from the meeting; the detectives "apologized" to him.

My take differed from his more than I let on; I noted caution in their manner. The apology was grudging, couched in meaningless terms which would cause the whole concoction to evaporate under scrutiny. But this may have been for CYA reasons: The case was becoming "cold" with a rapidity they must have found embarrassing.

We wondered if we'd run into the former female employee in Ashland; she lived nearby.

"I'm going to make sure they take away her baby," Mike announced, citing reasons I won't go into. As a mother, I was chilled. But I understood his logic: He blamed her for taking away *his* "baby," which was FTW.

Next stop on the itinerary was Eugene. Mike did the driving. I have a license but zero experience so my job was to massage his thumb to keep it nimble. Any restriction on his future mobility such as arthritis would affect his ability to shoot.

I'd built up a a sizable amount of anger at him over the months that he'd stayed at my apartment. As in the laws of physics, so in the laws of psychology: There is no action without a reaction. I'd swallowed some mega-insults; at first, because he'd been depressed to the point of suicidality. When he got stronger, I answered back, but rarely with the full force of the resentment I harbored. Only once did that righteous rage explode. I think it was when he grew angry at my reluctance to shoulder full responsibility for FTW by putting the fees on my credit card. For anyone who missed that post, the fees themselves weren't the issue; I'd be reimbursed. The issue was liability in the event of a copyright or any other kind of

---

[13] http://mikeruppert.blogspot.com/2006/06/urgent-message-from-mike-ruppert.html

lawsuit. Those damages can be in the hundreds of thousands, even if no money was made by the defendant or lost by the plaintiff.

Mike had responded to my outburst by thrusting out his stomach and using it to push me back as though to taunt, "I can knock you down;" atavistic cop behavior of the kind that provokes protesters to scream, "Pig!" and get themselves arrested.

He and I were alike in more ways than he knew. That, and not, as he maintained, my "unconditional love," was the source of whatever insight I'd provided when he was depressed. Did he have any idea how close he came to feeling me take advantage of his vulnerability at those moments when his thumb was in my hands? (Have a ball, Freudians.) If so, he put on a good show of obliviousness, letting out orgasmic shouts of relief from the massage. But I wasn't interested in giving him orgasms. Sometimes it felt as though only the knowledge of his breaking the drug addict's skull kept me in check.

Eugene

Lying on a fault line, we learned, Eugene has a 100% probability of seeing an earthquake at some point in the next century. So the building codes require heavy-duty reinforcement including, in one office block we passed, concrete Xs across the windows. The supermarket was even crowned with reinforced concrete parapets.

Mike knew that Eugene, like much of Oregon, was alert to the advent of societal collapse, in view of which those parapets didn't portend anything benign for the populace.

The elevator door at our hotel was doubled by a steel door, ostensibly as additional fire protection but it gave the place the feel of a detention center.

"Are you thinking what I'm thinking?" asked Mike.

I was. The architecture of Eugene would provide excellent sets for a movie that one of Mike's friends in LA was planning about the end of human industrial civilization with its attendant martial law and internment camps.

The idea turned him on. "Fuck Ashland; it's Eugene," he enthused. "It's more sustainable, a better transition for you. And something tells me I can be more dangerous from here." He was referring to his prospective lawsuit.

"You'll be more shadowy to the people in Ashland."

He also had a following in Eugene. An activist friend threw a potluck dinner in his honor where the guests were deferential and appreciative, one of them bringing an organic lemon cake that read, "Welcome Home, Mike."

Portland

We were staying in a hotel where everyone else was under thirty so there were cute gimmicks like a blackboard on each door with chalk for any artistically-minded guests. I drew a picture of Mike watching CNN.

"I didn't know you could do that," he said and took a photograph of it. (Mostly, I can't "do that," as witnessed by my illustrations in *Writer Wannabe Seeks Brush with Death*.) If anyone comes across that sketch on one of Mike's USB sticks, please let me know.

One night, we went to a packed bar, the hub of the Portland blues scene, and heard his friend, the petite powerhouse, Lisa Mann, belt, "You ain't nothin' but a hound dog." Mike was behind her on stage, dancing himself into a sweat. When, in a middle verse, she called out his name, he howled like a wounded hound. Afterwards, he showed everyone pictures of the pins in his thumb. Those who didn't spring back in disgust stared, puzzled.

"It's not a magic trick," I said. "They really went all the way through."

I was at the local coffee shop which offered free internet service with any purchase; twenty minute sessions requested, but if business was slack, you could stay all day.

I'd spent several hours there already, while Mike napped.

("How much do you love me?" he had asked with puppy-dog eyes.
"A whole lot."
"Enough to finish the laundry by yourself?"
"Fuck, no.")

I'd just ordered a bran muffin, my second interaction with this particular counterperson, a round-faced cherub (they were all college students) in a wool cap.

She handed me the muffin with an addendum: "If you need a place to stay, you can stay at my house."

I was taken aback. We'd had no prior conversation beyond the ingredients of various items on the menu. Was this androgynous-looking young woman lonely? Or were the people who hogged the computer there normally homeless?

Part 64: Spellbound

After we got back from Oregon, I was doing the shopping on Montague Street when I saw that our video store was going out of business. That was too bad but the silver lining was the resulting sale. I snapped up some bargains including *Spellbound*, a movie about — among other things —psychoanalysis and repressed memories. Gregory Peck is the troubled new director of a psychiatric institution in which Ingrid Bergman practices.

"You can take that back," Mike said, "I've seen it."

"I haven't."

A week later he said again, "You can take that back; I've seen it a hundred times."

On Christmas day, we had nothing to do until five when we were due at my mother's; Mike was on the computer so I watched the movie.

A while later, Mike came in, as he usually did, to watch TV while eating breakfast. Having seen how unsettled he'd become by the prospect of *Spellbound*, I offered to turn it off.

"No! Keep it on!" he said, staring intently at the screen.

The scene playing was a dream sequence with surreal sets designed, appropriately, by Salvador Dali. The dream figure (I don't remember if it was Peck himself, whose dream it had been) entered a casino where cards were being dealt for a game of blackjack. Two of the cards were blank.

Finished with his cereal, Mike cleaned the table.

"Do me a favor," he said on his way out, "Tell me how it ends."

I continued watching the movie as he went back to his backgammon game, cursing every so often. This was unusual but I didn't feel obliged to respond.

When the movie was over, I got up to make coffee.

"I'm having a panic attack,' he said. "The first in nine months. I'm not suicidal. What was the end? Who did it?" (There had been a murder.)

"The head of the hospital. Gregory Peck's amnesia was because he'd accidentally killed his brother when they were children."

"That was his mother," Mike said. "OK" (He had misheard; Peck's mother had nothing to do with it.) "What was the significance of the blank cards in the blackjack game, please? My parents were addicted blackjack players."

"The blank cards meant he felt guilty. And the number 21 referred to the 21 Club in New York."

Mike was relieved: No association with his parents; no one, including me, was messing with his mind.

"That movie stirred things up for me. I'm having a powerful reaction. I'm that character [the guilt-tormented Gregory Peck.] And you're my Ingred Bergman [who used her understanding of psychoanalysis to unravel the meaning of the dream.] I'm making notes on it for my novel. This is all going to Venice. And I'm going to find a good psychiatrist when I'm there."

"I'm having the biggest sense of activity that I've had in ten years," Mike said a few days later. Benazir Bhutto had been assassinated two days before, on December 27, ratcheting up the tension around the world. "Don't ask me what. I don't know. On February 3, I'm going to be fifty-seven and I plan to spend that birthday in Culver City and that will be the best birthday party I've ever had. I'll have a bike; maybe by then I'll even have a dog. A dog is necessary to my sanity."

"The superego, the ego, the id and the dog."

"Yes.

'I feel my powers coming back, like when I was a young policeman, able to shoot. I knew every street.

'Steve [Alten's] book is coming out; the 9/11 movement is furious but this will help Steve; those assholes have been ridiculed. [Mike later changed his position on Alten.] The only one that hasn't been is me.

'I'm going to write my novel and this time I will spare nobody, not [he named a prominent figure in the "9/11 Truth" movement;] nobody. I'll use X's emails; why the fuck not?

'I thought of a title: *The Ombudsman*. Do you know what an ombudsman is?"

"Of course. The EPA ombudsman was one of our greatest allies. But when Nabokov wanted to call his autobiography, *Speak Mnemosyne*, his publisher said, 'Never give a book a title people can't pronounce.' You don't want them getting embarrassed.

'I testified at a hearing for the Ombudsman; no two Congressmen pronounced it the same way."

"Things are happening very fast. I leave Thursday [for a brief trip to hire a private investigator in connection with his lawsuit and to prepare for his permanent move back] and I don't know how I'm going to stay in my skin until then. I expect to come back [here] having signed a lease on a house."

"I thought this trip was more about the P.I."

"And that's another wild card. [X] must be about seventy right now. He was damage control when I was at LAPD but he did it with love. He owes me one and he knows it.

'This is my way of letting the powers that be know what I'm doing. I'm not coming after them; just after those people. And with Rupert Murdoch's deep pockets, X could be interested.

'God may just have set this up. I'm coming back and if I do, it'll be like Lazarus.

'I'm going to behave very differently this time. I'm going to be very careful in the friends I choose. I'm going to have a moat around the house, with alligators.

'Lots of people are thrilled I'm coming back: [He named his LAPD friend and the guy who was involved in making a movie about the collapse of industrial civilization.]

'And don't ask me how, but I see me and Sean Penn colliding, not in a bad way. Maybe my job will be to protect him from the people who're trying to sabotage him."

Penn was in the process of divorcing his wife. Mike thought that in his midlife crisis, he would return to Santa Monica.

"And I'm going to miss you so much. In some ways, the dog will replace you."

"In some ways, you'll prefer the dog. But maybe you already know that and are too polite to say so."

"You're a package deal."

A tacit acknowledgment that I'd hit the nail on the head.

Part 65: Furnace

January 5, 2008

"Holy shit!"

"What?"

"It's gone! My email about B-. I looked in sent mail. Do you have it?"

"Yes." I found my cc'ed copy of the email and forwarded it to Mike.

"This is them. They're letting me know I have to back off."

He sat back, pondering. "I'm taking this very seriously."

"Why would they care more about that than about your helping Steve [Alten] or [the guy working on a movie about the end of industrial civilization]?"

"They're afraid of my brain."

The next day, I found the missing email in Trash.

"I didn't do that," he said.

"Well, it would make no sense for them to do that. I think what may have happened is: Larry Chin responded; after you read that, you put it in trash along with the whole sequence."

"That's possible."

But there was no doubt "They" *were* messing with him, as became clear on his reconnaissance trip to LA. It wasn't so much the missing luggage, leaving him to the elements during record-breaking storms, he said, as his seat companions on the flight:

"Aren't you the guy who smashed his own computers?" asked one. Another claimed Peak Oil is no problem because of the abiotic oil off the coast of Louisiana; a third had been to all the countries Mike had been to.

The first guy seemed to me the most convincing candidate for possible agent. As for the others, well... As soon as you raise the issue of Peak Oil, people have all sorts of facile comebacks of which infinitely-renewable-abiotic-oil-that-supplies-you-with-more-on-an-almost-as-needed-basis is a favorite. But Mike had long since lost his patience with this pipedream. And as usual when something happened that got under his skin, he interpreted the act as willfully directed towards him, just as when he heard someone use the phrase, "a voice from the wilderness" or, "crossing the Rubicon," he assumed they had read his website or his book. He forgot that he himself had plucked those phrases from ancient texts.

Both for better and for worse, this self-oriented interpretation of events was all part of that furnace of energy that burned so fiercely within him, propelling him into the heart of government wrongdoing to reveal the truth or, when that avenue was blocked, self-destruction. What he lost sight of in the process was other people; their histories and motives, whether innocent or otherwise. He saw them only in so far as they related to him; his efficient focus ("I am, after all, German,") dismissing anything else as chaff.

For instance, the third guy on the plane might have been to other countries as well. Anyway, it's not as though the countries Mike had been to were unusual.

On the other hand, we must never lose sight of the adage for which Mike was the poster-boy: Just because you're paranoid doesn't mean they're not following you.

 Nowhere was his Mike-centered stance more apparent than in his relationship with women, as witnessed by the following conversation about his life:

"Any regrets?"

"My girlfriend in high school. I dumped her when I went to college, moving on to bigger, better things. That was a mistake. She really loved me."

He used to describe me that way too: "She loves me unconditionally." Never mind that it's hard enough to do for one's own child and I sure as hell didn't do it with Mike; his descriptions of former relationships, if positive, were always about how much the woman loved him; never about how much he loved her.

Another time, we were watching a movie in which a flapper lolled atop a piano, crooning a torch song. She was dressed in a short, sequin dress and smiled beckoningly.

"That's what I call a real woman," Mike enthused.

No response from me.

"Not because she's blond," he hastened to add.

But of course, that wasn't the reason for my silence. The flapper was beautiful and sexy. Her manner said, at least to a man given to fantasy, "I'll do anything you want." But the one thing she assuredly was not was real.

One day when he was crying, I thought: It's two years since he left LA for Ashland. In that period he's moved four times, each time with a "Fuck you" attitude. Had that stance been cultivated so he wouldn't get attached? Is that why he never asked me anything, or got to know me apart from how I related to him? If so, I doubt he was aware of what he was doing, so instinctive had the behavior become. He had "more important" things to think about.

I did make him see the world from a different vantage point for a moment on January 11, 2008, shortly before he left. (I happened to record the date and thus offer it.)

"Do you think it's a man's world?" I asked a propos of a provocation, though I no longer remember what.

"No... But men have certainly fucked it up."

"They wouldn't have been able to do that if it hadn't been a man's world."

"True."

Another time, he betrayed a more expansive view without any prodding.

That vignette had an inauspicious beginning: I passed the bedroom where he was watching a show that seemed to be about modern gladiators. Two men in helmets were beating each other with what looked like clubs.

In the foreground, an earnest man explained, "There's been an assault on masculinity."

The scene might have been a reject, ("*Boys Gone Wild*," perhaps) from *Saturday Night Live*.

The next night, however, Mike unwittingly redeemed himself by watching *Nine to Five*, a movie about secretaries unionizing.

Although he could be gentle and kind as a lover, sex was the pre-eminent arena in which his tendency towards extremes worked itself into a frenzy. Undoubtedly, it was one of the reasons he was so antsy to leave.

I was practicing octaves on a keyboard whose keys, while silent with respect to pitch, clacked when pressed.

"I don't know why but that sounds very sexual to me," Mike said.

"Life is a Rorschach," I replied, quoting my friend the clinical psychologist.

Not long afterwards, I ran into him on the street. He didn't notice me because he was talking to a young woman who was staying with one of our neighbors.

I waved.

"We just got back from the bagel shop," Mike explained, gesturing to the bags they were each carrying. He adopted an attitude of nonchalance — which would have turned into defiance if challenged — as though to say, "You know that on a personal level, you're history anyway; when I leave in a couple of weeks, it'll just be official." I did know that so the meeting didn't faze me.

The young woman, however, did not know it and gave a wan smile.

January 12, 2008

Two weeks 'til he leaves, the morning of the 29th. Right now, he's watching the military channel. He says it gives him a sense of what the Powers That Be are working on. Having heard that, I sometimes watch with him but at the moment, the show is about different sorts of guns, a subject which means a great deal to Mike but nothing to me so I have immersed myself in research at the computer.

Mike comes in, settling into the wicker chair that I bought when a friend complained I didn't have an arm chair.

"We're going to have lots of long talks before I leave..."

Reminiscence? Reflections on life? The comment was a reference to the conversations we used to have when he first arrived and was in such a distraught state. He once complained to his shrink that they'd mysteriously stopped. I said it was by his choice; he no longer needed them.

"...Where I get down on my knees and thank you for saving my life," he continued.

"That'll take two minutes."

He laughed and got up to make himself a drink before returning to the bedroom.

That was the last of the "long talks."

Part 66: Leaving

Saturday, January 26, 2008

If we're going to go out or have another real conversation before he leaves, it's got to be today. Sunday night is *Sixty Minutes* and Monday night I work.

I had to work this morning too but I've left the afternoon clear, turning down an opportunity to teach another class, in case Mike wants to have a "last supper" together or see a movie.

I don't raise the subject, however. My purpose is not to go out per se; it's cold and I'm tired. I want to get a sense of where his mind is.

He doesn't mention anything but goes about his business, puttering between the TV in the bedroom and the kitchen, passing me at the computer without a word.

At seven, he puts on his coat.

"I need to get out. I'm going to see what's playing on Court Street."

And so he goes.

This confirms what I already know: To him, I am little more than a mirror that gives him back the image of a man who is accepted; a sounding board that responds with reasonable counsel. Mirrors and sounding boards do what they do because it is their nature, their function in life. They are not so needy nor so deserving of attention as he is. They have not suffered as he has. Or if they have, he doesn't want to know about it for they are certainly not so interesting.

Twenty minutes later he's back.

"There was nothing I wanted to see."

We watch *On the Beach*, the new one, which he says is crappy.

I agree. I'm most put off by the omnipresent *Waltzing Matilda* theme that metamorphoses cornily according to the mood of the scene.

But it's hard to maintain one's cynicism when the fate of the people in the movie so uncomfortably reflects where the real world is heading today, which is the reason he'd wanted us to watch it together.

Towards the end, the young wife weeps at the imminent death of her family, including her young child, by radiation or preemptive pill.

"Get over it, Bitch," says Mike. Then, figuring I might not feel the same, he says, "Sorry."

Tuesday morning

The time has come.

"Whatever's left in the closet, you can have. I can't fit anything else into this suitcase."

He puts down his bags — the carry-on and the behemoth — to hug me. "Good-bye, Moofie."

I cry, thank God.

"You saved my life." He cries also, redeeming himself for Saturday night. For a few seconds we hold each other.

"I've got to go. This is hard enough."

At some level too deep to do anyone any good, it almost seems true.

Part 67: Political Opportunity or Dog Park?

February 3, 2008

He calls. I wish him happy birthday which is no doubt the reason for the call. On my own initiative, I wouldn't have observed the occasion, even with an email. I've done my bit for him when he needed it. Any more would be sycophantic.

"I'm single-handedly upholding the American economy," he chuckles, referring to his buying spree for his new apartment, which included an HD TV for which his LAPD friend served as consultant.

The statement for our joint account confirms this. But he's exhilarated to be home and is providing background information for a movie about the FBI's harassment of two folk singers. If the movie is made, he'll get to play the "asshole FBI guy."

The only thing left is a "dawg." He's been to three pounds but hasn't found the right one.

A few weeks later

He has found his true love, a mutt who is going to require multiple treatments to rid himself of mange. But he's idolatrous and goofy which are the two sine qua nons. His name is Rags. To me, he looks like the canine incarnation of Mike.

March 14, 2008

My dawg snores.—MCR

March 16, 2008

don't sleep with him – JO

March 16, 2008 From Mike:

He sleeps in his new doggie bed on the floor, right next to my bed. Hewouldn't have it any other way.It must be love because I wouldn't either.Woof! I am a really good Daddy.Mioss you.Smooch.

One of Mike's politically-connected friends is in New York and we get together for drinks with some of that person's circle.

"Has Mike called you?" Mike's friend asks.

I hesitate before answering.

"He's calling every day?" the friend misconstrues my silence.

He's called twice: The first time, as relayed above, on his birthday; the second, to straighten out the Paypal account which was set up in my name because it was linked to the bank account.

"Are you going to go out to see him?"

"He doesn't want me in LA."

"Why not?"

"He says I'd slow him down there."

"I'm in shock. You saved his life."

"He's unique at what he does."

The friend later emails that I've achieved "serenity" but that is a rosy interpretation. I got the lay of the land a long time ago. It wasn't even Mike who taught me cynicism though in our relationship, it certainly came in handy.

April 15, 2008

Mike calls. He had dinner with the politically connected friend last night and gives me an update "on the QT." The *60 Minutes* Al Gore piece was a possible set-up to get him drafted at the Democratic Convention, Mike learned. Some sort of disaster is anticipated before the election — but what sort?

"Both Buffett and Soros have used the D word: Depression. It could be something with entitlements."

I go on Google alerts for Al Gore.

April 27, 2008

Two dreams:

1: Mike is invited to hell to interview Satan. (It's unclear who invited him.) I ask if I can come along, then have second thoughts (cold feet?) If I change my mind while in Hell, will I be allowed to come upstairs again? The answer is unclear. I decline the opportunity. Mike goes off.

2: Alex and I and about four other people are on a makeshift wooden boat in the ocean. A wave comes that is six storeys high. I take solace in the fact that we are in the curl of a less daunting part of the wave and try to calculate how long we'll have to hold our breath. The dream ends before we're overcome.

June 7, 2008 5 AM

The phone rings. I wake up but don't answer.

"Good. I hope you're out having a good time. Moofie, it's me. [He mentions a political opportunity — an extremely long shot — that has been offered to him.] I need to talk to you."

This isn't an I'm-about-to-strangle-myself 5 AM call; it's just an I'm-hyper-and-no-one-else-will-take-this-shit-but-you call.

Such are my thoughts until eight when I leave for work, still marveling at his sense of entitlement and toying with the idea of going righteous on him. But that would be too obvious; more to the point, it would cut off the information which only he can provide. As usual, the writer in me prevails; I call him back at six that night.

"Hi, Moofie. I was at the fortieth anniversary of Bobby Kennedy's assassination, so it was a public event. [He repeats the information about the political opportunity which was offered to him and about which he feels conflicted.]

'I have a good life, here; a dog I'm committed to. You'd love Rags.

'I don't want to get back on airplanes again. But we could get Peak Oil into the national conversation."

266

"That's not the problem. It's the danger. Correct me if I'm wrong but the Powers That Be be so powerful that you'll only be allowed so much success. If you really look as though you're having an effect, they'll make sure to put a stop to it."

"Those are the thoughts I've been having, too. Anyway, [the friend] is going to have to come here and sell me.

'How are you?"

"Tired."

"Sorry if I woke you..."

Sorry enough not to do it again? I think but don't say. (He never did do it again.)

"...but I had to talk to somebody.

'How's Alex?"

"His usual HUA self." I know better than to give more than one sentence. Unless there's an entertaining story, Mike, like many people, has little patience for listening to details about the lives of others. And for the record, at the moment that I was maligning him, Alex was in the process of doing first rate work at college and has since graduated from an excellent law school. "HUA" referred only to his stand on Peak Oil, but he's become more open-minded about that as well.

"Bobby's lawyer was at the anniversary, Paul Schrader. I talked to him for about twenty minutes. I told him, 'I didn't realize then that the people who were after me were the same ones who were after Bobby.' He was very moved by that.

'I haven't heard from Danni Tillman [Pat Tillman's mother] but she could still be on the book tour.

'She said she thought that by thanking Stan, [Stan Goff, who had written the Pat Tillman series] she was acknowledging FTW." (Mike had been upset not to have been thanked for that series in some public forum which I've now forgotten.)

"That's what I thought."

"I was right to let her know what that series did to me... I never realized how much of what I did was survivor guilt over Pat."

Another war hero, like Mike's dad. Then there's the guilt of having survived his own birth, possibly, he felt, against his mother's wishes.

"Well, Rags is here, lying on his back with his tongue hanging out to the side. You should see him at the doggie park. Oh, he heard me say, 'doggie park.' Now I'm going to have to take him. OK, I guess we'll go."

Part 68: A Presidential Energy Policy

Mike declined the political offer for sensible reasons boiling down to the likelihood that it would not be worth the risk. He ended his email to the friend who'd made the offer with, "I have a wonderful dog that I'm not willing to abandon to friends or a kennel. I am doing work that I like and I think my novel may well turn out to be the most important contribution of what feels like a very long life."

June 14, 2008
I am sending this to the two most powerful and wonderful women I have known in my life. I just wrote this as a note to go in the novel, which will be called "Ancestors". One of my (how fucking arrogant) characters will say it. I promise. Please save this if you think it worthy. Otherwise, I don't give a shit because I am writing to two true and great blessings who will love me no matter what. What a lucky, blessed man I have become through all of this bullshit. OK, NUFF OF THAT GIRLIE CRAP... Here's what I wrote that I think might actually be good: "I cannot go too near the music again. If I do, then all I have labored to understand -- for forty years -- becomes irrelevant. I know that from the first time I had to play a song five times in a row, I left my body, I understood the universe. I knew it from the first time I found myself dancing beyond the limits of human endurance, covered in sweat; devoid of breath; on fire with an energy that drove me through my body and into infinity. I found the same thing, though sadly neutered, in the military cadences we chanted and ran to endlessly at the LAPD Academy. And I knew that it was impossible to put that Power into words; a Power that could be used for good or evil."But I had to try."It was the ultimate translation."Jenna knows, and [the other activist] remembers "Thunder Road".I have sent out a lot lately. That's because big things are in motion-- agressively. I hold onto only a remote branch of these events, but I think what I have sent is worth the reading. I deeply wish that some day, somehow, Jackson Browne, Don Henley and the great Ben Tench could see this.Yeah, I'm toasted, and... as Hemingway might say: "It was good... I don't know why I know these things but I do."------- MCR

"And I knew that it was impossible to put that Power into words; a Power that could be used for good or evil."

Corroboration of what I wrote in Part 65 — Furnace: "Both for better and for worse, this self-oriented interpretation of events was all part of that furnace of energy that burned so fiercely within him, propelling him into the heart of government wrongdoing to reveal the truth or, when that avenue was blocked, self-destruction."

But putting aside the unctuous and patronizing "compliments" followed by the taunt which simultaneously negates them and blames us for eliciting them, (by being "girls,") what are we to make of this email? Are the other activist and I his groupies? Was this an ejaculation for our benefit? The only redeeming feature is that I'm in good company; he genuinely respects the other activist...

June 16, 2008

Rags took me out for dinner tonight at one of our fabulous local restaurants. This one's run by Harrison Ford's son. It's great. I could sit at the edge of the sidewalk and tie Rags to the railing..You'd think HE was Harrison Ford, the way people stopped. Cheez! I really miss my Dad. It's been three years.-- MCR********

June 16, 2008

Try this: The plan to partition Saudi Arabia has been in place for at least five years. That's when I described it. US air and naval assets are already positioned to secure the georgraphy, which is all in the east and concentrated. Special Forces are pre-deployed to assist Saudi factions behind the ruling family to secure just the oil fields. Like Iraq, the rest of the country be damned. That's been the plan for a long time. Jenna, you're using Mike Kane's old email address. I don't know if he checks it anymore. I put his new one in the address bar. I also added Matt. I stuck in Richard too.Mike

On Mon, Jun 16, 2008 at 7:32 AM, Jennakilt@aol.com wrote: "But think where this might lead: suppose we get tough with the Saudis and end up destabilizing the kingdom so that forces unfriendly to us take over. Then we will feel more or less forced to invade in order to maintain access to our national drug of choice. Where would it end? Does any of this help?"
http://www.richardheinberg.com/oil-and-politics http://www.alternet.org/story/85842/have_we_really_hit_peak_oil

270

Mike to Energy Investment Banker Matt Simmons:

[The email opens with an explanation of the political opportunity which Mike had declined but which had started him thinking about a presidential policy concerning Peak Oil]

...and I see a huge void here. I've also cc'd Colin.I am moving towards helping to devise a position paper with one of the best and brightest, [he names an activist who may or may not want to be mentioned here] which would be [the activist's] (not as candidate, of course) to put out there. To my knowledge, no one else has really addressed this. Then it hit that me this is a huge question that would have to look at Treasury, DoE, DoT and Interior at minimum. I know DC well enough, but not the specific policies within the Exec Branch. You may already be doing this for someone. But there are huge questions of interface with state and local that are essential. Most important, however, are the guts of the federal government. Like the Hirsch report this should be apolitical. Like the Hirsch report, it should be totally frank and honest. To your knowledge, has anything been done on this? Where should one start? My first thoughts: 1. Complete declassification of the Cheney Task Force report; 2. Complete inventory/evaluation of US infrastructure; 3. Global transparency on reserves; 4. Then the big one: immediate steps to be taken within the USG to address the real problem. I'm contemplating going to Sacto for ASPO-USA at the end of summer, just to spy on everyone. You going?Anything you might suggest is more than welcome since we're facing a blank page here. best, Mike-- MCR

After warning of a second leak from the BP disaster in the Gulf of Mexico, Simmons died in 2010 of accidental drowning following a heart attack in his hot tub.

Part 69: Follow the Leader

The following email was sent by Mike to an accomplished Peak Oilist, cc'ing me. The ellipses are placed to erase any trace of the recipient's identity.

Reread Matt Simmons's email again. McCain is "brain dead" on the issue [of Peak Oil] and Obama's camp is jumping into it. McCain ain't brain dead. He's the devil. And what do you want to bet Obama's answers are going to be half (or more) wrong? Who in the Peak Oil movement will even be prepared to comment, let alone offer something real? It doesn't have to be perfect, just honest and devoid of fantasy. (Fanatasies are good, but not around Peak Oil)... You are young and stupid like I was once and you believe you're not only the best qualified but maybe the only one out there. [In defense of the recipient of the email, it's highly unlikely that the person felt, much less expressed, any such thing.] You're right on both counts. You have a brain and you have eyes. It's time you stepped a little closer to the big spotlight because you are ready-- and because you are needed there. I and Colin Campbell were probably the only two with any charisma. X ain't got it; he's an egghead. [A sought-after one. In certain scenarios, the media need eggheads.] Y is not a writer or a speaker. [I've never heard Y speak but Y is a marvelous writer.] Z lacks the fullness of education and experience. No way would I ever put W on camera (God love him). [Leaving aside the questionable criterion, it's debatable whether Mike himself was any cuter than W. Colin Campbell, of course, is adorable.] You have it all. We can't let the business people at... define our stance without incorporating honest viewpoints, devoid of self-interest. That will be the real battle. That's why I'm going to Sacramento... Matt will help us draft and so will many others. Peak Oil needs a face and yours is ...articulate, trained and ready. What you walk out of here with will be your position paper. It will have your name on it. You can thank me and whoever contributes, but the world will need to see this as yours. It will be yours. Peak will be on the table before November and we need you to be on CNN and every place else, debating and teaching... There's nothing hanging on this except...-- MCR

He is back on his high horse, whether through his own chemistry or with outside help. How long before he gets himself thrown off again?

272

Of course what angers me the most is that I'm not even on the radar screen. Forget, "I want to write something with you," and, "You're eloquent." He's reverted to that Hollywood mentality which is at the core of our global problems in the first place: the star system, the notion of hierarchy.

I write the article below, later published in *The Moron's Guide to Global Collapse* and include Mike on the bcc list.

The Moses of a Post-Peak Oil World

"The trouble with the world is that the stupid are cocksure and the intelligent are full of doubt." Bertrand Russell

Peak Oil is here or close enough, thank you. Those of us who've been dreading this moment for years are now waiting for the other shoe to drop, ie: the shit to hit the fan. When that happens, who will be the leaders who will carry us kicking and screaming towards the sustainable way of life that we should have been leading all along? Will he be a Clint Eastwood type, far-seeing (you can tell from his squint), a man of few words? Or will he be possessed of that elusive quality, charisma, an Obama-type to whom people naturally turn because of his easy, loose-limbed command of the facts combined with that facility that Joe Biden kicked himself around the block for noting, "articulateness?" Will he be tall? Will he be a woman?

What is "leadership" anyway? Justice Potter might have said, you know it when you see it (or hear it.) As in the old E.F. Hutton commercial, when The Leader speaks, the rest of the room falls silent. Sometimes this is because he's making sense. Sometimes it's because he's wearing a suit. Sometimes it's because he's the loudest. Whatever the reason, people accord him authority. He's the closest thing around to Daddy. While everyone else is scared clueless about what to do, The Leader seems sure of himself so they figure his confidence must be based on something. Maybe he'll be an actor who played a leader in a movie. Knowing how to act the part, he will bark instructions. "Finally we're getting somewhere," the others will think, regardless of where Somewhere is.

A few years ago a band of New York City Peak Oil activists were discussing suitable crops to plant when they finally moved to their respective sustainable communities. Since New York City is in the Dark Ages when it comes to Peak

Oil, these activists were, by default, leaders in the field. But — and the activists were acutely aware of this — they were not farmers. They were novices, trying to scrape together what knowledge they could from the internet and the occasional bank-breaking weekend at an intensive Permaculture course. So the conversation, while earnest and, by New York City standards, enlightened, fell short of providing useful information.

Until a young woman called X spoke: "Potatoes."

Her voice lacked the high-pitched excitement (the charisma factor) of the others, leaders all. And they seemed not to hear her. But then a man who was sitting next to her said, "Potatoes! We forgot about potatoes!"

"Yeah, potatoes!" said another.

And so, by subliminal suggestion, X's idea took over the conversation. (A by-product of that evening is that I planted two potatoes on my windowsill in the hope of later writing an article called, A Potato Grows in Brooklyn. One turned into a slimy mess; the other disappeared which must mean it morphed into soil. But that's another story.)

However, X is not considered a leader either by the meet-up or by herself. She just happens, time and again, to have the information everyone's looking for.

The others know this. Sometimes they ask her for advice and she provides it, as when an adolescent ventures out on his own, only to turn back to ask Mom for money. The Peak Oil Leaders boldly go forth proclaiming X's information, having incorporated it into their rhetoric and made it their own.

"We must change the paradigm!" goes the cry of the few brave souls who have for a long time seen what's coming and tried to warn those bits of the world to which they had access.

They're talking about infrastructure and the economy and other vital issues. But so far no one's addressed the assumptions on which we base our decisions, the notion that for the sake of simplicity and streamlined organization, there must be one person to whom we all look for instruction.

So it seems that when the world goes belly-up and the meek, if they know how to farm, shall inherit the earth, one thing shall emerge unscathed: that citadel, the grand social pyramid with drones at the base, some knowledgeable folk in the middle and on top, the One, True Sun to whom all others turn for enlightenment; He or She who in Ancient Greece was a god, in 20th century America was a movie star and in the 21st century will be a Peak Oil activist — the Leader.

I played with the idea of including an addendum to Mike saying, "Don't bother writing a long. mollifying explanation. I cannot be schmoozed or fooled."

I need not have worried; Mike wrote back:

Oooh, you're so beautiful when you're angry.

Part 70: Spin-Off

The phone rang. After going through the usual niceties, Mike said, "Listen to this:"

He donned an orotund Russian accent.

"Dear George Bush and Dick Cheney:"

The letter continued, a fantasy — grounded in reality, as good satire must be — of the message the Russians were sending the U.S. with their latest signing of a cease-fire agreement with Georgia even as they set forest fires to prevent the installation of concealed troops and weapons, and bombed bridges between their former satellite and Europe.

"I'm writing well, huh?"

He was on a roll, getting into the character of a Russian potentate.

"The book's going well too. I told Kenny I bet it's going to be number one on the New York Times bestseller list."

"You set the bar high for yourself but sure, why not?"

"CNN's reading me."

"Yeah, I know. The powers that be are grateful for you these days. I don't think you have to worry about your survival."

"I feel like Galileo. They couldn't kill him because he'd figured out how to navigate."

"It's all about maps."

"It's all about maps. Right." Long time Mike aficionados will recognize that he spoke of FTW as providing a more accurate "map" than mainstream media with which to understand how global events had arrived at their current untenable position.

"You know, someone like Buckminster Fuller said, 'The paradigm changes a long time before anyone realizes it.' That's what's happening now."

"Another way of saying that is, we're the cartoon character who doesn't realize he's run off the cliff because he hasn't looked down yet."

The next call was to tell me about his new girlfriend. They knew as soon as their eyes locked that their relationship was pre-destined, just as he and I had at one time been pre-destined. Likewise he and his fiancée. If you went by resumés only, (one way or another, we were all involved in protecting the environment,) then any of these scripts was indeed plausible.

"I only wish you the same happiness," he closed, to rub in the hurt he presumed I felt. ("*I'm happily coupled and you're not. Nya nya nya nya nya. But I'll magnanimously send you best wishes.*")

I was not unhappy. I had wonderful friends and a fulfilling job. My book was progressing; my son, thriving. The only disagreeable aspect of my life at that moment was Mike's attempt to drive me towards yelling or slamming down the phone. Then he could tell his cohort, "Jenna went all psycho on me," and relay the conversation by way of illustration. After some time passed, he'd generously refer to the incident as my "breakdown."

I made sure not to give him that satisfaction.

(Of course, if he himself ended up in another breakdown, he'd regret the whole episode.)

I didn't expect calls to chat and there weren't any. Except one... several years after he left. He was not so inept as to make small talk, then switch to a desperate plea for money. That call came the following week.

I sent a couple hundred. The calls to shoot the breeze ceased.

(This is not to suggest his need for money wasn't genuine. It was and I am one of those who believe he was justified in asking to be paid for his unique insights into deep politics.)

By that time, he'd gone through his inheritance, spending $35,000 on legal fees fighting for his "good name" in the sexual harassment lawsuit. If he'd just told the same truth in public that is contained in the body of the suit itself — "Yes, I engaged in some, uh, unprofessional [read: farcical] conduct but she had 'unclean hands' by telling me about porn sites" — he would have ended up with the same result but $35,000 richer. Still, we all have those coulda-woulda-shouldas.

---------- Forwarded message ----------
From: Mike Ruppert <stgeorge119@gmail.com>
Date: Fri, Oct 9, 2009 at 8:14 PM
Subject: FOR BLOG -- ECONOMIC WARNING
To: Jenna <Jennakilt@aol.com>

ECONOMIC WARNING
Oct.9, 2009 -- For those of you who have listened for so long and for those who may be new. Do whatever you can to get out of dollar denominated assets and do it quickly. It is looking to me like the run on the dollar has begun in earnest. This is the one I have consistently predicted as far back as 2003-2004. I'm not going to write a long argument. Those who have been reading this blog don't need it. All the rest of you can just go back and read the terrific postings made here by Jenna Orkin over the last month. Those of you who have followed me and FTW for years will remember our only four previous warnings and you know how right those economic alerts proved to be. That's why I left a record of between two and three million words. Do it now. We're all reading the same map.
MCR

On October 10, 2009, at 10:47 PM, he continued:

It is not too late to buy physical gold. That is what will shield you the best right now. I'm laughing because I sold all my gold to fight the political persecution in Oregon and to live on while we made CoLLapse for eight months. (It wasn't just shot over two days. There were five shoots. And every aspect of my life was vetted with a microscope.) If I had money I would be running to buy gold first thing Monday morning and I'd keep it up until the wheels came off or the new playing field that's coming had opened other options.

Now imagine this: The dollar gets dumped (in progress) as the world's reserve currency. Oil is no longer priced in dollars and trillions of dollars come home to... do what? Sure, it may cost a thosand a month for phone service. But suddenly John Q will be told that his salary has gone up 50%... at first. But what about all those bullshit mortages (including the fraudulent ones), all those trillions in derivatives? Well if John Q suddenly finds he has a million worthless dollars in his pocket he could well go back and laugh as he pays off the $350,000 mortgage. But the books get cleaned and sanitized and some of the air leaves the derivatives bubble. A

278

*controlled-burn. Yeah, the only ones that are going to get burned are the people --
the New White Trash.*
MCR

October 11, 2009 From an email concerning the making of *Collapse*:

*...I had written about more than 100 suspicious military deaths. They asked for
the files on all of them. They asked me to go through each death while Chris decided
what he did or didn't want to use. That triggered my survivor's guilt and I almost
crashed and burned behind it. [I had to] pull all the Tailwind files, all the
Tillman files, the Carone files, the Vreeland files, the CIA-drug files and all of
many other files. I had to explain all of them and relive all of them, all over again.
...It was utterly gureling at times. Once I was on set for 14 hours...*

As Mike settled into his life out west, he "went all spiritual" and
knew I wasn't interested in going along for that ride. He involved
himself with the sort of writers whom he would have avoided
like kryptonite back in the FTW days, and could not have done more
to damage his earlier reputation for journalistic integrity if he'd been J.
Edgar Hoover.

FTW had been founded on the principle of hard evidence. We
may have believed that more was going on in a given situation than
met the eye but if we had nothing to back up our hunches, we often
kept silent. (That assertion is not foolproof; spare yourselves the time
and energy of digging up the numerous instances when Mike did go
out on a limb. Most of those relate to the timing of disaster; in his
intensity, even desire, for a "fast crash" as opposed to a "slow burn"
for human industrial civilization, — in order to preserve more of the
natural world — his most frequent sin was to ratchet up the calendar.
He had been told of, and acknowledged, this foible but couldn't stop
himself.)

But he was back in "risky behavior" mode, as his Bellevue
psychiatrist might have said, and speculated or opined with abandon
on matters which were, shall we say, outside his area of expertise. For
instance, there may or may not be a life after death or "spirits"
communicating with us now. But the essence of that field of inquiry is

that no one can ever know, much less prove it. It's the opposite of everything FTW stood for. These are the reasons I don't spend time thinking about it; the endeavor is even more fruitless than arguing about whether there were explosives in the twin towers and WTC 7, an aspect of 9/11 Mike left alone since the Kennedy assassination had taught him that physical evidence, no matter how compelling, will always come down to, "He said, she said." Only in this case, he and she are Ph.D.s. The physical evidence from 9/11 has been dispatched to India, China, South Korea and Fresh Kills, Staten Island; the debate can never be resolved. In the case of spiritual matters, there's no physical evidence to begin with; only phenomena we can't otherwise explain.

Perhaps Mike told himself I wasn't sufficiently evolved to see the light, if he even gave the matter that much thought. I thought, "What are you smoking?" and eventually got the answer: Apart from weed, he'd taken up peyote and assorted mushrooms, along with prescription medication.

The only regular contact we had towards the end was through the news dispatches I sent out every day to a list of interested readers, primarily at Collapsenet. Often, Mike extracted one or two for his Facebook page.

He wrote an all-purpose blurb for my book, saying I could amend it as needed. (I didn't.) But he had a whole circle of new best friends (several generations' worth, in fact, between Los Angeles, Sebastopol and Colorado) so that I'd essentially become history, which boiled down to being my choice anyway.

I was shocked at his suicide, of course, but didn't have the same sense of tragedy that newer friends felt. I'd gone through that grief when he disappeared to Venezuela. And I'm not sure the person I grieved for then existed outside my own wishful conjuring.

But it's not quite time to wrap up this story. By current estimates, (I haven't yet written the next section) two more parts are needed.

Part 71: In Defense of Matt Stroud

(Written after reading a comment at Collapsenet.com but before reading Wes Miller's brilliant response to the original Matt Stroud article in the Verge.)

Let's start with the observation that apart from two smearing "Conspiracy Theorist" headlines in some of the less reliable media, The Verge is the only mainstream outlet thus far to have acknowledged Mike's death. The reasons for this are best summarized by the following passage from Nathaniel Blumberg's *The Afternoon of March 30:*

*...the American news media have been deeply penetrated by our intelligence community. Confirmation of everything I have been saying on that score came less than two weeks ago, and I've been waiting for just the right moment to pass it on. It comes from no less a source than the New York Times. I would like to say that it was the lead story on page one but, alas, as usual it was buried at the bottom of the fourteenth page of the second section on June 9. That story, my good and patient friends, reports that the Central Intelligence Agency, in order to settle a lawsuit under the Freedom of Information Act, reluctantly disclosed – those are the words of the good gray lady herself – that journalists have been used in a variety of roles and missions. Among other duties, journalists provided cover or served as a funding mechanism, some provided nonattributable material for use by the CIA, some collaborated in or worked on CIA-produced materials or were used for the placement of CIA-prepared materials in the foreign media. Some journalists had even served as couriers and as case officers who secretly supervised other agents. And some – oh, it's been a long time a-coming – provided **assistance in suppressing what the CIA termed a media item, such as a news story.**"[1] [emphasis mine]*

Nathaniel Blumberg, THE AFTERNOON OF MARCH 30: A Contemporary Historical Novel

So you may assume that the only way Mike's story will get into the public arena is sideways, via a highly skeptical view. This is a major reason that my own memoir of his time at my apartment is so unsparing.

While it's true that most people read superficially in the sense of reading only the words on the page, for any who might probe more deeply, Stroud's exposé includes a link to Mike's critical article, *Oh Lucy! – You Gotta Lotta 'Splain' To Do*. Anyone who checks that out will see that there's more to this story than just a crazy guy with an oddly consistent world view which, unlikely as it might seem, happens to coincide with reality.

Mike's always been controversial but as we're not talking about art, it doesn't suffice to shrug off the argument by saying, "Ya love 'im or ya hate 'im." On one extreme are followers who may believe, as he himself wrote in his suicide note, that he sacrificed himself for mother Earth, a sort of latter day Christ figure dying for our sins. This group sees his "flaws" as mere imperfections to be brushed away, allowing the humane spirit within to shine through.

But our mistake may be in thinking of Mike's impatience, intolerance etc. etc. as "flaws" at all. It is impatient people, intolerant of the status quo, who get things done. Anyway, those who knew Mike well saw how essential the "flaws" were to him. They were the flip side to his accomplishments, motivating him in complex ways.

On the other extreme are those who delight in his internal demons including the accusation, which he did not deny, that he appeared in his underwear in the doorway of a young female employee's office. It was this sort of behavior of which he sought to purge himself by fleeing to Venezuela. That is not speculation; he told me.

It was not the only reason for fleeing to Venezuela, of course. The "vandalism" of the FTW offices which The Verge refers to included the smashing of all seven of the company's computers. Mike justifiably saw this as a warning: "Next time, it'll be you." He came to understand that he'd be allowed back in the US only on condition that he "get out of the game," meaning investigative journalism, an "agreement" he stuck by.

Complicating the feud between Mike's defenders and his detractors is that he gave the latter group so much rope to hang him with. In the last years of his life, he publicly aired the sort of views about extraworldly affairs (aliens, the symbolism of the appearance of an eagle at a particular time) which can never be substantiated. He's not alone in believing that a spirit or god communicated with him or others in these ways. But they're the sort of beliefs that anyone staking his reputation on concrete evidence would be advised to keep to himself.

One fact cited in the article, which I'd like to clarify is the date of Peak Oil. Extrapolating from a graph in *Crossing the Rubicon*, the article implies that global peak took place in the 1960's. The graph, however, was referring to the peak of discovery. There's a significant gap between that and the peak of production, which may have taken place c. 2008 or is taking place around now.

This observation refers only to easy oil, which is what the Peak Oil movement is concerned with. Fracking, shale and tar sands do indeed extend the life of oil supplies but at intolerable cost to the environment.

Also, while it's true that Mike was originally a mainstay of the 9/11 Truth movement, he later broke with them irrevocably for their promulgation of the "No Plane at the Pentagon" meme and other less reliable evidence such as witness testimony of explosions before the twin towers fell. First of all, any potential physical evidence of bombs was expeditiously dispatched to Fresh Kills, SI, or to China, India and South Korea for recycling. But even if you did find evidence of bombs, Mike pointed out, what would that prove about who had placed them? Mike stuck with incontrovertible evidence of US government involvement in the attacks such as the warnings from multiple foreign intelligence agencies which went unheeded; the wildly anomalous put options on United and American airlines which got "overlooked" although the government monitors the stock market in real time; and the at least five war games taking place the morning of the attacks which diverted planes away from the east coast.

(There's also a slight inaccuracy referring to my personal relationship with Mike, which I mention only as a shield in case someone later accuses me of lying to the reporter.)

Saints are not interesting. Stroud's article will undoubtedly peak interest in Mike, thereby bolstering the case for the adage, "There's no such thing as bad publicity." Thus, however circuitously, it will help promulgate the invaluable information and insights Mike provided into our current global crisis.

Part 72: The Beginning

I first met Mike at a symposium to observe the third anniversary of September 11. I'd been invited to speak on the environmental disaster that had ensued from the collapse of the buildings and which I'd come to know intimately because at the time, my son had been a student at Stuyvesant High School, located four blocks north of Ground Zero.

Through attending, and often testifying, at hearings at all levels of government as well as at blue-ribbon scientific panels, I'd become familiar with the infinitely inventive, mercurial ways in which the government lies. They would announce they found no asbestos but neglect to add they did find exorbitant amounts of some other contaminant; use a test intended for a hard surface on a soft surface where its effectiveness was greatly reduced; not test in a place where they knew they'd be likely to find bad news; use outdated monitors which found 1/9 the asbestos detected by independent scientists; neglect to turn on a critical piece of equipment; allege, in the face of weighty evidence, that particles of a certain size were not dangerous; and in the unfortunate case where they managed, in spite of all precautions, to find anomalies, either bury them under mountains of meaningless data or "average them out" over an extended time or space until they disappeared. In one case, they downgraded the pH level of the air by a seemingly insignificant one point, neglecting to explain that the scale is logarithmic, so the reduction is not one of approximately 10%, which is how it might appear to the untrained eye, but of a factor of ten.

They also manipulated the message that filtered out to the public by refusing to testify at a hearing unless they could speak first, knowing that deadlines would preclude the press' being able to hear the truth from independent scientists or citizens later in the day.

So when Mike spoke at that anniversary convocation, giving an encapsulated version of The Truth and Lies of 9/11, his revelation of corruption at a still deeper level and to a global extent resonated. It wasn't a stretch to believe the Bush administration not only passively benefited from the attacks but actively abetted them, particularly given the massive amounts of evidence supporting the thesis and the unlikelihood that such a coup could have been pulled off without inside help.

Said evidence, some of which has been referred to by Senator Daschle and former Senator Clinton, includes a document by PNAC, the Project for a New American Century, asserting that the US needed to rev up its military program but that the generation of Americans who remembered the Vietnam war wouldn't support that prospect, absent "a new Pearl Harbor;" numerous warnings — which went unheeded — from French, Russian and Israeli intelligence agencies, among others, of an attack the week of September 9; highly anomalous put options on United and American Airlines which the CIA monitored in real time, thus putting the lie to allegations they were clueless that anything was up; and war games which drew planes away from the East Coast the morning of the attacks and introduced chaff onto the radar screens, confounding pilots who might have felt impelled to intercept the hijacked planes. In direct contradiction of later testimony by National Security Advisor Condoleezza Rice to the 9/11 Commission that no one expected a plane to fly into a building, one war game included just such a scenario: A plane flying into the National Reconnaissance Office at approximately the same time as the real hijacked plane was flying into the Pentagon.

Mike's talk that day culminated in the accusation: "Richard Cheney was not only a planner in the attacks but also... on the day of the attacks, he was running a completely separate command and control and communications system, which was superseding any orders being issued by the National Military Command Center — that's the Pentagon or the White House Situation Room."

The audience gasped. And the next chapter in my post-9/11 life began.

There was a room backstage where speakers hung out, partaking of a box of chocolates with vodka centers. Mike spent most of the day there talking to Congresswoman Cynthia McKinney while intermittently pursuing — both professionally and personally — Indira Singh, a computer analyst who had conducted an investigation into PTech, a Saudi software company. According to Singh's presentation that day, PTech had infiltrated numerous branches of the U.S.

government including, Congresswoman McKinney observed, the House of Representatives.

Mike had not focused on economics in his presentation but I sensed that his Weltanschauung — his way of looking at the world — might give him insight into a question that had been nagging me for years, waiting for the right person to come along.

"They always talk about economic growth. Can the economy keep growing forever?"

"No!" he exclaimed, bouncing slightly on the balls of his feet in frustration at our economic system as much as at the naiveté of the question.

In view of his stand on the matter, which I would come to know inside-out, as an introductory question, mine was ironic. For a fundament of Mike's world-view is that, "Until you change the way money works, you change nothing." And the basic reason for this is growth.

Other writers substantiate this idea: Our economic system is based on interest, a notion that was initially condemned by all three major Western religions — Judaism, Christianity and Islam — when it was introduced. (Islam is the last holdout but even Shari'a banking has reconciled itself to some compromises by replacing the term "interest" with "commission.") All three understood the unethical nature of profiting from a business while undertaking no risk oneself and doing no work beyond putting up front money. (In the case of the Federal Reserve, even that front money was not earned; it was simply printed because of an unconstitutional gift bequeathed by Congress when it set up the Fed in 1913.) But also embedded in the system is the implication that infinite growth is possible in a world with finite resources.

Money, particularly paper, is the currency of a faith-based economic system. Every year, the United States digs itself a trillion dollars deeper into debt which it has no intention of repaying because to do so is impossible. Instead, it simply inflates the system outside the view of the American people, since as of a few years ago, it stopped publishing the M3 money supply.

Mike's answer to my loaded question was the first of two times he

286

would confirm a suspicion I'd had my whole life. (The second would also be about economics, I'd always wondered: When everyone was thrown into poverty after 1929, where did all the money go? At a press conference held during a break at Petrocollapse, the Peak Oil conference which took place the following year, Mike said, "The Depression was not a loss of money; it was a transfer of money.")

After the conference I returned to Google, that ever wakeful, impassive eye, as well as to Mike's website, fromthewilderness.com, to educate myself in yet another field which was, as far as I was concerned, virgin.

His book, *Crossing the Rubicon*, was hard to take in with only one reading. Each sentence represented a lifetime of work so that when 9/11 took place, his decades of experience paid off in that he knew where to look, whom to call for clarification. But having read it twice, I'm convinced that few of the people, whether sincere or malicious, who write him off as an alcoholic/kook/conspiracy theorist, have bothered to read it. (He openly admitted to having been an alcoholic as well as having been hospitalized for suicidal depression. But when director Chris Smith asked him about conspiracy theories in the movie, *Collapse*, Mike replied, "I don't deal in conspiracy theory; I deal in conspiracy fact." At his best, he minimized speculation in favor of just the facts, Ma'am.)

The main motive for the attacks, Mike and his cohort alleged, was Peak Oil, the point at which the maximum amount of easy, conventional oil is produced on a global scale. The projections for the date of this watershed event tend to range from 2008 to 2015 but such distinctions are infinitesimal in comparison to the event itself, whose arrival changes everything as it necessitates a reversal of economic growth. (The introduction of technologies such as fracking, as well as shale and tar sands extraction extends our current economic paradigm of infinite growth but at intolerable cost to the environment.)

Einstein spent his life looking for a Unified Field Theory which would tie together gravity and other laws of physics that explain the universe. It seemed to me that Peak Oil was the Unified Field Theory of global collapse, tying together the increasing volatility in the economy and the climate as well as the environmental destruction wrought by desperate efforts to mine the earth for resources.

I sent FTW an article on the environmental disaster of 9/11. Apart from an expose by Juan Gonzalez in October 2001 and further revelations by Andrew Schneider in the St. Louis Post-Dispatch, by 2004, there was still little understanding among the general public of the cost in lives and health of the aftermath of the attacks. FTW published the article.

Then, studying the website's daily dispatches, I developed a sense of what they were looking for and began sending them articles from the mainstream media that might be up their alley. They featured many of these finds as well.

As with my research on the contaminants of 9/11, I also emailed this new information to allies from the battles of Lower Manhattan. Some were as hostile as they'd been three years earlier — when they had asserted that the government would never lie to the American people about the air quality — only now the jeers were muted by years of bitter experience.

In July of 2005, while speaking at the 9/11 Truth Convergence conference in Washington D.C., I saw Mike again when he served on a panel of questioners at a 9/11 hearing chaired by Congresswoman McKinney at the House of Representatives.

Among the witnesses were several of the "Jersey girls," whose testimony conveyed outrage and the sort of exhaustive research that is fuelled by a determination I understood only too well. Although they didn't explicitly accuse the Bush administration of having a hand in the attacks, they appeared to have read *Crossing the Rubicon*, referring to the stone-walling of investigations by Dave Frasca of the Radical Fundamentalism Unit of the FBI and other red flags that Mike had investigated.

A couple of weeks later, I got an email from Jan Lundberg of Culture Change who'd read an article I'd written following a brief email correspondence with Robert Hirsch, the lead writer on a report on Peak Oil which had been commissioned by the US Department of Energy. Lundberg asked if I'd moderate Petrocollapse, the first Peak Oil Conference in New York City, for which he would obtain the seed money.

Organized with five weeks' notice, (for the last two weeks of August, we could do nothing but wait for the manager of our first choice venue to return from vacation,) the conference took place October 5.

It was a stark, tell-it-like-it-is event. Although we had some Permaculture experts who offered advice on how society could get itself out of this mess, the over-all impression left a number of volunteers and audience members depressed. In an effort to dispel the gloom, the next NYC Conference, organized by Phil Botwinick and the NYC Peak Oil Meetup the following April, optimistically called itself Local Solutions.

But Petrocollapse afforded an opportunity for Peak Oil experts such as Mike and James Howard Kunstler, who'd previously known each other only through their writings or even by appearing in the same documentaries, to meet in person.

Now part of the regular FTW circle, I let it be known that I'd be interested in a permanent job. A while later, in February, the phone rang.

"Is this the wonderful Jenna Orkin?" a male voice asked with an audible grin.

I affirmed in a neutral tone, not engaging in whatever game this was.

"The beautiful, intelligent, sexy Jenna Orkin?" the voice continued.

I would have hung up except that the confidence of the caller suggested he knew me personally. Whoever he was hailed from an era when such an overture might have been thought of as flattering rather than sexist. The approach carried the aura of Hollywood. Perhaps it was one of my father's friends, some of whom held such attitudes towards women though, God knows, they kept them in check with their colleagues' daughters.

"Who is this?" I asked.

"This is Mike Ruppert... Did you think it was a crank call?"

"Yes!" I sighed with relief. How close I'd come to hanging up on the man I currently held in highest esteem.

The ensuing eruption of laughter was slightly forced, as though at the absurdity of the notion that his approach generated overtones of an obscene phone-call.

He offered me the job of managing the FTW blog which would be launched some time in the next few months. Naturally, I accepted. (The blog would become the only remaining functional part of FTW after mid-2006 so that it was later contacted by Julian Assange of Wikileaks before he came to world prominence.[14])

Two months later, Mike was in New York again for the Local Solutions Conference. We hung out together the whole weekend, the first time we were "intimate" as the current euphemism has it. I recited to him my poem, *King George and the Knights of the Oval Office; or: 9/11 for Dummies*, which he fully appreciated. (His compliments were as generous as his insults could be maddening.)

"I feel so lucky," Mike said. "Remember Calvin and Hobbes? There's one cartoon where Calvin's standing at the top of a hill and he trips over nothing and goes tumbling down. Then he picks himself up and says, 'Tada!' After all I've been through, that's how I feel."

"Will I see you again?" I asked. From the way everyone at the conference talked about Peak Oil, it sounded as though the collapse of society was imminent.

"You?! Of course! Come to L.A. I'll show you the sights, the old FTW office, where I went to High School... I'll play you all my favorite music and you can play me yours."

"Do you know anyone with a piano?"

"I'm sure I do."

He mused about how well we got along. "But there are some formidable obstacles," he observed wryly.

On the last day, Mike, his Office Manager, Monica Psomas, and I were in a cab heading west on 34th Street when, without saying anything, Mike pointed out a sign on the second storey of an office building: Spy Store.

I laughed at the irony of happening upon such a store while in a

---

[14] http://mikeruppert.blogspot.com/2009/03/from-jenna-orkin-oil-price-cannot_08.html

cab with Mike, of all people.

"Sorry, driver," I said. "I'm just laughing because...." It was impossible to give an accurate explanation. "I used to be a spy."

Later, when I knew Mike better, I understood how that comment must have spooked him, in every sense of the word. (He did once ask what it had meant. It was nearly impossible for him to wrap his head around an upbringing like mine in which the intelligence world is simply the stuff of movies. From my end, I couldn't imagine how he could think a real spy would risk joking about her métier and arousing suspicion.)

Once Mike got back to L.A., I elaborated on the fantasy in an email:

I went to the Spy Store yesterday. My poison-tipped umbrella was broken. The poison tip works OK but the umbrella leaks.

Mike called on his way to Mary Tillman's house to copy thousands of pages of documents for Stan Goff's series on the death of Pat Tillman in Afghanistan from friendly fire. Then he replied to the email:

On a poison-tip umbrella scale, the danger involved is about a four. When it gets to seven is when I start worrying.

Perhaps he was closer to seven than he realized. Within two months, the FTW office was burglarized and all seven computers, smashed.

Epilogue

Art is born of humiliation - W.H. Auden

It would be fatuous to muse about why Mike might have killed himself. Maybe it was indeed "the state of the world," his despair over human destruction of the planet, as so many of his fans fervently believed. Maybe he really did it "for the children," as he undoubtedly told himself. Maybe his return to poverty had something to do with it. Maybe he'd ingested some combination of substances that "triggered" the act. He'd made sure always to have at least one gun on hand. Maybe, as per the Chekhov quote I posted at mikeruppert.blogspot.com: When the interior of Act One of a drama displays a gun on the wall, then by the end of Act Three, it must go off.

But there's another factor to which I've alluded previously, concerning Mike's "dark side." Here's a more complete version of our conversation on that topic:

"There is a flaw in me that's always been there but that has allowed me to accomplish what I've accomplished."

"You were trying to compensate."

"When I was writing the war games chapter of Rubicon I was masturbating three, four times a day. That's how I wrote that chapter. I was deeply ashamed but that made me work harder."

Of course, it was not the masturbation that shamed him, but his "unholy" obsessions, such as the later one with his 25-year-old employee, which the masturbation exorcised.

"You couldn't eradicate the dirt in yourself so you dedicated yourself to tracking down bigger dirt in the government."

"That's a thought."

He believed the government knew of his psychological weakness (beyond what he'd disclosed publicly or even to his closest associates) but also said that Venezuela had burned it out of him. That turned out to be wishful thinking; his destructive behavior, whether of self or others, eventually resurrected.

Perhaps it is this fatal flaw that Mike had been referring to when he had said in an AA meeting, "I was always one step short of perfection and one step ahead of the devil." And perhaps Stgeorge119@gmail.com, as Mike was known on email, needed to slay the dragon of US imperial policy ("I understand him too well," he had explained, referring to Cheney, as he exited the bedroom during a State of the Union address,) as propitiation for the more intimate, and therefore dangerous, dragon within.

Against the Dying of the Light

My mother, Gisella Orkin, did not go gentle into that good night.
There weren't many things she did do gently; caring for her babies was
about it, although she could also melt in the presence of a stranger's
suffering. We once attended a party where she spent the better part of
the evening talking to a stroke-afflicted guest whom everyone else
politely ignored.

But more often, she was a force to be reckoned with as few people,
even her closest friends, understood.

Her family, however, understood it all too well. The first decade of
her marriage to my father, Harvey, was punctuated by explosions,
accusations fired from both sides, (they were well-matched in this
regard,) the scene invariably culminating in a door slam which left both
her and me quaking and wondering if he'd ever come back.

But ten years into this Strindbergian danse macabre, we all moved
to England and the turmoil abated. I reflected, from the filtered
information available to a child, that perhaps my parents were
absorbing some of that well-known British restraint.

That doesn't seem to have been it. In 1983, my brother, Anthony,
learned of the existence of our half-sister, daughter of the woman with
whom our father had been carrying on an affair. It would appear that
whatever needs our mother had not been meeting had found an outlet
elsewhere.

One of those needs was for a drinking buddy. Unlike everyone else
in my parents' circle, my mother neither smoked nor drank. She wasn't
sanctimonious about it; she had initially fallen for my father because
with his Scotch in one hand and cigarette in the other as he opined
wittily on the subjects of the day (he was a writer on the Emmy
Award-winning *Sergeant Bilko* series and went on to appear on British
television with David Frost and the Beyond the Fringe crowd,)
he fit her image of sophistication. She just didn't cotton to alcohol
herself.

She tried, once, in an effort to become the easy-going sort of
woman with whom Dad got along.

For ten minutes, madcap fun reigned.

"Wanna do a belly-whopper?" she yelled from the bedroom as she
hadn't in years, since I'd grown too big.

"Yes!" I ran in excitedly as she, a former **Broadway dancer** who exercised every day of her life until, at eighty-one, she simultaneously grew too weak and forgot, lay on the bed and kicked up her legs to balance me on her feet.

But twenty minutes later, she bolted for the bathroom and threw up everything she'd eaten that day, spending the rest of the night curled up in fetal position in the tub.

My father never raised the subject again.

There was one notable exception to the reprieve provided by England to my parents' Sturm und Drang: I walked in on the tail end of it when I came home from a friend's house one mild afternoon. My mother was wracked with sobs as in the old days; my father took my arrival as his cue to exit for the pub (or so I assumed at the time.)

I asked my mother what was going on.

"Harvey told me that he was married before... when he was in the army. It lasted eight months."

"Were there any children?" I asked, aghast at this bombshell going off in my placid view of the distant past.

"No," said my mother reassuringly.

This scene took place, I had occasion to figure out in retrospect, about two months after my half-sister, whom I will call Barbara, was born, which was right around the time my father learned of her existence.

There are a couple of possibilities as to what my parents' conversation had actually consisted of:

1. My father told my mother of his affair as well as of its result. My mother could not bring herself to tell me so she substituted a tale which, whether accurate or not, would satisfy my curiosity while also being, in her mind, not too far from the truth.

2. My father did not come clean that day. Instead, he told my mother of his earlier marriage in order to test the waters. The consequences were so dire that he realized he couldn't reveal the real dilemma he was in.

Whatever happened that day, my mother never acknowledged the affair although everyone else in my parents' circle knew about it. For one thing, the birth of the baby in question was all over the news as the Other Woman, who has since died, was renowned at the time. "But who was the father?" the press naturally wanted to know. They never found out.

Barbara, who has asked for reciprocal secrecy in this account, has told me some of the reasons for her mother's sealed lips beyond the obvious one of not wanting to be seen as a home-wrecker while our father might be portrayed, more, as a hapless oaf who was seduced: Not only was she having an affair with a married man, but he was a foreigner! And not just any foreigner, but an American!! And not just any American, but a Jew!!!

As for my mother, how was it possible for a woman as canny as she was about human foibles, (her most powerful weapon in argument was her ability to skewer the heart of her opponent's weakness) to remain oblivious to my father's philandering?

She must have known at some level, or else why find it necessary to account for his unusual chumminess with so many women? When my father lay dying of a brain tumor at the age of fifty-seven, my mother allowed a private visit from the actress Patricia Neal. Complimenting her on the trust this showed, Pat said, "Not many women would have done that."

"Harvey's not like other men," my mother asserted confidently, and not for the first, or last, time. "He has many women friends." (Neal maintained in her autobiography that her relationship to my father was platonic.)

When Barbara was twenty and I was still unaware of her existence, much less her relationship to us, she came to New York.

Anthony, who had learned about her while doing a junior year abroad in England, called and said, "I have something to tell you but you have to promise not to tell Mum."

Not having any idea what the secret might be about, (Was he ill or in trouble?) I couldn't promise.

Thus I didn't learn about Barbara for another ten years.

But that summer, she made the trip, in part, to look up members of her family. When she called Anthony, my mother took the message, later musing to Anthony, "I wonder why she wanted to meet you." Then she added, in the conspiratorial whisper of gossip, "You know, when she was born, it was quite a scandal."

Anthony mumbled something about a mutual friend who'd thought he and Barbara would get along.

The point of this anecdote is that whatever my mother had once learned or suspected about Barbara's origins, by the time of their phone interchange, she had made herself forget. Did the acting classes with Sanford Meisner (among her classmates were Grace Kelly, Leslie Nielsen and Robert Duvall,) enable her to feign ignorance so well, she ended up fooling herself? However she managed this feat, I have wondered if the effort contributed to her eventually contracting Alzheimer's or whatever it was that claimed first her mind and then her life.

The saga of dementia (the initial test for Alzheimer's so traumatized her, even possibly exacerbating her symptoms, that her doctor didn't make her undergo another) is on its way to becoming a literary genre in its own right. For like Tolstoy's unhappy families, each story is a nightmare in its own, unique way.

In my mother's case, it's impossible to say when the illness began. A loss of spatial sense is supposed to be a symptom but she never had such a sense to begin with.

Perhaps the first sign was heightened dissatisfaction.

This quality did not appear out of nowhere either. She had always had idiosyncratic peeves which she expressed with unusual conviction. For instance, she abhorred popular culture. Any actor less than Pacino was dismissed, though when a performance struck her as worthy, (an event which could take place in a tiny, ramshackle theater as easily as on Broadway – she responded to quality rather than brand names,) she shouted the loudest, and sometimes the only, "Bravo!"

But with advancing age, her tastes, like other people's arteries, narrowed and hardened further. When she could no longer find a new writer worthy of sustained attention, she retreated to the two giants of her literary pantheon: Proust and Fitzgerald. Alas… They, too, had lost their luster.

So, also, went her former pleasure in food.

This was still another arena in which she'd always been particular. Rare was the restaurant that could meet her standards: The vegetables were overcooked or the sauce, heavy; the dessert too sweet; the coffee, stale.

On the flip side, she could wax rhapsodic over a fresh roll or perfect summer melon.

The sicker she got, however, as with Proust and Fitzgerald, the more her old enthusiasms lost their appeal, as though she had developed a virulent form of, "Familiarity breeds contempt." She'd fallen out of love and like any romantic who wakes up one day to a hard reality, she turned her attention, instead, to accumulating grudges.

It was a skill at which she excelled. When a spoonful of mashed potatoes – long a savored appetizer – struck her as too salty, then in spite of all her mental losses, she diabolically retained a sense-memory of the event and refused ever to touch the dish again.

So followed a pageant of other former favorites: Nut butter of any flavor, (which I'd been counting on to provide some protein and calories,) turkey chili, Moroccan soup, guacamole, watermelon, plums, peaches, cheese, tzadziki. As for staples like tuna or potato salad, they'd never made it onto the list in the first place.

It didn't matter how hungry she was; she would rather starve than eat something she didn't like. Sometimes she gobbled the meatloaf sandwich I'd brought after which I'd find its cousin – lamb rather than meatloaf – uneaten, but for a gingerly bite, in the fridge.

One of the few up-sides to her new tastes was that she forgot she hated chocolate.

Also, for the first time ever, I could take her out for dinner.

Every Saturday, we went to a different neighborhood restaurant. If I'd dared suggest that three years earlier, she would have accused me of courting bankruptcy. But now I got to give her pleasure without incurring any morning-after-buyer's-remorse and resultant scorn. And since the outings were infrequent enough, the restaurants retained their allure.

There was a glimmer of the old Gisella at one Italian bistro where she cased the joint suspiciously and said, "This looks expensive."

"No, it's not," I shrugged and that was that. She took my word for it; we went back often and each time she marveled at the bargain.

Even as her aesthetic tastes became more difficult to satisfy, her sense of wonder for simple pleasures lingered: A ramble through Central Park the day after a snowstorm; in the summer, a trip to the zoo where she cocked her head at a bird of Paradise perched on a nearby branch and said, as she had used to greet my brother or me after school, "Hello, darling." The last complete phrase I heard her say, when she was in the hospice and I told her for the hundredth time that my son was getting married, was, "How wonderful!"

Whenever its onset, her illness took a long time to unfold.

Many years before her death, she would grow agitated when I helped her complete a sentence because she couldn't find the right word.

"Don't interrupt!" she'd lash out. Or, "No-o-o!" and then continue her train of thought, adopting the word I'd suggested.

This went on until a few years before her death when she could no longer disguise her deficiencies. But even then, on good days, her underlying condition became history and whoever she was talking to was the idiot.

In a way, she was right. Incapacitated though she was, some of the people who took charge of her were wrong-headed in their approach. It was infuriating to her to recognize this while remaining helpless to combat it because she lacked the words.

Thus the geriatric care manager who, in my mother's view, barged into her kitchen uninvited and talked about her airily in the third person to her aide, ("She can go out after lunch,") instigated a scene that surely made that care manager feel she'd earned her $175 per hour.

Once the illness took hold, however, my mother's deterioration proceeded with the inexorability of a Greek tragedy. I responded by putting off as long as possible the inevitable move to a home.

For she had always loathed the thought of ending up in one. She had never worried about it, though, since she planned to kill herself before the prospect became an issue. Like any good student of suicide, she had a way: She would take plane trips to Spain (at the time, the site of an above average number of plane accidents) until one of them crashed. When I pointed out that she could thus outlive her savings, she revised the M.O. but not the goal. She was thrilled when she took a cruise on the Queen Elizabeth II and the ship ran aground. What an elegant way to go! But then the lifeboat was lowered, she instantly redirected her enthusiasm and leapt in, going on to delight in her grandchildren and throw countless more dinner parties.

Anyone who knew her understood that moving her from her apartment would precipitate the transition from gradual to sudden decline, ushering in the denouement to her death. So when she became more absent-minded than usual, I simply had the gas turned off, kept the fridge stocked with dishes from Citarella that had thus far avoided the blacklist and set up an account at the corner coffee shop so she could have her favorite broccoli cheese soup even when she forgot to pay.

Some involved in her care, however, thought the move to a residence had been put off long enough. ("She should be in a home," muttered her G.P., sotto voce. "That would kill her faster," I muttered back. He nodded with a sigh. "Well, then," he resumed his full voice for my mother's benefit, "you can be tottering along now; see you in two weeks.")

Of course, the antsiest faction to get her out was the co-op board of her building, who instructed the staff to call 911 whenever she seemed "upset."

Thus the local police became regular visitors.

The first time they took her to the hospital, I arrived to find her sitting on her bed, rolling her eyes at all the fuss. The doctor on call agreed with her assessment of the situation and released her the same day.

Then she took up what is known as "sundowning."

"This apartment is so gloomy," she would complain at dusk, before going downstairs to talk to whoever was hanging out in the lobby.

But when the encroaching dark seemed to grow still more ominous, she ran down the hall, screaming.

On the rocks

With her sister Susan, also a dancer

With the author, age about two

With her second husband, screenwriter Albert Hackett

If her aide, Elizabeta, (some names and identifying details have been changed) was there, she'd run after her but as often as not, the presence of the aide was the horror from which my mother ran. At a deep level, she retained her Sartrian conviction, often voiced when her mind had been intact: Hell is other people.

"Your mother's been having night episodes, as I'm sure you know," a sympathetic British woman said when we met outside the elevator and at the sight of the woman's two wide-eyed children, my mother became her old fun-loving self. "Whenever I hear her, I let the children out; seeing them calms her down."

The children, one of whom was less than two, seemed to understand their role and take it seriously.

What was it about the dark? Did it presage that final, all-encompassing night? For my mother's screams were those not only of protest but also of terror; the final "No-o-o!" of Don Giovanni as he descends into Hell.

The second time she was hauled off to the hospital, she resisted the aides who led her from the ambulance to an examining room. She was injected with a narcotic that knocked her out for hours.

This was in the Emergency Room where, five years earlier, the 99-year-old mother of a friend, having fallen, was catheterized, although she had not broken any bones and was not incontinent. The procedure was performed by six people, none of whom was a nurse, much less a doctor. In the process, they tore the woman's bladder.

From the Emergency Room, she was sent to the ward where my mother had now been admitted. There, while in the hands of residents and interns, though no attending physicians, she was scheduled for thoracic surgery without the consent of my friend, who was her mother's Health Care proxy; this, on the pretext of an unexplained cough. My friend put the kibosh on the surgery which she learned of only because she happened to be present when her mother was about to be wheeled away to the operating room at 8:30 P.M.

A month after admission to the hospital, having bled continuously from the catheter which the hospital had insisted on keeping inserted, my friend's mother died.

The story of this institution, into whose hands my mother had now been delivered, kept me hyper-alert.

Mum remained in the hospital over the holidays, uncatheterized, as per instructions which were repeated until they appeared on the computer screens of all relevant personnel, but heavily sedated while her doctors titrated her medications.

Meanwhile, she was not given food orally on the grounds that she wasn't hungry, a mantra which would be repeated at every institution where she subsequently sojourned. However, she ate most of the croissant as well as decaffeinated coffee and milk brought by me or Elizabeta.

It was later explained that the actual reason she was denied food was the fear that because of her sluggish state, she might choke; a standard procedure which makes sense. However, it set in motion a vicious cycle in which she became too weak to eat as a result of which she became even weaker.

On Christmas morning, the whiteboard next to her bed read:

Nurse: *Karen*
Attending: *Merry Christmas!*

I added below, "You mean, 'Nobody.'"

After ten days or so, the hospital, having somehow consulted with the co-op board (or vice versa?) said she could go home so long as we hired a geriatric care manager to supervise her care. As a matter of fact, they worked with one who was available for an interview the following day.

The woman, a polished rep with a Southern lilt, explained that her agency, which I will call Happy Days (the other names I concocted in irony all turned out to be real geriatric agencies somewhere or other,) would send someone over to assess the apartment, then send a nurse who would be in charge of my mother's medication. This involved putting her pills into a box that had a separate compartment for each day so as to be able to keep track of which medications had already been taken. An aide from the agency would do the hands-on care. That aide could not be Elizabeta, with whom my mother got along (a rare enough phenomenon) because Elizabeta had come from a different agency.

I told Happy Days that my mother did not take kindly to strangers. If there was not at least a transition period between Elizabeta and the new aide, we'd all be back in the hospital and one step closer to my mother's having to go to a home, which would not be in the agency's interest, let alone my mother's.

My mother was released from the hospital; the agency assessed the apartment and sent the nurse; then a rep arrived with the aide.

My mother had had it with strangers; she didn't let them in and as was her wont, she accomplished her goal with all due drama.

The agency did what their protocol required: They called 911. And back we all were at square one or rather worse: We were one step closer to having to place Mum in a senior residence.

I went to the hospital where Mum was in the waiting room, hiding beneath the brim of her cap with a mischievous grin as though to say: "I was really bad but boy, was it fun."

Next to her sat an agency rep, one whose services cost $180 per hour rather than the aide whose fee was an order of magnitude less.

Mum was admitted while the doctors, in consultation with me and Anthony, worked out a Plan B.

When I got to the hospital the next morning, Mum was sitting up in bed, her breakfast pushed aside, untouched. She beckoned me to come closer, gripped my arm, using it to hoist herself out of bed and started walking purposefully (if with the miniscule steps of a Chinese woman with bound feet) down the hall. She was blowing this joint and going home.

We proceeded in silence so as not to give away the plan, our only communication, Mum's firm tugs this way or that on my arm. Besides, she was occupied keeping a lookout for the exit. I had neither the heart nor the guts to argue with her. Instead, as we hustled past the nurses' station, I said out of the corner of my mouth, "My mother's trying to escape."

A moment later, a voice came over the loudspeaker which, in the overall din, Mum didn't notice: "Patient at large." The staff watched our progress in silence until we reached an intersection. Mum looked down the endless linoleum hallway that stretched before us as in a

Kubrick nightmare, turned around in confusion and shuffled back to her room; her failure, forgotten.

Happy Days retreated gracefully into history. Enter Geriatric Care Manager Number Two: Ms. Competent.

Because Happy Days had from the outset expressed doubts about their ability to handle the co-op board, they had, in fact, mentioned Ms. Competent early in their discussions with us. (Translate: They knew they were out of their depth and would soon lose the case. Perhaps they specialized in elderly patients who behave themselves. But their awareness of their limitations and of the likelihood that this would be a brief encounter may shed some light on their frenzied activity as soon as we signed the contract; activity which would surface when their bill arrived several weeks later.)

In addition to an impressive bravado with the co-op board, (and, lest someone accuse me of trying to hide something, Adult Protective Services who had been paying the occasional visit,) Ms. Competent's great advantage over her predecessors was that she understood the value of Elizabeta, mum's aide. Ms. Competent, in other words, was willing to play ball.

She put Mum on the waiting list for a residence known for its flexibility. Meanwhile, since Elizabeta was not available 24/7, having an ongoing dental problem as well as a teenage daughter; and since Ms. Competent was unable to find a suitable person to fill in; and since Mum already "knew" her as she had been by to make her own assessment of the apartment and set up the all-important pill-box, it would be best if Ms. Competent herself did the supplementary care; this, at the rate of $175 p.h., the same rate to be applied also to her travel time.

The clock had been set for a move to a senior residence; it was only a matter of months at the outside. Since the idea of Ms. Competent's acting as aide at approximately eight times the usual rate would, in happier times, have outraged my mother, (particularly as it had been Ms. Competent who had triggered my mother's epic outburst with the talking-past-her incident,) I went looking for a residence with more immediate availability.

My students chastised me for not taking care of my mother myself.

In their cultures, the elderly are looked after, by all accounts without resentment, sometimes even by non-blood relatives. One student, from Tajikistan, had a friend who'd taken care of her husband's grandmother for fifteen years until she (the grandmother) died at the age of 112. And in Tajikistan, "taking care of" is no simple matter, even if the oldster is able to manage her own "toileting;" in that case, it involved hauling in wood for the fire and water from the well.

In the eyes of my students, therefore, I was a sorry excuse for a daughter. I bit that bullet and found a senior residence that was nearby and boasted expertise in Alzheimer's.

The close atmosphere, with cozy lamps that cast a sepia tinge over the furnishings while show tunes from the 40's played in the background, (surely audible only to visitors,) – wasn't my mother's style but would, if she remained at all sensitive to her surroundings, bemuse her. The place evoked the gentility of the deep South, as in the final act of Streetcar, when Blanche gets carted off to the loony bin. But, lifting my hopes, a large calendar on the wall was scribbled over in magic marker with the month's activities: Movies, Ballroom Dance, Art Class and so on.

If Mum overcame her prejudices, (most likely through forgetfulness,) she could end up getting a kick out of this place. It was, after all, not unlike a cruise, but for the condition of her fellow passengers which she might be too out of it herself to notice.

I packed her a couple of suitcases: Night clothes, comfortable track suits and a few elegant blouses in the hope – pathetic, as it turned out – that they'd earn her some respect.

On the morning of the move, Anthony and Elizabeta took Mum out for breakfast before strolling down the street where they "happened" to run into the residence director who, as had been arranged, was standing at the entrance. She invited them in for tea. Charming conversation ensued; Mum must have been tickled.

Then it was time to leave.

Or so Mum thought.

When she realized the truth of the situation, Anthony said, "She tried to bite me," only calming down when a nurse (in my imagination, the six foot tall one with the androgynous name) wrestled her into submission and injected her with a sedative.

Ms. Competent had wisely opted out of taking part in this scene. But, she had said, "I'll come by when it's over to introduce myself and make sure everything went smoothly."

In other words, Anthony and Elizabeta would do the heavy lifting *after* which Ms. Competent would use the occasion to network with the residence director.

However, Anthony did not object. Indeed, he was relieved by the participation of Ms. Competent; when it came to people in charge, I, like my mother, had not been known, recently, for playing well with others.

The next day, I visited around lunch time. The floor was dark; the curtains drawn.

Most of the residents were women. But there was one squat man who waddled over to Mum and felt her up. She waved him away, not interested but at the same time, sympathetic to his desire. Unfazed, he moved on to a Frenchwoman who, with the same degree of absence as Mum, permitted his caresses as she talked a stream of surrealistic fragments to no one in particular.

"What's today's activity?" I asked the attending aide.

She stared back blankly. A few residents were sitting in front of the TV, intermittently glancing at it before returning to their thoughts or absence thereof. One snored on the couch. Another walked around, sat down for a while, got up and went back to her room while a third came out of her room, walked around, sat down for a while... This seemed to be how they spent most of the day, like zoo animals who've become habituated to captivity.

At two PM, an activity director came by to round up participants for Ballroom dancing.

"Do you want to come dancing, Gisella?" she asked Mum.

"What? No!" said Mum, not understanding the question and recoiling in fear.

"All right," responded the woman pleasantly, before returning to the elevator with the sole resident who'd expressed interest. She already had enough takers from the early-stage Alzheimer's floors.

"It's dancing, Mum!" I protested.

But all Mum knew was, I was there and she didn't want the visit to end. I made a mental note not to come at activity time.

During our initial interview, the director had said that there were regular trips outside but somehow, once Mum was enrolled, the weather was never quite right.

I hired an aide to take her across the street several times a week for decaffeinated coffee and a sandwich (she wasn't eating much here, either) and kept her on the waiting list for the residence recommended by Ms. Competent.

It was when a bed became available there that we learned that what we had taken to be a routine deposit at Mum's current residence was, in fact, a "community contribution" and therefore had to be forfeited.

Apparently, this graciously furnished human warehouse had anticipated family reactions to the real, day to day routine and devised a novel way to keep residents from jumping ship.

No matter – she was outta there.

The next home was cheerier – the dining-room, awash in sunlight – and quirky; the Montessori of senior residences. When Mum acted up, the nurse took her into her office where she stayed for hours, talking while the nurse took care of paperwork.

Also, the staff made an effort to include the less competent clients, of whom Mum was one. She attended a sing-along where most members were, in fact, chiming in. But either Mum couldn't hear or she was too drugged to participate; she slept through the entire session, like the kid in school who ends up dropping out.

She was not the only lost soul in that residence. Another woman, a former public school music teacher who could no longer speak, was crying every time I saw her.

Meanwhile, Sunshine sent their bill: $1720.

"Care management; Visit; Care management; Coordination of Services; Communication with Client/Family or Other Social Support: 2.00 Hours; $360." "Care Management; Coordination by X.Y. [someone I never met in person:] 3.00 Hours; $540."

By "coordination of services," they meant agency employees who had spent whatever percentage it was of the five hours on that portion of the bill conferring with each other, then calling me to find out what

310

each other had said.

"Care Management; Visit; Supported caregiver: 4.0

This last item referred to the fact that the aide had been escorted to my mother's apartment by the agency rep.

I sent $442, for two hours of "coordinating/management/visiting" services and a full day's pay for the aide who had been hired and, through no fault of her own, not allowed to carry out her duties.

Needless to say, the bill was resent. I forwarded my previous email which read in part: "I am not sure why the caregiver needed support. She was capable of calling 911 herself. That ability is surely included in the job description. In any case, if the caregiver is the one being supported, she should be the one paying [the agency rep.]" The dunning letters ceased.

Mum's new residence called. She was "not responding to medication," residence-ese for "screaming her lungs out and driving us all crazy." The doctor had tinkered with her meds to no avail; it was time for her to be hospitalized once again.

She was there for several weeks before the doctors determined that they had no medical cocktail adequate to control her enough to meet the standard of a senior residence; she must go to a fully staffed nursing home.

Only one of the homes they recommended in New York City was both able and willing to take her.

Anthony and I visited.

"The sheets are changed every day," said the guide, "and if the resident has a bowel movement in bed after that, we change them again."

"That's good to hear," said Anthony. "Once."

"And this is the Activity room," said the guide.

The residents were sitting in two rows in front of the television where a frenetic game show erupted in applause. There was no response from this audience; everyone was either asleep or unable to hold his or her head up to look. The back row wouldn't have been able to see anything anyway. As usual in these homes, only the aide was watching and that, only desultorily.

The advantage of this home was that it was near enough for me to visit frequently. However, it was more important for Mum to be someplace where the staff would pay more attention to her.

She went to a home in New Jersey that had an excellent reputation for working with dementia patients.

It was two and a half hours away by public transportation, too far for Elizabeta. But there was one aide there who was able to induce Mum to eat. Probably she smiled or said a few phrases that allowed Mum to feel she was engaged with another human being.

It wasn't long, however, before Mum made trouble here too. Once again, she needed to "have her meds revised," code for "sent to the psychiatric ward."

Here, the Activity Room was aptly named: It was a hive of activities. The TV was on, of course, but at the same time, directly in front of it, was a music class. An aide led the patients in a song, regularly sounding a triangle by way of accompaniment.

Anyone actually watching TV would not be able to hear while anyone paying attention to the music class would be distracted by the TV. The word "bedlam" came to mind. (Deriving from "Bethlehem," this was, in fact, originally the name of a lunatic asylum.) Any resident who wasn't crazy already soon would be.

Out in the hall, other patients lay on cots; some, groaning, as in a scene from Dante's *Inferno*. Soaring above the general din, at regular intervals came a cry from a patient at the far end: "Help me!"

The staff walked past her, oblivious as figures in a dream where you're screaming and no one hears.

Another patient took up the lament, like a bird recognizing the call of her own species.

"Help me!" cried the first patient.

"Help me!" echoed her soul-mate.

Since Mum was dozing, I went over to the first crier.

"What do you need?"

"They haven't got, well, you know…," she said, with a covert look as though I was in on whatever she was talking about. "It was… the other one… didn't go there."

I nodded knowingly until the woman had had her say. And the "Help me's" went quiet, for the moment, from her end of the hall.

But "Help me!" Number 2 was still going strong.

"What do you need?"

"What time is it?"

"A quarter to three."

"Afternoon or night?"

"Afternoon."

The woman lay back in despair. "I'm so tired. I want to go to bed."

She was *in* bed but had, if not miles, then hours to go before she could get a night's sleep.

Mum was on one of these cots too. A versatile contraption, it can function as a wheelchair when necessary. An aide unlocked the device so after rousing Mum, I took her for a walk through the halls where we toured the impressionistic reproductions on the wall. More importantly, we talked to anyone who was up for a chat. Mum was starving for a social life and I introduced her around in the hope that these people would greet her also when I wasn't there.

In between visits, she got Physical Therapy as well as Occupational Therapy for her wrist which was curling in with the atrophy of her muscles. I'd signed her on for whatever the nursing home offered on the theory that if nothing else, she'd benefit from the contact with people. Even the visits from the pastor were welcome although in her coherent days, she would have been appalled.

"What's her religious affiliation?" he asked.

"None." Then, lest that be misconstrued, "N-O-N-E."

The social worker had said that if the nursing home learned that my mother was born Catholic, she might end up with some heavy duty religious talk as well as last rites.

If she understood any of it, this would be sure to set off a fit of despair.

One day, I arrived to find Mum in her room, rocking back and forth. A string about six inches long was clipped to the shoulder of her gown at one end; at the other, to the back of her chair. She had been trying to "escape" again; this time, simply to go to the bathroom. But that was not allowed because it was dangerous for her to get around unassisted and there was no one available to escort her. Therefore, like a child in a classroom, she had to stay seated.

If I were a twenty-something, I would have had one of those smartphones to record the moment. The video would not have revealed Mum's face; this was not her finest moment and in her finest moment, she would have detested the record. But posted on Youtube, it might have had some effect.

However, I am not a twenty-something with a smartphone.

I summoned the nurse.

"You wouldn't do this to a dog."

"I'll call the supervisor," said the nurse, smelling trouble, and left the room ASAP.

"She was trying to get out of the chair," explained the supervisor with faux patience, as though the act were equivalent to attempted jailbreak. Did she think that settled the matter? ("Oh, well then, of course you must tie her down. For $560 per day, you couldn't possibly be expected to help her walk around the room a few times.")

"You can't restrain her all day," I objected.

"It's not a restraint!" responded the supervisor with unaccustomed vigor. "We don't restrain patients. It's not attached to her; it's attached to her nightdress; she can get out if she wants to."

"No, she can't; she's not strong enough. She's been trying for the last half hour. And anyway, if she could get out, then it wouldn't be effective, would it?"

However, with the word "restraint," I had unwittingly hit a nerve. It is against the law, I subsequently learned, to restrain patients. The following week, the tether was longer and Mum, unaware of it and therefore, at peace.

In the interim, her doctor had been informed of The Situation (Read: Irate Family Member) and called to discuss it (Read: Placate Said Family Member.)

"The whole time I was there, she was trying to get out," I said.

Agreeably enough he replied, "Yes, I know. I'm trying to find a medication to stop her moving so much."

Why don't you just kill her? That'll stop her moving so much. Her movement, however potentially dangerous, is a sign of the life-force.

She was also continuing to lose weight. A lean 119 pounds for most of her life, she was down to 98.

"Her appetite is poor," said the nurse, evoking a line from a Ring Lardner story: "'Shut up,' he explained."

My mother's second husband, the screenwriter Albert Hackett, (with his first wife, Frances Goodrich, he co-wrote *It's a Wonderful Life* and *The Diary of Anne Frank*, among other films,) died at ninety-five after a "battle with" Alzheimer's and anyone else who was around at the time. For the last five days of his life, he closed up shop which is to say, he refused to eat.

In her "right mind," my mother had admired the expeditiousness of this exit and said that when her time came, she would follow suit.

A casual observer might assume that her time had indeed come. Mum, who was raising Cain whenever the staff bathed or even moved her, also shook her head when they offered her food, refusing the white roll, the gray beef, the boiled spinach. (I didn't understand how anyone could stomach that turgid green mass but the nurse, a trooper for the institution, stalwartly asserted, "I don't see what's wrong with it.") However, she gobbled up the papaya or mango I brought and smiled enchantingly at anyone who behaved not as though they were clinicians doing their job but friends who were happy to see her. Although, God knows, she could be implacable, there were times when she was not rejecting food so much as authority or simply being treated as a job rather than as a human being. (The nurses and aides are not to blame for this; they are victims too, overworked and underpaid; but the reality remains.)

Each of her residences had asked for any information the family would like to add about the patient. Each time, I'd provided a list of her preferred foods, especially the fresh fruit she craved.

"We can't keep food like that on a large scale," said the woman in charge of meals. "But," she smiled as though the bright idea had just struck her, "you're welcome to bring it yourself if you wish."

I brought those foods but not a week's worth of groceries. Mum's weight continued to drop – to 95.

I fed her Ensure and applesauce; she wanted more.

"Sometimes patients don't like to be fed by a stranger," explained the nurse. "They'll only eat if a family member gives it to them. You're welcome to come at mealtimes."

"Elizabeta used to feed her; she was no more family than you are. And there was an aide in [the first branch of the nursing home] who also got her to eat." The implication being, "She'll eat if you keep trying."

The nurse busied herself with another patient.

This ward had an Activity room too but this was an Activity room with a difference; it was the end of the line. Even the TV didn't pretend to keep patients entertained; it was set to screen saver – a palm tree bending slowly back and forth.

Probably this was to keep the more agitated patients from going berserk. The rest were so zoned out on whatever medication they were taking that they didn't notice anyway. Or if they did, they soon gave up and retreated to sleep.

Despite the subdued atmosphere, one week, a fight broke out.

It started when a patient got out of her seat.

"Siddown," snapped the aide.

"No," retorted the patient.

"Siddown and shuddup!" snarled the aide, pushing the patient back towards her chair.

"No, you shut up!" returned the patient.

Now everyone joined in: "Yeah, you shut up!"

They were in their element, a dysfunctional family; the aide, wielding power only because she was in better physical shape, for now, at least. The scene brought to mind an article which claimed that people who take care of Alzheimer's patients are six times more likely to get the disease themselves.

Mum's weight continued to fall. "Appetite: Poor," noted the nurse on her chart before wheeling the food away.

Again, I asked for Ensure and after a few protests from Mum (weaker now, like a mewling cat) she ate half the container.

Again, I reported that with respect to feeding my mother, the staff needed to keep trying.

"As they reach end stage, they lose the ability to swallow," explained the nurse.

Mum had not lost the ability to swallow but the phrase "end stage" triggered the thought: She is now eligible for hospice.

We transferred her to her final stop: a hospice in New York.

Like its predecessors, this home was a place which Mum, in better days, would rather have died than end up in.

But as with its predecessors, now that she was there, *she changed her mind*. She still intermittently fought off the staff, refusing to eat, then wolfing down Ensure when Elizabeta or I offered it to her.

She was in hell. But she didn't want to die; she wanted to go home. She was fighting for her independence.

Everyone does, observes a friend who used to be a Clinical Psychologist.

Only when she lost the ability to swallow did she clam up her mouth firmly and consistently, as she had always maintained she would.

Since a feeding tube was not an option and I didn't want her to suffer hunger pangs, (despite the assurances of a nurse that endorphins make the whole experience more pleasant,) I instructed her doctor to up her morphine.

Three days later, at 5:30 AM, the call came that she had died.

Other books by Jenna Orkin

The Moron's Guide to Global Collapse
Writer Wannabe Seeks Brush with Death

Author's Biography

Jenna Orkin is a writer and journalist whose work has appeared in Counterpunch, Fromthewilderness.com and other publications. One of the first to question the US Environmental Protection Agency's assertions that the air in Lower Manhattan following the 9/11 attacks was safe to breathe, she went on to co-found the World Trade Center Environmental Organization as well as other Lower Manhattan activist organizations that revealed and testified to the government's lies. It was while speaking on the issue at the third anniversary of the attacks that she met Mike Ruppert.

16084792R00185

Made in the USA
Middletown, DE
03 December 2014